America's New Low-Fat Cuisine

Leslie L. Cooper

America's New Low-Fat Cuisine

Quick & Easy Menus for Today's Health & Fitness Excellence

ILLUSTRATIONS BY MARY C. MARTINEZ

Houghton Mifflin Company

BOSTON

1991

The information contained in this book is not intended as a substitute for consulting a medical doctor. The intent is to provide the reader with information and ideas to be used along with medical advice from a physician.

For information about permission to reproduce selections from this book, write to Permissions, Houghton Mifflin Company, 2 Park Street, Boston, Massachusetts 02108.

Library of Congress Cataloging-in-Publication Data

Cooper, Leslie L.
    America's new low-fat cuisine : quick & easy menus for today's
health & fitness excellence / Leslie L. Cooper.
        p.   cm.
    ISBN 0-395-51605-6.
    1. Cookery.   I. Title.
TX714.C674   1991
641.5′63 — dc20   90-28278
                                CIP

Text design by Anne Chalmers

Printed in the United States of America

AGM   10   9   8   7   6   5   4   3   2   1

ACKNOWLEDGMENTS

THIS COOKBOOK began as a vision about twelve years ago. Many people have been involved over the years as the book went through its long metamorphosis, ending with the pages you hold in your hands. I'd like to thank everyone who has been a part of my life and work from then until now. And I would like to give a special heartfelt thank-you to the following people:

◆ Robert K. Cooper, my loving husband, best friend, business associate, and lifemate, whose hard work, determination, and courage have become my guiding star
◆ Christopher R. Cooper, my son, and personal taste-tester, whose love and support make my kitchen and my life shine
◆ Chelsea S. Cooper, my daughter, for helping me learn to be able, at any moment, to sacrifice what I am for what I can become
◆ Roberta and Daniel Marsh, for their love and support
◆ Gerald and Ana Loecher and Family: Although the distance between us is great, my heart and thanks remain warm and sincere.
◆ Debbie Eisner, my sister, for our long talks and family bond
◆ Clayton J. Loecher, my brother, for the memories of togetherness that will last a lifetime
◆ The Loecher and Friedlieb Families: Murray, Ginger, and Daryl Loecher; Corinne, Eric, and Lysa Friedlieb; Freda and Frank Kaplan; for all the laughter, talks, tears, and love we've shared over the years
◆ Hugh and Margaret Cooper, for their unconditional love and support and for being a shining example of goodness
◆ Mary Martinez, whose illustrations bring warmth and life to this cookbook
◆ Ruth Hapgood, my editor, whose wisdom and gentle ways are a grand inspiration

- Jayne Yaffe, whose insightful hand has brought out the best in this book
- And all those who have supported me over the years, while eating, writing, and living my way through the completion of this cookbook

Contents

Indexes

Foreword

ALL THE NUTRITION GUIDELINES in the world won't result in better health if you can't bring these dietary principles to life in your kitchen and when dining out. "What we need," says Dr. Jean Mayer, the internationally known nutritionist and president of Tufts University, "are practical cookbooks that educate us in the preparation of delicious light cuisine. . . . And a well-written cookbook can give consumers all the information they need to do this, right down to the portion sizes."

You hold in your hands a shining example, a cookbook for the 1990s and beyond. This is your guide to the new era in delicious eating. With the right recipes — and this book is filled with them — you can quickly and inexpensively implement wise nutritional guidelines: eating frequent, small meals and light snacks; cutting back on fat, cholesterol, and salt; increasing complex carbohydrates and fiber; and so forth. At the same time, you can preserve the delicious flavors you know and love — and introduce new ones.

My wholehearted endorsement of *America's New Low-Fat Cuisine* goes beyond the fact that it was written by my wife, Leslie, a talented fitness instructor and exceptional chef, who has spent more than a decade studying nutritional science and testing recipes and meal plans. My enthusiasm for this book is confirmed by the many people who have attended Leslie's courses and who have tested the menus and recipes in this book or have sampled them at our educational center.

This cookbook complements and expands on the dietary recommendations I presented in *Health & Fitness Excellence* and offers practical suggestions for meal planning and food preparation. It took Leslie countless hours to create the sample 28-day menu, with its unique 14-day cool-weather and 14-day warm-weather meal/snack plans and its more than 250 recipes.

On these pages you'll also find up-to-date information on a variety of foods, herbs, and spices; and guidelines for cooking with whole grains and legumes, fruits, vegetables, and low-fat and nonfat dairy products. Consistent with the latest recommendations of leading health organizations, most of the recipes are vegetarian, but Leslie has included delicious options for meals with seafood and poultry. There are chapters on shortcuts for baking your own whole-grain breads, suggestions on packing lunches for children and adults, and the best nutritional bets for where and what to eat when dining out. Each individual recipe, meal, and snack has a full nutritional analysis.

In short, this is not just a special cookbook. It's a bright and timely invitation to begin a lifetime of better nutritional health for you and your loved ones. And that's one of the best investments you can make.

—Robert K. Cooper, Ph.D.,
author of *Health & Fitness Excellence*
and *The Performance Edge*

America's New Low-Fat Cuisine

◆◆◆◆◆

1

◆◆◆◆◆ **An Invitation to the New Era of Delicious, Healthful Eating**

AT THIS MOMENT, how many cookbooks are lining your kitchen shelf? How many do you really *use,* day in and day out? All of us who realize the importance of good nutrition are faced with the discomforting fact that more and more of our favorite cookbooks and recipes fail to meet the latest nutritional guidelines.

And in today's hectic world — where both parents work and single-parent families are more common than ever — chances are, your busy schedule leaves you little time or energy to cook at home. There's a growing concern that our diet, and that of our family, is falling short.

The "New Era" Cookbook

As our knowledge of nutrition has changed dramatically in recent years, it has become obvious that we need a very different kind of cookbook, one that:

◆ Is filled with lighter, more healthful, low-fat foods that haven't lost the satisfying, family-style touch or hearty, special flavors that so many of us know and love

◆ Provides a wide range (more than 250 kitchen-tested recipes) of pleasantly gourmet, fast but sophisticated, heart-healthy, inspired entrees, accompaniments, snacks, and desserts drawn from culinary tastes and traditions around the world

◆ Is immediately practical for busy, two-career families on the go, providing a variety of taste-tested options for "meals in minutes" and sensible shortcuts to save time in the kitchen

◆ Meets the very latest nutritional standards for low-fat, high-carbohydrate, high-fiber meals and snacks — with each recipe backed by a complete nutritional analysis, listing calories, fat, cholesterol, protein, carbohydrate, fiber, sodium, and calcium

◆ Provides well-designed seasonal menus, for cool weather and warm, with a light breakfast, midmorning snack, light lunch,

1

midafternoon snack, and moderate evening meal — arranged in simple, taste-coordinated meal plans

◆ Features easy-to-use indexes, so you don't waste a single minute finding the recipes you want

◆ Offers simple, proven guidelines for gently transforming favorite traditional recipes into more healthful versions that meet today's important new dietary standards

◆ Gives a variety of options for packing heart-healthy, fun-to-eat children's lunches and brown-bag meals and snacks for adults

◆ Provides a detailed how-to section, complete with kitchen strategies and shortcuts for baking delicious whole-grain breads and preparing a wide range of recipes that include whole grains and legumes

◆ Gives clear, helpful guidelines for dining out, with fresh advice on the most healthful foods to choose at a variety of today's most popular restaurants, including Italian, French, Mexican, Spanish, Oriental, vegetarian, and American.

America's New Low-Fat Cuisine is designed to meet all of these requirements and more.

Taking Charge of Your Diet

Many of us work, run households, raise children, and still need to find time for ourselves. We also need to eat! And making it fast and simple is key. As a working mother and wife, I know that it's a real challenge to put great-tasting, well-balanced, healthful meals on the table day after day. My goal with America's New Low-Fat Cuisine is to help make home cooking efficient, convenient, healthful, and pleasurable — without distress.

The Nutritional Revolution Enters the Kitchen

Healthful eating is an important step in preventing major diseases, such as coronary heart disease and cancer. According to the latest discoveries in nutritional science, for best health and performance we each need to eat a wide variety of fresh, high-quality, wholesome foods. Overall, our meals and snacks should be low in fat (20 to 25 percent of total daily calories), low in cholesterol (100 to 300 milligrams per day), low in salt (between 1000 and 3300 milligrams of sodium per day), and low in refined sugars; moderate in protein (9 to 13 percent of total daily calories); and high in complex carbohydrates (65 to 68 percent of total daily calories) and fiber. This cookbook supplies up-to-date information in a practical, easy-to-use format that transforms these guidelines into meals and snacks that are great tasting and that put to rest, once and for all, the common notion that healthful eating is bland, boring, or unsatisfying.

It's also important to remember that while good nutrition is crucial for best health and fitness, it's only one part of the picture. Exercising regularly, controlling stress, reducing excess body fat, improving posture, and maintaining a positive environment and mental attitude are also key concerns.

America's New Low-Fat Cuisine is designed to complement and expand on the dietary recommendations provided in the book *Health & Fitness Excellence: The Comprehensive Action Plan* (Houghton Mifflin, 1989), written by my husband, Robert K. Cooper, Ph.D. The dietary guidelines in *America's New Low-Fat Cuisine* are consistent with those recommended by the U.S. Senate Select Subcommittee on Nutrition and Human Needs, in a report entitled "Dietary Goals for the United States"; the Food and Nutrition Board, National Academy of Sciences – National Research Council; the American Cancer Society; the American Heart Association; and the National Cancer Institute.

Complete Nutritional Analysis of Each Recipe, Meal Plan, Snack, and Dessert

It's become essential for all of us to know the details of our daily diet — how much fat, cholesterol, fiber, sodium, and so on, are in each meal and snack. Chapter 2 gives detailed guidelines for understanding, interpreting, calculating, and using these nutritional analyses. Each individual recipe and meal plan lists calories, grams of fat (monounsaturated, polyunsaturated, and saturated), protein, fiber, and carbohydrate, milligrams of cholesterol, calcium, and sodium, as well as percentage of total calories from fat, protein, and carbohydrate. This takes the confusion out of healthful eating and gives you the advantage of knowing, at a glance, the precise nutritional profile of your diet.

Step-by-Step Advice and Shortcuts

In accordance with the latest scientific guidelines for optimal nutrition, I've kept the fat content of the recipes and meal plans at an ideal level of 25 percent — or less — of total daily calories. Every recipe and menu is designed to fulfill the United States Recommended Daily Allowances set by the government. In the upcoming chapters, I'll share my suggestions for saving time in your kitchen. Many recipes in *America's New Low-Fat Cuisine* are vegetarian, featuring a variety of whole grains, legumes, fruits, vegetables, and low-fat or nonfat dairy products. Options are also included for heart-healthy seafood and poultry. And fabulous guilt-free desserts, ranging from old favorites to new creations, include everything from low-fat, whole-grain Brownie Pudding to the richest-tasting low-fat, low-cholesterol Lemon Meringue Pie you have ever enjoyed.

If you love good food *and* care about best health and performance, then I've written this cookbook for you.

With warmest wishes for best health and happiness,

Leslie L. Cooper

2

♦♦♦♦♦
♦♦♦♦♦

Getting the Most from This Cookbook

IT'S THE LITTLE THINGS that make a difference in healthful eating. This chapter can save you time in the kitchen and increase your ease and enjoyment in preparing delicious new meals and snacks.

Nutritional Analyses

Each recipe and meal plan in *America's New Low-Fat Cuisine* includes a computerized nutritional analysis for calories and a variety of nutrients. Dietary fat, cholesterol, heart disease, cancer, high blood pressure, and excess body fat are issues that affect every family in America. This cookbook makes it easy to see at a glance how much cholesterol, fat, fiber, sodium, or calcium a recipe or meal contains. And if body fat control is one of your goals, then choosing meals and snacks that are low in fat — and knowing how much dietary fat you consume in a day — can mean the difference between success and failure.

The exact amount of nutrients in food is influenced by a wide variety of factors, including the weather, water, soil, season, method of processing, length of storage, method of cooking, method of analysis, and so on. The source for nutrient information in this book is the United States Department of Agriculture (USDA), and I have used the latest available calculations. (See "References" on pages 333–334.) Where an analysis is incomplete because of missing government research data, a "+" is indicated next to the nutrient.

The United States government and leading research centers have developed average daily nutrient requirements for adults. Look at the following examples. I have included estimated daily requirements for myself and for my husband, Robert, to give you a more practical view. It's important to note that as your activity level increases, so does your caloric requirement. Children, teenagers, and pregnant and lactating women require more of some nutrients, too. Don't get trapped in the math, though. Remember that these figures are just helpful guidelines. These suggestions can be extremely useful in taking the guesswork out of eating a healthful diet. And factors like stress, exercise routine, general health, environment, air pollution, and so on, are not figured into these calculations. Perhaps in the not too distant future researchers will gather the data so they can be.

Examples of Estimated Daily Nutrient Requirements

"Typical Adult": Average daily allowance for adult men and women combined

Calories 2350

Cholesterol 250 milligrams

Total fat 52 grams

Protein 45–65 grams

Carbohydrate 408 grams

Dietary fiber 30 grams

Calcium 800–1000 milligrams

Sodium 1100–3300 milligrams

Fat = 20% of total calories

Protein = 9–13% of total calories

Carbohydrate = 65–68% of total calories

Leslie L. Cooper: Female, age 31, height 5'7", weight 115 pounds, moderately active

Calories 2000

Cholesterol 250 milligrams

Total fat 45 grams

Protein 44 grams

Carbohydrate 340 grams

Dietary fiber 20–30 grams

Calcium 800–1000 milligrams

Sodium 1100–3300 milligrams

Fat = 20% of total calories

Protein = 9–13% of total calories

Carbohydrate = 65–68% of total calories

Robert K. Cooper: Male, age 40, height 5'10", weight 160 pounds, moderately active

Calories 2800

Cholesterol 250 milligrams

Total fat 62 grams

Protein 56 grams

Carbohydrate 465 grams

Dietary fiber 26–30 grams

Calcium 800 milligrams

Sodium 1100–3300 milligrams

Fat = 20% of total calories

Protein = 9–13% of total calories

Carbohydrate = 65–68% of total calories

In *America's New Low-Fat Cuisine,* each recipe and meal plan is followed by a nutritional analysis that looks something like this:

Nutritional Analysis: 1 serving
cal 129; chol 24 mg; fat-total 2.8 g; fat-mono 0.8 g; fat-poly 0.3 g; fat-sat 1.5 g; protein 3.67 g; carbo 23.3 g; fiber 1.45 g+; calcium 148 mg; sodium 107 mg; fat 19%; protein 11%; carbo 70%

The serving size is determined by the number of portions that a recipe makes — listed at the top right-hand corner of each recipe. If the recipe lists four servings, the food total for the meal is divided into fourths and the analysis applies to one-fourth.

Calories: The average number of daily calories required for men is approximately 2500 to 3000, and the average for moderately active women, about 2000. Some weight loss programs recommend cutting to less than 1000 calories per day. This may be dangerous, and *any* diet plan calling for 1200 calories per day or less should be undertaken only with a medical doctor's supervision. To lose excess body fat, a number of experts also recommend limiting fat to approximately 20 percent or less of total daily calories and increasing activity levels, preferably with regular aerobic exercise.

Cholesterol: The National Institutes of Health Consensus Conference on Lowering Blood Cholesterol suggests that individuals consume no more than 250 milligrams of dietary cholesterol per day. For those with high blood cholesterol levels, a family history of heart disease, or those who have previously suffered from a cholesterol-related problem, some authorities are suggesting a diet with less than 100 milligrams of cholesterol daily.

Cholesterol is found only in animal products. This includes dairy foods, whole eggs, poultry, fish, and meat. The recipes in this cookbook that include butter or whole eggs have low-cholesterol substitution options. Where suggested, replace butter and eggs with margarine and egg whites or egg replacer. A separate nutritional analysis is provided for these low-cholesterol options.

Fat: Excess dietary fat in general, saturated fat in particular, have become leading health concerns. In each nutritional analysis, fat is broken down into four separate figures — fat-total, fat-mono, fat-poly, and fat-sat. Total fat is the combination of monounsaturated fat, polyunsaturated fat, and saturated fat. Fat quantities are presented in grams and as a percentage of total calories. A healthful diet should not include more than 20 percent of total daily calories from fat, including about one-third as polyunsaturates, one-third or less as saturates, and the balance as monounsaturates. Infants and toddlers need more dietary fat than older children and adults. In *America's New Low-Fat Cuisine,* meals generally have 20 to 25 percent or less of total calories from fat. Average Americans consume 40 percent or more of their calories in the form of dietary fat. If you have a history of, or are prone to, heart disease, your physician may recommend consuming even less saturated fat. The total amount of dietary fat in one serving of a recipe or meal is indicated by the fat-total.

What does it mean when we say 20 to 25 percent of total daily calories from fat? For most of us, this amounts to about 45 to 70 grams of fat per day, depending on caloric intake and activity level. And how do you calculate how many grams of fat are in your foods? This cookbook makes it simple. Basically, you need to think in terms of grams of fat *and* percentage of calories from fat in your diet.

Let's say you choose to eat a light lunch at a restaurant and begin by ordering a beverage — mineral water or iced tea — and a vegetable salad with a tablespoon of dressing. Some people — especially those of us who are weight-conscious — tend to make this the entire meal. At first glance, this might sound like a low-calorie, healthful lunch — high in fiber, low in grams of fat (if only a small amount of the dressing is used) and calories. But there's a problem. Because the salad and beverage are very low in calories, the majority of your dietary calories are coming from the salad dressing, which by itself is usually high in fat. This means that the meal is very high in its percentage of calories from fat. But it's easy to change that by limiting the amount of salad dressing to less than a tablespoon (or, better yet, choose a low-fat or nonfat dressing) and then by adding a slice of whole-grain bread to the meal and perhaps a small amount of legumes to the salad. These wholesome foods will raise the carbohydrate and protein level of the lunch.

It's also important to go beyond caloric percentage to the actual *quantity* of fat, in grams. If you overeat — by consuming huge portions or eating second and third helpings at each meal — the percentage of fat in your diet may be 20 to 25 percent of total calories, but since the total calorie count is excessively high, the number of *grams* of fat will be too high. Try to keep in mind that anguish over exact numbers is not the answer. Instead, focus on keeping dietary fat low and increasing the complex carbohydrates in your diet.

Some foods are very deceiving when it comes to fat content.

Although they may be acceptable if consumed on occasion in small quantities, it's very important to be aware of them.

For example:

◆ There are 30 grams of fat in one avocado. That can be more than half a day's worth of total fat.

◆ All of the calories in olives are from fat. They contain no calories from protein or carbohydrate.

◆ One glass of whole milk provides 8 grams of fat and has 49 percent of its calories from fat, as opposed to skim milk with just a trace.

◆ One tablespoon of oil has 14 grams of fat.

◆ Tempeh and tofu (made from soybeans) are good vegetarian protein sources, but they are also relatively high in fat. Tempeh has 8 to 10 grams of fat in a 4-ounce serving (that's about 44 percent of calories from fat) and a half cup of tofu has 4 grams of fat (48 percent of its calories from fat).

◆ One tablespoon of regular mayonnaise has 12 grams of fat. Some "light" varieties have about 5 grams.

◆ One tablespoon of peanut butter has 8 grams of fat, or 69 percent of calories from fat.

◆ Most nuts are between 74 and 86 percent fat.

Remember, the key is combining small amounts of these higher-fat foods properly with low-fat and nonfat ingredients in meals.

Protein: Protein deficiencies are extremely rare in America today. In fact, statistics show that most of us eating the "average American diet" get too much protein, especially if we eat meat, dairy products, seafood, and poultry. Unfortunately, computer programs do not yet take into account *complete protein* (containing all essential amino acids — found in animal products or in the combination of certain grains and legumes) as compared to *incomplete protein* (missing one or more essential amino acids). Our bodies much more efficiently use complete protein. The Recommended Daily Allowance (RDA) for protein, set by the National Academy of Sciences, does not distinguish between complete and incomplete protein. So some protein quantities in the computerized nutritional analyses in this cookbook and others may seem a bit higher than they actually are.

Carbohydrates: Until recently, complex carbohydrates were known as "starches" and were considered fattening. This view has changed dramatically in recent years. Researchers at national health organizations now recommend that carbohydrates be the mainstay of our diets — about two-thirds of total daily calories. Complex carbohydrates include most vegetables and all grains (including pasta, bread, and so on). Simple carbohydrates include sugars and sweeteners and are considered "empty calories" because they provide little nutritional value to meals or snacks. It's important to minimize simple carbohydrates in the diet, using them to enhance the flavor of more healthful foods. When buying packaged foods, read the ingredient labels to be sure you're getting foods containing low-fat, high-quality complex carbohydrates.

Dietary Fiber: Adequate dietary fiber is essential to good health. There are two general types of dietary fiber, soluble and insoluble. Receiving enough of both types is easy if your diet includes a wide variety of whole grains, legumes, vegetables, and fruits. While there is no official recommended daily intake for dietary fiber, the National Cancer Institute suggests that adults consume about 20 to 30 grams per day, or approximately 1 gram of fiber for every 100 calories. The fiber content and type of dietary fiber in some whole-grain foods has not yet been fully analyzed by researchers. Therefore some of the recipes in this cookbook have a "+" next to the fiber analysis, indicating that the fiber content, a combination of soluble and insoluble, is a low estimate. Whole-grain pasta is one of the foods that is missing in government data on fiber. Because whole-grain pasta is quite high in fiber, the analysis will show less fiber than is actually present in that recipe.

Calcium: This mineral is found in dairy products and in smaller quantities in other foods. It is necessary for bone growth and maintenance. A few of the meals in this cookbook have a relatively low calcium level because they are dairyless. To ensure that you receive the full daily calcium requirement, have a bowl of cereal with skim milk for breakfast or a snack that includes low-fat or nonfat dairy products. The Food and Nutrition Board, National Academy of Sciences–National Research Council, has set the recommended dietary allowance per day for calcium — 800 milligrams for the typical adult, and 1200 milligrams for young adults and pregnant or lactating women.

Sodium: A variety of wholesome foods contain small amounts of naturally occurring sodium. This cookbook usually lists salt as an option. In a few recipes, such as yeast bread, a small amount of salt is necessary. I prefer sea salt. If you are used to the flavor of salt, foods made without it may taste a bit bland at first. As you begin to reduce the amount of salt in your diet, the natural taste of food will be enhanced. Begin by reducing the quantity of salt in your cooking and leave the salt shaker on the table for each person to add a dash as desired. A secret to cooking without salt is in the addition of herbs and spices. The National Academy of Sciences–National Research Council's Food and Nutrition Board has specified "safe and adequate" intakes for sodium from 1000 to 3300 milligrams per day.

Wines Used in Cooking

Certain types of alcoholic beverages — the most common of which are dry white and red wine — can be used in cooking to enhance flavor and add subtle yet unique brightness to a recipe. When wine or another alcoholic beverage is heated above 175 degrees Fahrenheit, the alcohol evaporates, leaving a special taste behind to mingle with your dish. When the recipe is heated as directed, there will be no alcohol flavor. The "Resources" section in the back of the book contains two sources for purchasing organic wines.

Portion Sizes and Cooking Times for Convenience

Each recipe gives portion sizes or number of servings. Most recipes serve 4 to 6 people and can be cut in half or doubled, as needed, without altering flavor. Taste to adjust seasonings before serving. Save leftover food for a snack or lunch the following day, or freeze it for future fast meals.

Each recipe lists estimated times for preparation, cooking or baking, and, where appropriate, chilling, soaking, or marinating. This will help you plan your time effectively. Preparation, or "prep," time is the time it takes to prepare the ingredients — wash, cut, sauté, and so on. "Cook" and "bake" times refer to the actual baking or cooking needed to complete the dish.

Planning Ahead

It's a familiar scene. You find yourself hungry, standing in front of an open refrigerator, staring, waiting for the perfect food to jump out and say "cook me." Occasionally, I still catch myself without a plan, and my head in the fridge.

Planning your meals and snacks in advance can save you time and energy. I usually find it easiest to take time each evening, once the day has slowed down, to plan the next day's menu. If certain ingredients are frozen, I take them out to thaw. This is also a perfect time to write out a grocery list for upcoming meal plans. Then I have the foods on hand that I need. Once I decide on my family's lunches and snacks, I don't have to be concerned about it again until I prepare the food. Planning can certainly make cooking more pleasurable.

Foods Prepared in Advance

One tried-and-true way to save time in the kitchen — and still have nutritionally balanced meals — is to use leftovers. But instead of using the word *leftovers*, let's say "foods prepared in advance." It sounds better. And besides, that's what all the new low-fat, gourmet frozen or deli snacks, appetizers, and entrees are these days — fresh foods prepared in advance.

Those of us who work all day can use advance meal planning to choose quality breakfasts, a variety of snacks, and put dinner on the table efficiently and conveniently. But what about lunch? Eating out, ordering in, or brown-bag lunches are the usual choices.

But more and more people are finding convenient ways to expand their lunch choices with foods prepared in advance. When cooking soups, stews, chilis, casseroles, pies, marinated salads, even pastas, burgers, or kebabs — make extra. Then you can store the additional food in airtight containers and refrigerate it for the next day's lunch, or label it and freeze it for a future meal.

Microwave ovens are now available in most lunchrooms and in three-quarters of all American homes. By dividing the leftover food into individual portions and storing it in microwave-safe containers, you and other members of your family can heat up delicious and nutritious, quick homemade meals during work hours. Even if a microwave oven isn't available, you can use a thermos container to keep cool foods cool and preheated foods warm. When you're prepared, doubling a recipe takes no extra time, and it can provide you with additional meals or snacks.

In *The Enchanted Broccoli Forest* (Ten Speed Press, 1982), Mollie Katzen gives a wonderful pep talk about improvising in the kitchen. Her message: If you love food, you can be a good improvisational cook! So next time you look into the refrigerator and see ingredients that may begin growing if you don't use them soon, lay them out on the counter and use your imagination to create a dish that incorporates these still-fresh odds and ends. Pasta dishes and casseroles are likely candidates for these miscellaneous foods. And who knows, you may even create a new recipe that becomes a favorite.

Making Healthful Choices in Your Grocery Store

Reading food product labels has become much easier in the past decade. New labeling requirements have benefited every health-conscious shopper. Once you know what you want — and don't want — in the foods you buy, you can read the ingredient list on a product and make a decision as to whether or not to buy it.

American consumers are sending food manufacturers a message. Light foods are not only appearing on grocery shelves, but they are selling very well. As long as it tastes good and is in some way better for us, why not? But be wary. Consumers must keep a discerning eye out for advertising ploys and erroneous claims. Reading between the lines and really understanding what to look for on a product label is key.

"Light" foods seem to be popping up everywhere. Read labels carefully. Light mayonnaise actually is light in fat — 5 grams per tablespoon, as compared to the usual 12 grams. Light cream cheese is also a good substitution for the regular variety — 5 grams of fat, as compared to 10 grams in regular cream cheese. Several companies now offer reduced-fat and low-sodium Swiss and Cheddar cheeses. These lower-fat cheeses are made with part–skim milk as are the familiar part–skim milk mozzarella and farmer cheeses. Look for cheeses that have only 5 grams of fat or less per one-ounce serving. Some tortilla and potato chips even come in "light" varieties these days, with approximately half the amount of fat that's in the original variety. But be aware that these foods can still be very high in fat, so quantities *must* be limited. "Light" means only that the product has less fat, salt, sugar, or calories than the original variety.

Another product that has come under scrutiny lately for the use of the term "light" is "Extra-Light Olive Oil." This product doesn't have less fat, sodium, or calories, but it is lighter in taste. This can be an asset for those who want to use a monounsaturated fat in baking and other foods, where the flavor of regular olive oil may be too strong.

Reading food product labels gives you a good head start on choosing the best foods for you and your family. The following list of resources can help you learn more about specific foods, preservatives, and unfamiliar names on food product labels.

Resources: Where to Learn More about Specific Foods

The Catalogue of Healthy Food by John Tepper Marlin, Ph.D. (Bantam, 1990).

The Complete Eater's Digest & Nutrition Scoreboard by Michael F. Jacobson, Ph.D. (Doubleday, 1985).

Composition of Foods: Raw, Processed, Prepared (Handbook No. 8) by the Agricultural Research Service (United States Department of Agriculture, 1975). For sale by the Superintendent of Documents, U.S. Government Printing Office, Washington, D.C. 20402; (202) 783-3238.

Food Facts by Evelyn Roehl (Food Learning Center, P.O. Box 402, Winona, Minnesota 55987; 1984).

The Goldbecks' Guide to Good Food by Nikki and David Goldbeck (Plume, 1987).

Health & Fitness Excellence: The Comprehensive Action Plan by Robert K. Cooper (Houghton Mifflin, 1989).

Jane Brody's Good Food Book by Jane Brody (Norton, 1985).

Jane Brody's Nutrition Book by Jane Brody (Bantam, 1987).

Kitchen Science by Howard Hillman (Houghton Mifflin, 1989).

Nutritive Value of Foods (Home and Garden Bulletin No. 72) by Human Nutrition Information Service (United States Department of Agriculture, 1981). For sale by the Superintendent of Documents, U.S. Government Printing Office, Washington, D.C. 20402; (202) 783-3238.

On Food and Cooking by Harold McGee (Macmillan, 1988).

The Wholefood Catalog by Nava Atlas (Fawcett, 1988).

The Whole Foods Encyclopedia by Rebecca Wood (Prentice Hall, 1988).

Additional Tips

◆ The measurements in this cookbook are for *rounded — not level — spoonfuls.*

◆ *Al dente* literally means "to the tooth." It is often used in reference to pasta that is cooked until it is firm to the bite or chewy.

◆ When a recipe tells you to "lightly oil" a pan or dish, use the smallest possible amount of butter, margarine, oil, or a nonstick cooking spray.

◆ When sautéing, heat the suggested amount of oil in the pan first (be careful not to let it overheat and smoke), to prevent the foods from absorbing much of the oil.

◆ Whenever possible, look for products that are unsalted.

◆ To reduce the sodium content in salted canned legumes, fish, and feta cheese, rinse them under cool water and/or soak in cool water for 15 minutes and then rinse and drain.

◆ Salt is listed as optional throughout this cookbook. If you are accustomed to salty foods, begin by adding salt to recipes as needed to meet your personal preferences or those of your family. Then gradually decrease the amount of salt you use in cooking.

◆ Fructose, honey, and maple syrup are the preferred sweeteners in some recipes. Equal quantities of sugar may be substituted for fructose.

◆ Wine is used in cooking in some of the recipes. Choose a dry, inexpensive variety. See the "Resources" section for companies that sell organic wine.

◆ Low-fat cottage cheese is used in the recipes, and nutritional analyses is 2 percent fat. If you have access to a good-quality 1-percent-fat cottage cheese, choose it instead.

◆ Cultured nonfat buttermilk is available in many markets. Low-fat buttermilk may be substituted if nonfat is not available.

◆ In recipes that call for whole-grain flour, any type of whole-grain flour may be used. I have a favorite mix: equal parts oat flour, barley flour, brown rice flour, and millet flour. You may also use whole-wheat pastry flour. Refer to the "Whole-Grain Cooking Chart" in Chapter 7 for more information. When recipes call for whole-grain flour, the nutritional analyses are calculated using whole-wheat flour.

◆ Commercial breads may be substituted for homemade. Choose a whole-grain bread made without added fat. I prefer French, Italian, or Vienna. Bagels are also a good choice.

◆ Olive oil is recommended over other cooking oils because it is a mostly monounsaturated (75–80 percent) fat. A number of health authorities believe that monounsaturated fats may be a better choice than either polyunsaturated or saturated fats. You can also use canola oil, another oil high in monounsaturated fat.

◆ When called for, potatoes should be washed well and not peeled unless otherwise stated in the recipe. Be sure to avoid green spots and sprouting eyes.

◆ When called for, cucumbers should be peeled unless they are homegrown or unwaxed.

◆ All herbs and spices used in the recipes are *dried* unless *fresh* is specified.

◆ Sprouted seeds and grains may be added to any of the recipes in this book. They are especially good in sandwiches, salads, and with Mexican food. Try growing your own sprouts at home. Be sure to eat sprouts while at their peak of freshness (before they are about eight days old).

◆ Yeast breads have no preparation times listed. Exact baking time is determined by many variables. Refer to Chapter 7 on baking bread.

◆ A large clove of garlic should be approximately the size of a quarter. Garlic is used extensively throughout this cookbook. It is a wonderful flavor enhancer, and some studies suggest it is a very positive addition to healthful meals.

◆ The yogurt used in the recipes is nonfat plain yogurt. If nonfat is not available, low-fat may be substituted.

◆ The flavor and quality of freshly ground black pepper is superior to preground. A variety of peppercorns can be mixed for a special seasoning. My favorite is a mix of black, white, green (dried), and pink (or rose). Some companies now offer these peppercorns already mixed — see "Resources" at the back of the book.

◆ Cayenne pepper is a hot pepper and may be used in *small* quantities to add a spicy, not-too-hot flavor.

◆ Regular canned tomatoes may replace canned Italian-style tomatoes if necessary. Look for the unsalted variety containing only tomatoes and juice. Tomato purée and crushed tomatoes are interchangeable.

◆ Dried fruits are best when unsulphured and unsweetened.

◆ Parmesan cheese tastes best when freshly grated. This cheese may be stored in a tightly covered container in the refrigerator. Although Parmesan cheese is relatively high in fat and sodium, you need only small amounts because of its strong flavor.

◆ In recipes that call for vegetable broth, use 1 teaspoon of vegetable broth powder mixed with 1 cup water. Chicken broth may be substituted for vegetable; look for a low-sodium, reduced-fat variety.

◆ Some recipes call for eggs, or egg whites, or egg replacer. This option is for those who choose not to eat eggs or whole eggs. For use in recipes, two egg whites equal one whole egg. There are also several egg replacers available. Choose the one that best suits your needs.

◆ Reduced-sodium soy sauce contains less salt than regular brands of soy sauce and can add flavor to a number of recipes.

◆ Mustard is noted in the recipes in this book in several ways: Dijon-style mustard is a wet mustard that has wine added and is finely ground. Prepared mustard is any style wet mustard. Dry mustard powder is dried, ground mustard seeds.

◆ When margarine is used instead of butter, the nutritional analysis is calculated using regular hard, 80-percent-fat margarine.

I wrote this cookbook as a guide to the new era of delicious, healthful eating, and I've included a variety of recipe options so that each meal will reflect your personal touch.

Because I live a good distance from a grocery store, when I don't have all the ingredients I need, I improvise. With a bit of thoughtfulness, you too can create a variety of new recipes.

The 28-day meal plan has been designed to help you eat a well-balanced diet that meets the latest nutritional guidelines. I have combined various recipes to create balanced menus. When you choose not to follow the designed meal plans, pay attention to the fact that some recipes are higher in fat and protein than others. For example, avoid serving a higher-fat salad or dressing with an entree that is also higher in fat.

If some of the foods or meals in this cookbook are new to you, please make a slow transition, especially if you are feeding a family. Successful changes take time. This is not another fad diet that will come and go. Make a gradual move toward a lifelong way of healthful eating. At first, be sure to choose those meals and snacks that you feel will get the best response. Then slowly begin adding new tastes. This is the best way to step into the new era of delicious, healthful eating.

3

Meals in Minutes: Preparing Fast Meals at Home

CHANCES ARE, your busy schedule limits time for meal preparation. But fixing fast meals doesn't mean you need to compromise on food quality. In the time it takes to cook a TV dinner in the oven or drive to a fast-food restaurant, you can prepare a variety of healthful, fast meals. And your best ally in the kitchen is organization.

Many of the recipes in this cookbook can be completed in just minutes, and these are listed in the "Fast-Meal Index." Each of the meals takes forty-five minutes *or less,* from start to finish.

Be sure to plan ahead. Many legume dishes, for example, need advance preparation, such as soaking legumes overnight. Delicious legume recipes (such as Caribbean Black Bean Soup) need to soak and cook quite a while, yet the actual work time in the kitchen is minimal.

Getting Organized

When it comes to cooking, being organized gives you the feeling that you are in control of your kitchen and your diet.

If you have a family, delegate kitchen responsibilities — setting and clearing the table, washing the dishes, and so on. There's no reason that the cook should do all the work. One of my biggest pleasures is creating a special meal and being finished in the kitchen when the meal reaches the table. Then it's time for *me* to relax.

If you work outside the home, organize your time so that when you arrive home you can accomplish a sequence of kitchen tasks. Keep a pen and paper available to write things down — your grocery list, recipe changes, whatever. When I run low on an ingredient I add it to my grocery list. Changes, additions, or personal notes should be written down *in* cookbooks so you remember your thoughts the next time you choose that recipe.

Several books do a particularly good job of sharing helpful kitchen advice for the interested cook. *Jane Brody's Good Food Book* and *The Joy*

18

of Cooking by Irma S. Rombauer and Marion R. Becker are good examples.

Stocking Up

Keeping things stocked up means fewer trips to the store, saving both time and money. First, appraise your kitchen space. If you live in a small apartment, pantry and freezer space may be limited. Consider rearranging your kitchen, putting up some additional shelves, and getting rid of items you haven't used in a long time. Then stock up on the things you find essential from day to day.

Here's a listing of the ingredients I keep on hand — for meals in minutes and for other recipes throughout this cookbook. Once you try a variety of recipes, you can create your own "stock up" list.

Grains and Flours (Keep flour in the freezer for extended storage.):
Brown rice (I prefer short grain for *paella* and *risotto* and long grain for most other dishes.)
Hot cereal grains (My family's favorites include: millet, cream of brown rice, corn grits, cream of rye, as well as oatmeal, and oat bran. Try combining several grains for a mixed whole-grain cereal.)
Hulled barley
Popcorn
Oat bran
Rolled oats
Whole-grain flours (barley, oat, cornmeal, rye, buckwheat, millet, brown-rice, or other)
Whole-wheat flour and whole-wheat pastry flour

Bread and Pasta Products (Breads can be stored in the freezer and thawed as needed.):
Rice cakes (Lundberg rice cakes have more flavor than most.)
Rye crackers (Wasa Crispbread, Finn Crisps, Kavali, or others without added fats.)
Whole-grain bread (Ezekiel bread by Food for Life has no added fat and is great for sandwiches. Look for other breads without added fat.)
Whole-grain pastas (Some of my favorites: linguine, fettuccine, spaghetti, angel hair, ziti, mostaccioli, shells, macaroni, spirals.)
Whole-wheat pita bread
Whole-wheat tortillas or *chapatis* (Indian whole-wheat flat bread)

Dry Goods:
Active dry yeast
Arrowroot (Use instead of cornstarch.)
Baking powder
Baking soda
Carob powder
Cold cereals (Choose those that have no added fat and are low in, or
   have no, added sugar.)
Dried fruits (raisins, currants, dates, and others)
Nuts and seeds (Stock and use in small quantities: almonds, walnuts,
   pine nuts, pecans, pumpkin seeds, sunflower seeds, poppy seeds,
   hulled sesame seeds, and others.)
Peanut butter (without added oil)
Tahini (sesame seed butter)

Sweeteners:
Fructose
Honey
Maple syrup
Molasses (Barbados is my favorite.)

Herbs, Spices, and Dry Seasonings:
Allspice
Basil
Bay leaves
Caraway
Cayenne pepper (Various "hotness" ratings are available.)
Celery seeds
Chili powder (There are many varieties, from hot to mild. Some are
   made from ground chili peppers, and some include other herbs.
   Experiment to find your favorites.)
Cinnamon
Cloves
Coriander
Cream of tartar
Cumin
Curry
Dill weed
Garlic, granulated or powder
Ginger
Marjoram

Mustard powder
Nonfat dry milk powder
Nutmeg
Oregano
Paprika
Peppercorns (Black or a variety of peppercorn types makes a wonderful seasoning. Freshly ground is much more flavorful than preground. My favorite is Nouvelle Mix from G. B. Ratto & Company. See "Resources" for catalogue address.)
Red pepper flakes
Rosemary
Saffron (This is a very expensive spice, but a little goes a long way. Make sure you get real saffron, which is made from crocus stigmas, not safflowers.)
Sage
Sea salt (Many people prefer its flavor to that of standard iodized salt. Try sea salt from the French Mediterranean, available from G. B. Ratto & Company. See "Resources" for catalogue address.)
Tarragon
Thyme
Turmeric
Vegetable broth powder

Oils, Condiments, and Wet Seasonings:
Canola oil (or another high-quality, mild-flavored monounsaturated or polyunsaturated oil)
Flavored extracts (especially vanilla, lemon, and almond)
Jam, jelly, conserves, preserves, fruit spreads
Ketchup (Some varieties are now made with honey instead of corn syrup, or have less sodium.)
Mustard (Dijon-style and country or stone-ground)
Olive oil (Extra-virgin is best.)
Soy sauce (Reduced-sodium is best.)
Tabasco hot pepper sauce
Vinegars (Balsamic, white wine, red wine, champagne, raspberry, apple cider, or others. Good-quality, well-flavored vinegars can reduce the amount of oil needed in salads and dressings.)
Wine, red and white, dry (for cooking)
Worcestershire sauce (Some natural foods stores carry varieties without anchovies or preservatives.)

Canned Goods:
Artichoke hearts (packed in water)
Beans (navy, pinto, kidney, garbanzo, etc.)
Chilis, green
Evaporated skim milk
Fruit (packed in fruit juice only, without added sweeteners)
Fruit juice
Italian-style tomatoes (or substitute regular whole tomatoes)
Olives, black
Pimientos (G. B. Ratto & Company has the best quality I've ever
    seen — from Spain.)
Refried beans (without lard or other saturated fats)
Salmon, pink or red
Salsa or picante sauce
Tomato and/or vegetable juice
Tomato paste
Tomato sauce (without added fat is best)
Tomatoes, crushed or puréed
Tuna fish (packed in water)

Dairy Products:
Butter, unsalted (substitute margarine if necessary)
Cottage cheese (1- or 2-percent-fat)
Cultured buttermilk, nonfat or low-fat
Hard cheeses, low-fat (Swiss, Cheddar, mozzarella)
Parmesan cheese
Ricotta cheese, low-fat or light
Skim milk
Yogurt, nonfat plain

Other Perishables:
Carrots, peppers, celery, lettuce (and other fresh vegetables)
Eggs (or egg replacer)
Garlic
Lemons and limes
Mushrooms
Onions (red and yellow)
Parsley (and other fresh herbs)
Potatoes
Poultry (fresh or frozen)
Seafood (fresh or frozen)

Tempeh (store in the freezer until ready to use)
Tofu

Some Indispensable Utensils

Many cookbooks devote a great deal of space to choosing the perfect kitchen utensils. Here's a short listing of the utensils and equipment I find indispensable in my kitchen. These tools make cooking tasks less time consuming.

Knives: Every section on kitchen tools should start with the advantages of a good-quality set of kitchen knives. Once you've chosen a set, keep them sharp! A wood block that holds the knives can be a good investment. The knives stay in much better condition than if they were clanging against each other in a drawer. Use a chef's sharpening steel to keep them razor sharp.

Food processor: Shop around to choose the kitchen marvel that best suits your needs and budget. There are many sizes, styles, brands, and price ranges available. A food processor can save you time chopping, slicing, puréeing, and so on.

Hand-held electric mixer: This low-cost item comes in very handy. I like to use mine to beat the yeast and a little flour when making homemade whole-grain bread; this procedure helps develop the gluten and creates a better texture. Also handy for beating egg whites, creaming butter (or margarine) for cookies and snacks.

Lemon juicer: For about two dollars you can get a little contraption that squeezes juice from lemons while screening out the seeds.

Lettuce spinner: Available in most kitchen and hardware stores these days, this unit is a big help. After washing lettuce, spin it dry in this container. No more wet towels and time wasted on hand drying each leaf before making a fresh salad.

Garlic press: This could very well be the tool I use most often in my kitchen. Remove a clove of garlic from its head and lightly crush it under a cutting board or your palm to crack the skin. Peel, place inside the press, and squeeze. The traditional method of chopping the garlic into fine pieces takes minutes longer.

Certain kitchen tools, such as a *hot-air popcorn popper* and *nonstick pans,* can really help lower the fat in your diet. Since low-fat cooking is important for good health, consider using a nonstick pan for certain recipes so you don't have to add extra fat to keep food from sticking.

New kinds of nonstick surfaces are popping up on the cookware scene, including Corning's Pyrex Clear Advantage bakeware with

Invisi-Clean coating and Le Creuset's cast-iron skillets with Glisse-mail enamel coating. Another old favorite found in nature is soapstone.

Quickening the Cooking Time

A microwave oven and pressure cooker can both help you cook certain foods faster. If speed is of the essence, you may want to consider incorporating these items into your kitchen.

Surveys show that 70 to 75 percent of all homes now have a microwave oven. A microwave can quicken the defrosting and reheating of some recipes in this cookbook. And you can reduce preparation and cooking times with a microwave, especially in long-cooking items such as casseroles, sauces, squash, and some legume dishes. Certain recipes and foods are not particularly well suited to microwave cooking. These include baked products, especially those made with whole grains, and baked potatoes seem to lose their crispy jackets and light, fluffy centers. If microwave cooking is popular in your home, a good book on the subject is the *Microwave Gourmet Healthstyle Cookbook* by Barbara Kafka (Morrow, 1989).

A pressure cooker is a valuable addition to the kitchen in any busy household, shortening cooking time by a third or more. There is no faster way to cook legumes, which take approximately thirty minutes in a pressure cooker, instead of a couple of hours. Slow-cooking sauces, soups, chili, even brown rice, can be cooked to perfection in a third of the normal cooking time, without loss of flavor. Most pressure cookers come with detailed instructions. For more insights on using a pressure cooker in a variety of ways, refer to *Cooking Under Pressure* by Lorna Sass (Morrow, 1989).

Advance Preparation

The evening meal may be the one time of day we can get together as a family. And with today's hectic lifestyles, the family meal may soon become obsolete. Many of us find ourselves so busy during the week that finding the time and energy to cook a well-balanced meal is difficult. The average American now eats at least four meals a week in restaurants. For all of us in this situation, advance preparation becomes a big help in providing healthful meals and snacks. Weekends are an opportune time to do some meal planning and preparation for the upcoming week. And choosing to spend some extra time cooking at home on the weekends may even help maintain or bring back family mealtime.

For example, if you plan to make a recipe during the week that calls for cooked legumes, try preparing them on the weekend and freezing them until needed. Even raw bread dough can be frozen and thawed, raised, and baked when you want a quick, fresh loaf of homemade bread.

Double the Recipe: Two Meals Instead of One

I always prepare a double recipe when I cook soup, casseroles, chili, legumes, and other recipes that freeze well. Purchase some containers with tight-fitting lids. I put half the dish in these containers or wrap it very well. Mark the container top, noting the contents, the date, the approximate number of portions, and then freeze. On a day when you won't have time to cook, remove one of the containers from the freezer that morning, or the night before, and thaw. Add a quick salad and some bread, and you have a healthful, homemade, and delicious meal in minutes.

If you forget to remove something from the freezer and come home wishing you had, choose a soup or stew that can be heated in a double boiler while still frozen. If you have a microwave, you can thaw any dish in minutes.

Other Quick Tips

◆ Presoak legumes, as suggested in the "How to Cook Legumes" section in Chapter 7. If you rinse, sort, and soak beans overnight in the refrigerator, then they are ready to be cooked when you arrive home from work. Legumes require only about twenty to thirty minutes in a pressure cooker.

◆ Keep healthful loaves of bread in the freezer. Being able to defrost a loaf of bread quickly can round out a fast meal nicely, adding extra carbohydrates.

◆ Many of the quick breads in this cookbook are easy and fast to prepare. Whole-Grain Irish Soda Bread, Whole-Grain Buttermilk Biscuits, Onion Rye Flat Bread, Pita Chips, and many of the muffin recipes are also the perfect addition to a fast meal.

◆ Many new commercial products are lower in fat, sodium, and sugar than their predecessors. Even some old standbys like Campbell's tomato soup can be made with skim milk for a fast and easy soup choice. Progresso makes some vegetarian soups that are good-tasting and relatively low in fat. And some of the tomato sauces on the market are made with little or no fat or salt added and can be poured over pasta for a quick meal. Many companies have a nutritional analysis right on the package, including grams of fat, milligrams of cholesterol, sodium, and so on.

Fast Recipe Ideas for Meals in Minutes

Pasta is a popular fast-food standby in my kitchen. When I need a quick meal, I reach into the pantry for any of the dozen pasta varieties — spaghetti and linguine to rotini or wagon wheels — that I keep stocked in my pantry.

There are so many options with pasta, from uncooked pesto sauce to slow-cooked homemade tomato sauce, each lending its own flavor to this wonderful food that cooks in less than ten minutes.

Open a can of tomato sauce, toss in appropriate leftovers, a can of cooked beans, cooked chicken, seafood, tempeh, tofu, or vegetables, and you have a main course. I often put up a pot of water to boil for pasta while I heat a little olive oil in a skillet and sauté some garlic and onion, then look around for whatever else may work in the sauté. Add a bit of tomato sauce and skim or evaporated skim milk to make a creamy red sauce. Cook the pasta and toss with Parmesan cheese and the sauce.

It's so fast and easy to improvise with pasta. The more you experiment, the more recipes you'll create.

Oriental dishes are another fast-meal option. Cook a little brown rice or soba (buckwheat) noodles and top them with a sauce of quickly sautéed vegetables — with or without chicken, seafood, tempeh, tofu, or legumes.

Seafood can also be a fast-meal option. It needs to cook only ten minutes per inch thickness of fish.

Chicken breasts can cook in minutes to form the basis for a variety of fast meals.

Turkey breasts are sold in many markets. Look for a fresh split breast to quickly grill or broil, and serve with a grain and vegetable for an easy meal.

Beanwiches are a favorite standby in my house. Heat up homemade or canned refried beans and spread a thin layer inside a whole-wheat pita pocket. Top with salsa, tomatoes, lettuce or sprouts, a little low-fat Cheddar cheese, and some sliced onion, green chilis, Cottage Cream (page 319), and olives. Now you have a great sandwich.

Mexican food can be fast and simple, too. Use whole-wheat tortillas and make burritos, soft-shell tacos, or tostadas with the same fillings as listed for beanwiches.

Turkey burgers can be made quickly if the ground turkey breast is defrosted. Make extra burgers and store them in the freezer. They thaw and cook quickly.

Pita pizza has become my husband's favorite fast food. Heat the oven to 350°F and bake whole-wheat pita bread until slightly crisp. Spread tomato sauce on the top, sprinkle with chopped vegetables, a little low-fat mozzarella cheese, and a crumble of oregano. Bake until the cheese melts.

Fast Doesn't Have to Mean Furious

Preparing a healthful, well-balanced meal doesn't have to be stressful, even in today's busy world. Let the "Fast-Meal Index" in the back of this cookbook help. If you have some personal favorite fast-meal recipes but aren't sure whether they meet the latest nutritional guidelines for good health, turn to Chapter 4, "Recipes You Know and Love: Gentle Ways to Make Them More Healthful." Remember, fast food can be healthful food if chosen carefully and prepared well. And fast doesn't have to mean dull. Many delicate and sophisticated dishes can be prepared in just minutes.

4

Recipes You Know and Love: Gentle Ways to Make Them More Healthful

MANY OF US have vivid memories of enticing aromas wafting from our mother's or grandmother's kitchen. My grandmother's home-made chicken soup is one of my favorites. The wonderful scent lingered in her house for hours. When I made my first batch of homemade chicken soup, the aroma brought back wonderful child-hood memories.

There is something so special, so loving, about the passing down of recipes and traditions from one generation to another. Throughout history, food has been used as a symbol of caring, sharing, and providing. As our country's economy and technology advanced, so did the manufacturing and development of refined food products and prepackaged convenience foods.

Many of our parents' or grandparents' recipes originated at the start of this wave of food technology and refinement. Therefore they often don't meet today's dietary guidelines. So how do we keep the essence and tradition of these family favorites? By substituting more healthful ingredients, lowering the quantity of fat and salt, and fitting these special recipes into well-balanced menus.

Essentially, we are creating modern versions out of old traditions. Whether they are current family favorites or one of Grandma's special recipes, changes can produce a more healthful variation. Some recipes may not be easy to transform, and therefore should be eaten just on occasion as a special treat. But many traditional recipes can be converted without greatly altering flavor or the memories that go along with them.

Substituting with Wholesome Ingredients

Here are some gentle ways of making the recipes you know and love more healthful by substituting ingredients.

Recipe Ingredient	Healthful Substitution
Brown sugar	Equal amount of fructose with the addition of a little honey or molasses
Butter	For a no-cholesterol option, use an equal amount of margarine, extra-light olive oil, canola oil, or other cold-pressed polyunsaturated vegetable oil.
Buttermilk	Cultured nonfat or low-fat buttermilk
Cheese, hard	Choose part–skim milk cheeses that contain only 5 grams or less of fat per ounce. Cheddar, Swiss, mozzarella, farmer, are most readily available.
Cocoa	Equal amount of carob powder. Carob is sweeter, has less fat, and has no caffeine.
Cottage cheese, 4%	Substitute 1% or 2%.
Cream, heavy	Equal amount of evaporated skim milk. There is no really good substitute for fresh whipped cream.
Cream cheese	Substitute light cream cheese or drain low-fat cottage cheese and blend until smooth. Chill well.
Eggs	For a no-cholesterol option, use two egg whites to equal one whole egg, or substitute with egg replacer, according to package directions.
Flour, white	Substitute whole-wheat pastry flour and other whole-grain flours in baked goods other than yeast breads; use whole-wheat flour for these breads. Depending on the flour, use approximately three-quarters as much whole-grain flour for white, or add ¼ cup more liquid.
Ground beef	Equal amount of freshly ground turkey breast. Be sure to have the skin and all the fat removed from the turkey breast before grinding.

Recipe Ingredient	Healthful Substitution
Half-and-half	Equal amount of evaporated skim milk
Lard	Equal amount of unsalted butter, margarine, olive or other oil
Mayonnaise	Choose light varieties with half the amount of fat.
Milk, whole	Equal amount of skim milk or evaporated skim milk
Oil	Olive oil, canola oil, or other polyunsaturated oil
Pork	Chicken breast, or tempeh for a vegetarian option
Ricotta cheese, whole-milk	Equal amount of low-fat, part–skim milk, or light ricotta cheese
Salt	Use sea salt, no-salt seasonings, or increase herbs throughout recipe.
Shortening	Equal amount of butter or margarine
Sour cream	Combine three parts low-fat cottage cheese with one part nonfat yogurt in a blender and cream until smooth. And light varieties of sour cream have less fat than regular.
Sugar	Equal amount of fructose. In cold, acidic foods use half the amount of fructose. For 1 cup sugar, substitute ¾ cup honey or maple syrup. When using liquid sweeteners instead of sugar, reduce liquid in recipe by about ¼ cup for every cup liquid.
Veal	Pounded chicken breast, or tempeh for a vegetarian option
Vinaigrette	Traditional vinaigrette is three parts oil to one part vinegar. Slowly begin adding more good-

Recipe Ingredient	Healthful Substitution
	quality vinegar than oil. Stir in a little nonfat yogurt for a creamy vinaigrette.
Yogurt, whole-milk	Nonfat yogurt

Cutting Back the Fat

Reducing fat content in a recipe may take some experimentation. Some recipes are better suited to little or no fat than others. In some sauces, virtually eliminating the oil will not alter the flavor much. But cutting back the fat in baked goods can render them dry and tasteless if you're not careful.

Ground turkey breast is a great substitute for ground beef. Preground turkey found in grocery stores includes dark meat, skin, and fat all ground together, and has about the same fat content as ground beef. Ask the butcher to grind only the breast, without the skin, and with all the fat removed. Have it divided into one-pound packages. Buy several and freeze what you aren't using right away. This ground turkey is a great low-fat substitute for beef in meat loaf, burgers, stuffed cabbage, meatballs, meat sauce, and on pizza, in lasagna, in Mexican food, in dumplings, and so on.

Fat and salt are flavor enhancers. When these two ingredients are reduced or eliminated, recipes tend to be a bit bland. But increasing the amount of herbs and spices, sweetener, and other seasonings will help bring out more flavor. Whole-grain products bring their own unique flavor to recipes too. As I mentioned earlier, if you are used to using salt in cooking, don't cut it out completely right away. Begin gradually to decrease your salt intake until you have adjusted to the taste of other flavors.

Many traditional baked goods — cookies, cakes, pie crusts, quick breads — contain large amounts of fat. Unfortunately there is no good substitution. In these cases, quantities just need to be decreased. For many recipes, you can easily cut the fat in half with good results. Let's say a muffin recipe calls for a ½ cup butter. Use only a ¼ cup butter and add 2 or 3 tablespoons of skim milk, fruit juice, or other liquid to make up for the loss of fat. If the muffins have a good flavor and texture, try cutting back the fat even more the next time. If they lack flavor, add more sweetener, vanilla, lemon, or spices (cinnamon, nutmeg, etc.), according to the ingredients included in the recipe. For a moister texture, add a little more liquid and bake the muffins either at a lower temperature or for slightly less time.

When making recipe substitutions, always watch the cooking times — and especially baking — carefully. Cooking times may vary according to the type of ingredients being substituted. If you substituted honey or maple syrup for sugar, lower the oven temperature by 25 degrees. These sweeteners brown faster than sugar.

New Traditions to Call Your Own

Transforming your favorite recipes or culinary heirlooms to meet today's nutritional guidelines is a way to combine the best of both worlds. Keep the old recipes for sentimental value (I staple them to the back of the newly transformed version). Each time you prepare this updated recipe make sure you have a pencil to add any revisions. When you hand these special recipes down to the next generation, you're not only passing on a tradition but sharing a recipe that you know is wholesome.

◆◆◆◆◆

5

◆◆◆◆◆ **Dining Out:
From Fast-Food to
Continental Cuisine**

CHANCES ARE, your busy lifestyle often makes it necessary to eat meals and snacks away from home. Dining out was, until recently, considered a luxury or treat for special occasions. But today, Americans spend more than 40 percent of their family food budget at restaurants.

Making healthful meal choices, in almost any restaurant, is easier than you may think. With some knowledge and foresight, you can enjoy, in moderation, all the world's great cuisines. Knowing which foods to savor or avoid can turn a potential dietary disaster into a well-balanced culinary delight.

A recent Gallup poll suggested that nearly half of adult Americans have changed their habits in some way to eat more healthfully in restaurants. Many restaurants, following the trend of increased health awareness, are adding more fish, salads, low-fat dishes, and whole-grain breads and pasta to their menus. Even many fast-food chains now have salad bars, baked potatoes, sliced turkey breast, or grilled chicken breast sandwiches. By learning to choose meals that are generally high in complex carbohydrates and fiber, moderate in protein, and low in fat, you can dine out healthfully.

Selecting a restaurant can be challenging. The yellow pages of your phone book is often a good place to start. Call ahead and ask about the menu and special orders. Don't be shy about making requests — you'll be surprised by how accommodating many places are these days. It's easy for most restaurants to eliminate the salt, cook with half the amount of fat or no fat at all, and cut back on the cheese. If you eat at a particular restaurant regularly, tell the chef and waiter your preferences and see what they'll do for you. Once they know your dietary preferences, you can usually leave the rest to the chef.

Watch your weekly eating patterns and try to select a wide variety of meals — to help improve your overall health. When ordering, ask about portion sizes to make sure you don't overeat. A serving of fish

33

or poultry, for example, may be too much protein for one sitting, or more than you choose to eat. On the average, four ounces of fish per person is plenty of protein for good health. Ask the restaurant personnel to wrap up any leftovers so that you can take them home for lunch the next day. Or consider sharing the protein portion of the meal with someone else at your table, and then enjoy more potatoes, vegetables, and bread — maybe even a light appetizer. This will give you a chance to sample new dishes and help balance your nutritional intake for that meal.

Making the Best Choices

Making the right restaurant food choices can be easy if you know the basics. Start by avoiding fried foods. Keep a watchful eye on junk foods disguised as appetizers and conveniently placed at the opening of a menu. They're a common downfall when we're famished and want "just a little something" to tide us over until the rest of the meal arrives. Tempura, potato skins, deep-fried zucchini, mushrooms, and mozzarella tempt us with a crispy jacket of solid fat. Next time these appetizers start calling your name, quickly ask the waiter to bring some bread — preferably whole-grain, without the butter. Contrary to popular myth, bread is *not* fattening, and can be a top-rate, high-carbohydrate addition to almost any meal.

Like most Americans, I don't usually enjoy plain raw veggies, particularly when they're cut up a day or two before they arrive on my platter. The exception is when fresh vegetables are served with a low-fat dip. If you have chosen a light-protein entree, then a small appetizer portion of seafood salad (without mayonnaise and very light on any oil) or a shrimp cocktail can be a good low-fat choice. Another smart option: suggest that the people you're dining with select a light pasta entree to split as an appetizer.

It pays to be a bit of a culinary detective when ordering salads. No matter what type of dressing you choose, ask for it on the side. Watch the fat content: 1 tablespoon of oil (any kind) has 14 grams of fat; mayonnaise weighs in at about 12 grams per tablespoon; and an avocado has 30 grams of fat. Ask for salad dressing ingredients. One of the best options is to request oil and vinegar, separately and on the side. Then you can choose to go very light on the oil and have control over how much fat you're consuming. If you enjoy the flavor of gourmet vinegars (balsamic, champagne, raspberry, white or red wine, and so on) or lemon, you can delight in a salad that's basically fat-free. French dressings with a heavy tomato base can be relatively low in fat. With the dressing on the side, you can sprinkle on a tablespoon and regulate the amount of fat you consume. Remember that although vegetables are predominantly carbohydrate, they are very low in calories. Therefore most of the calories in a salad are from the dressing — and with traditional oil or mayonnaise-based dressings, most of that is fat.

On to the entree. When dining out, the major dietary pitfalls are large slabs of meat, fried fish, poultry with skin, and dishes swimming in cream, butter, cheese, or oily sauces. Instead, ask for your food prepared in the manner *you* choose — sauces on the side, fish and skinless poultry cooked without added fat, light on the cheese and oil, and without cream.

Ordering pasta dishes can also be a bit of a challenge. High-fat sauces are often made with butter or cream. Tomato-based sauces are a far better choice. Some sauces list wonderful ingredients, but have an olive-oil base. How much oil? At 14 grams per tablespoon, a pasta dish with an oil-based sauce can be loaded with fat. Ask the waiter to have the chef go especially light on the oil. Good chefs will make certain the dish still has wonderful flavor, and you've saved yourself unnecessary added fat.

What happens if the meal winds down and you're still a bit hungry? Eat another piece of bread. The extra carbohydrates will fill you up and not add unnecessary fat calories. And as the dessert cart or menu arrives, you may feel fine about forgoing high-fat treats. Fruit sorbets, some sherbets, and low-fat or nonfat frozen yogurt are deliciously light ways to end a meal. Fresh fruit is always a good choice, and is especially delectable when the restaurant serves it with a special nonfat topping such as balsamic vinegar or Grand Marnier. On occasion, a piece of fresh fruit pie can be a savory treat, because the filling is usually low in fat (unless it's coconut or banana cream). But skip the crust, or eat just a few bites, since traditional crust recipes tend to have significant amounts of fat. And if you choose to have your pie à la mode, it pays to know that a scoop of Häagen-Dazs contains about 18 grams of fat, whereas the same portion of frozen yogurt has only 1 to 4 grams of fat.

It's All in the Asking

One of the keys to dining out healthfully is knowing how the foods in a particular restaurant are prepared and what your options are. Here are some examples of what to ask for while dining out:

Skim milk or low-fat milk, instead of whole milk

Baked potato served plain. Ask if plain low-fat yogurt or low-fat cottage cheese and chives are available instead of butter and sour cream.

Baked or broiled seafood or skinless poultry. Ask for this dry or cooked with a little lemon or white wine and herbs, rather than butter and salt. Cancel cream sauces or ask that they be served on the side so you can have a taste.

Vegetables, if not precooked, can be served plain, steamed, or boiled, with lemon and freshly ground pepper on the side. Avoid butter, margarine, oil, and cream sauces.

Salads and salad bars can be wonderful choices for an appetizer or main course, depending on the items you choose. Prepared salads with a cream, mayonnaise, or heavy oil base are usually quite high in fat. Instead, choose fresh raw vegetables or fruits, legumes, and whole-grain bread. Try using oil and vinegar or lemon instead of creamy dressings, and always ask for the dressing on the side. Keep a light hand when using salad oil.

Soups can be very deceiving. Unless you ask for a list of ingredients, it's hard to know what's in them. Many vegetable soups have a beef broth base, and legume soups may contain cream or meat. Ask about ingredients. Most establishments are happy to share this information. Tomato-, bean-, and vegetable-based soups are usually lowest in fat.

Pasta is an excellent food choice if made with tomato, wine, or other low-fat sauces. Avoid sauces made with cream, butter, or lots of oil.

Breads are a good source of complex carbohydrates. Ask for whole-grain breads, and skip the butter or margarine. Yeast breads are usually low in fat and have little sweetener. French and Italian breads are often made with only wheat flour, water, yeast, and salt, and are a good low-fat bread choice, especially if made with whole wheat.

Cereals. The best are made with whole grains, little or no sweetener, no added fats, and no artificial flavors and colors. A wide variety of whole-grain, high-fiber cereals is now available. Be sure to read package labels. Ask for skim or low-fat milk. Oatmeal and cooked hot cereals are good breakfast choices when served with skim milk and fresh fruit.

Desserts are a treat. When you choose them, select those lowest in fat. Fresh fruit is a good choice. If you crave something extra-sweet, fruit sorbet, sherbet, and low-fat or nonfat frozen yogurt are fine as occasional treats, although they may be high in sugar.

Top Food Choices at Restaurants

Italian: From a culinary perspective, Italy can be divided by its use of fats and pasta — butter and soft homemade egg noodles in the agriculturally rich north, and olive oil and eggless macaroni in the south. Far north, by the Alps, rice (for *risotto*) or cornmeal (used in polenta) may replace pasta. Vegetables play a major role in Italian cuisine — artichokes, eggplant, peppers, zucchini, and spinach are very popular.

If you order carefully, Italian restaurants are a good choice when dining away from home. Part–skim milk mozzarella cheese is frequently used and is lower in fat than many other cheeses. Avoid cream, butter, and oil sauces. Dishes with tomato and wine sauces are good choices and are relatively low in fat. Choose fish or chicken breast that is not fried or in a butter or cream sauce. Nonmeat lasagna is another popular, healthful choice. Ask for it, and other dishes, with half the usual amount of melted cheese. Ask for fresh salads with a dressing on the side — oil and vinegar, or lemon, are best. If you love pizza, choose a deep-dish pizza with a whole-wheat crust and order it vegetarian-style (go light on the olives) with extra vegetables. Request half the usual amount of cheese.

Mexican: Mexico has a rich culinary history, including more than two thousand dishes, but most Americans know only north-of-the-border versions of Mexican food. Poultry and fish are popular, although pork is the most common meat. Mexican recipes include some distinctive vegetables such as jicama (a tropical root that looks similar to a rutabaga), squash blossoms, tomatillos (similar to small green tomatoes), avocado, *chayote* (a pear-shaped squash), nopal cactus, and an extensive variety of delicious peppers. Tortillas, legumes, and salsa are staples, and frying (usually in lard) is a common preparation method.

When chosen carefully, Mexican food is relatively low in fat and high in complex carbohydrates and other nutrients. Beans, rice, corn and wheat tortillas, fish, and salads are common staples in Mexican restaurants in America. A good practice when selecting a new Mexican restaurant is to call ahead and ask if the refried beans are made with lard. Many establishments have switched to small amounts of polyunsaturated oil or no added fat. Avoid sour cream, guacamole (not only is the avocado high in fat, but it's usually mixed with other high-fat ingredients), meat, egg dishes, and fried foods. In dishes that contain cheese, request no more than half the usual amount.

French: France can be divided by its culinary riches. Olive oil prevails in Provence and the Riviera, pork and goose fat in Alsace-Lorraine and Périgord, and what we in America usually regard as French cooking comes from the heartland of dairy country, with reliance on butter, eggs, and cream. French cuisine offers a wide range of seafood, vegetables, fruits, meats, and cheeses. In the past several years, the food from the warm and sunny region along the Mediterranean has become popular in America. Rich in seafood (especially grilled), olive oil, vegetables, garlic, and spices, this fun, informal style offers a variety of heart-healthy menu choices.

Most French restaurants pride themselves on using high-quality foods, but watch out for the fat. Avoid cream sauces, heavily buttered items, red meat, and other high-fat ingredients that many French restaurants are famous for. Nouvelle cuisine is a generally lower fat version of French cooking. Look for meals with fish, potatoes, fresh vegetables, wine sauces, and bread.

Spanish: Spain, like the French Mediterranean, has a cuisine based on olive oil, poultry, and seafood, as well as beans, rice, pork, eggs, lamb, and sausage. Although potatoes, peppers, and garlic are staples, other vegetables are usually served as part of a main dish.

Spanish restaurants are not yet common in America, although *tapas* (Spanish appetizers) have become popular. Like most Mediterranean countries, Spain offers a wonderful variety of healthful dishes. High-fat foods to avoid are sausage, meats, eggs, and fried dishes.

Oriental: The cuisines of China and Japan are light and varied. Vegetables, seafood, soybean products, and white rice are central to most dishes. Very small amounts of meat are used — mostly pork and chicken — and dairy products are almost nonexistent. Salt plays a major role in both Chinese and Japanese cuisines. Most flavorings, sauces, and broths are sodium-based, including soy, miso, teriyaki, black bean, oyster, and others. The Japanese consume a good deal of pickled, smoked, and highly salted foods. Stir-frying is the most common method of preparation, although deep-fat frying (as in tempura and egg rolls) is also popular.

Oriental restaurants can offer some good low-fat food choices if you stay away from the meat and fried foods. Most dishes are high in sodium. MSG (monosodium glutamate) is an artificial flavor enhancer that you should avoid. Ask the chef to eliminate it. Upon request, many Oriental restaurants will also reduce or eliminate the oil and sodium from some dishes. Fish, vegetable, poultry, and tofu recipes are often good choices.

Vegetarian: Although vegetarian restaurants serve nonmeat and even nondairy meals, many vegetarian dishes are high in fat. Limit cheeses and avoid heavy oil, butter, and cream items and all fried foods. Vegetarian restaurants make whole grains a regular option. Take advantage by choosing whole-grain breads, cooked whole grains, legumes, and pasta. Ask the waiter for help in choosing the best meals for your personal nutritional concerns. Don't hesitate to request information about ingredients and preparation methods. You may even find a delicious low-fat dessert on the menu, such as the ones presented in this cookbook.

Indian: Geography is responsible for the variety in Indian cuisine. In the north, rice, lamb, and greens are common. The south is primarily vegetarian, although fish is plentiful, along with rice, vegetables, and legumes. Coconuts, coconut milk, coconut oil, and ghee (clarified butter), all high in saturated fats, are common. A dizzying array of spices, cooked and combined in a variety of ways, is the unique backbone of Indian cuisine.

Vegetables, legumes, grains, yogurt, and spices can make Indian food a healthful choice for dining out. Avoid dishes with large amounts of coconut (in any form), ghee, and meats such as lamb. Grains and legumes, yogurt, greens, vegetables, seafood, and lean poultry are all good choices, provided they are cooked with only small amounts of oil. Ask how specific dishes are prepared and request that they be made to your liking.

American: Traditional American food is not all burgers and fries or meat and mashed potatoes. East and West Coast seafoods, Cajun dishes, salad bars, and grilled foods are part of American cuisine. The light and beautifully presented California cuisine has become popular in recent years. Spa cuisine carries this concept a step further by offering a low-fat, low-cholesterol bill of fare.

As you would at other restaurants, choose foods low in fat and cholesterol. Order dressing and sauces on the side, choose seafood or lean poultry, and limit or eliminate unnecessary butter, high-fat dairy products, oil, and fried foods.

Delicatessen: There are more and more delis around today, the majority in New York and other major cities along the East Coast. A deli is anything from a bagel shop to a full-service restaurant.

Delis usually have a wide selection of sandwich fixings and beverages, plus junk-food snacks and the best pickles you've ever tasted. Many delis are small take-out places where you can get a quick sandwich on the run. Here the best choices include turkey breast, tuna fish, or seafood salad (light in mayonnaise), chicken breast, or other low-fat choices on a whole-grain bun or bread with lettuce, tomato, mustard, and possibly a slice of onion or cheese. Don't forget the pickle. These days, many delis with health-conscious customers also provide a variety of fresh salads that are light and wholesome.

Travel Foods

When you travel — for business or pleasure — preplan meals and snacks to reduce stress and keep your energy high.

If you're driving, take some spring water or fruit juice and snacks like pretzels, bagels, rice cakes, rye crackers, homemade popcorn, dried and fresh fruit, and other treats that are low in fat. Consider where you'll be stopping for meals along the way. If your restaurant options are limited, consider preparing meals at home which can serve as picnic food in the car or when you stop at a scenic spot. I like to pack a cooler with sandwiches — bean spread in pita, turkey breast, or tuna fish with lettuce, tomato, mustard and so on, and I often prepare a salad (pasta, marinated beans, or vegetables) — and store it in a tightly covered bowl in the cooler. Be creative. Picnic food is great travel food.

If you travel by plane, call the airline ahead or ask your travel agent to request a special meal. Most airlines offer a number of choices, including seafood, vegetarian (dairy and nondairy), kosher, low-sodium, fruit plates, or even cold seafood platters. If airplane food doesn't please your palate, pack your own travel food. Remember to drink plenty of fluid on the plane, since cabin air rapidly dehydrates your body. Alcohol and caffeine drinks will also contribute to dehydration. Many airlines serve a variety of juices and some have spring water.

◆◆◆◆◆

6

Lunch Box Suggestions and Menus for Children and Adults

AS THE MIDDAY MEAL, lunch sets the tone for the afternoon hours. When you're away from home, a brown-bag lunch is both economical and time-saving. Whether you're packing a meal for yourself, your spouse, or your children, making it tasty and nutritious can be easier than you think.

Children: Making Lunch Healthful and Fun

How do we get our children to eat foods that are good for them? First, we set good examples in our own eating habits. Second, we begin teaching our children about good nutrition at an early age. But what if we didn't? We can encourage older children to enjoy, and even ask for, healthful foods instead of high-fat hot dogs, hamburgers, french fries, soda pop, and candy.

The key to creating healthful eating habits is gradual change. Abrupt alterations tend to trigger rebellions. Begin exchanging tasty, health-promoting versions of old favorites. Read food labels carefully. When you shop for groceries, make basic changes first. For example, switch to a brand of peanut butter that's made with only peanuts instead of brands containing sugar, added fat, and preservatives. Choose jams sweetened with fruit juice rather than sugar. Choose whole-grain bread, pasta, and rice instead of refined versions. If you usually buy whole milk, switch to 2-percent, then 1-percent, and finally to skim milk. Buy 1-percent- or 2-percent-fat cottage cheese and look for low-fat, nonfat, or part–skim milk cheeses, yogurt, and other dairy products. Scan the recipes in this cookbook and begin with those you think will appeal most to your family.

Give everyone time to adjust their habits and develop new tastes. Be careful not to get carried away by trying too many new-tasting foods at one time. *You* know your family best.

THE LUNCH THAT WILL BE EATEN

Packing a child's lunch box is an important assignment. There are a number of ways to make lunches for kids fun and exciting.

First, buy some small containers that fit inside the lunch box, allowing you to pack a wide variety of foods each day, making meals and snacks more fun than simply a sandwich and an apple. Review the suggestions and menus that follow. Be careful not to pack foods that are likely to cause teasing from other children. There are plenty of healthful foods that look and taste appealing to most kids.

Remember that a good-quality breakfast will help children start the day right. And a good-quality lunch will help children stay alert and focused throughout the day. Substituting skim milk for whole milk, for instance, will leave some room for the ever-popular peanut butter and jelly sandwich.

Does your child have a long bus ride? Why not pack some snacks for travel time to and from school? Nutrition experts recommend healthful between-meal snacks. Have you ever noticed on weekends, holidays, and vacations how often children choose to eat? It's about every hour or two in our house.

More than just a time for eating, the lunch break is a social time for children. Help them enjoy it. Choose a lunch box or bag *they* like. Let them help you plan their lunches. Before your next shopping trip, ask your children which sandwiches, fruits, and snacks they'd like. Suggest new options and ask for daily feedback. It's surprising how much better a lunch tastes to children when they've helped choose and prepare it.

Kids love to trade and share food. Every once in a while, give your children something extra to share with a good friend — make certain it's a food they are proud of and love. Homemade cookies are a big hit (especially Chewy Oatmeal Raisin Cookies). Don't forget an occasional surprise treat. All of these things can help youngsters eat healthful foods and enjoy their lunch more.

There's no reason that school lunches need to be limited to sandwiches and items that fit into plastic bags. You can fill small plastic containers with flavored yogurt, low-fat cottage cheese with fruit, applesauce, and homemade pudding. It's also a great idea to tuck an occasional note inside that says "I love you," "Enjoy lunch," or just "Hi!" A little extra effort really makes a difference.

Older children may be harder to please. Talk with them about changes in the family diet which you would like to make and explain why. Let them be part of the discussion and decision making whenever possible. Appeal to their personal interests — the desire to be a good athlete, dancer, student, and so on — and use this to help promote the transition to more healthful foods.

SAMPLE LUNCH BOX MENUS

Here are a few lunch menus and a list of some healthful, easy-to-pack foods that most children like. At first, emphasize your child's favorites. Then slowly introduce new items. Remember that these are sample menus. Add or omit food according to your child's age, appetite, and preferences.

Tuna fish on whole-grain bread
Low-fat or nonfat yogurt
Fresh fruit
Carrot sticks
Whole-grain cookies
Skim or low-fat milk

Part – skim milk cheese with lettuce and tomato on whole-grain bread
Whole-grain cupcake
Unsweetened applesauce
Sweet red pepper strips
Skim or low-fat milk

Peanut butter and jam on whole-grain bread
Cucumber sticks
Unsweetened pineapple chunks
Whole-grain muffin
Skim or low-fat milk

Low-fat ricotta or light cream cheese with jam on whole-grain bread
Homemade popcorn
Whole-grain cookies
Fresh fruit
Skim or low-fat milk

Seafood or chicken salad sandwich with lettuce and tomato on whole-grain bread
Part – skim milk cheese cubes
Pita chips
Raisins
Fruit juice

Bean spread (hummus or tofu) on whole-grain bread
Celery sticks stuffed with nut butter or low-fat cottage or ricotta cheese
Fresh fruit
Homemade pudding
Skim or low-fat milk

ADDITIONAL LUNCH BOX SUGGESTIONS

Sandwiches:
Peanut butter with honey and bananas on whole-grain bread
Sliced turkey or chicken breast with lettuce, tomato, and mustard on whole-grain bread

Part – skim milk cheeses with lettuce, tomato, and mustard on whole-grain bread

Grilled tempeh or tofu with lettuce, tomato, and pickle on whole-grain bread

Cinnamon, Raisin, and Nut Spread on whole-grain bread or pita bread

Vegetable-tofu spread with lettuce or sprouts in a whole-wheat pita pocket

Fruits and Vegetables:
Canned unsweetened fruit
Cherry tomatoes
Natural pickles
Homemade salads (see index)

Other:
Rice crackers, rice cakes, or rye crackers (best with spreads)
Low-fat cottage cheese, plain or with chopped fruit or vegetables

Brown-Bag Lunch Suggestions for Adults

For adults, smart brown-bagging can save money, improve health, and enhance performance during the workday. Here again, there are many options. Some work sites have lunchrooms with a refrigerator, hot plate, stove, or microwave oven. Take advantage of these if they are available to you.

Don't forget that small between-meal snacks also play a significant role in how you think, feel, and perform during the day. Review the snack recipes in this cookbook, and make some for coffee breaks. If you commute to and from work, consider bringing an extra-light snack for the trip home, so you aren't "starving" when you arrive home for dinner.

Leftovers — what I call "foods prepared in advance" — can be a wonderful brown-bag lunch idea. You can reheat casseroles, loaves, pies, soups, stews, grain and legume dishes, and even leftover pasta at work on a hot plate, stove, or in a microwave. A set of containers in various sizes will make packing these lunch entrees fast and easy. If cooking isn't feasible, use a thermos to keep cold foods cool and hot foods warm. And if there's no refrigerator on site, try packing your lunch in a mini cooler.

Eating at work or away from home can be as healthful and inexpensive as you choose to make it. You can brown-bag just about any food if you have the proper containers. For some fun sandwich ideas, refer to the lunch-box menus and suggestions for children.

7

The Basic How-To's for Cooking and Baking with Whole Grains and Legumes

MOST OF US don't realize how many delicious grains and legumes are available. But nutritional experts now recommend that a variety of whole grains and legumes are essential to best health. Part of the problem is that most of us are trapped by habit, and it's an effort to try new foods and recipes, such as baking homemade bread or cooking brown rice or legumes. This chapter is designed to arm you with step-by-step directions for cooking with whole grains, whole-grain flours, and a variety of legumes. You'll also learn my strategies for baking homemade bread.

How to Cook with Whole Grains and Flours

The most commonly used grains in America are white rice, white all-purpose flour, and small amounts of rolled oats for an occasional bowl of hot oatmeal cereal or an oatmeal cookie.

Unfortunately, as modern technology has grown, so has the availability of refined, denatured foods. Nutritious whole-wheat flour is milled into white flour by grinding off essential nutrients like the outer fiber-rich bran and highly nutritious germ. Then it is chemically bleached, eliminating nearly all of its original nutritive value. And this is the only flour many Americans use. Brown rice travels a similar refining path, reaching most kitchens as white rice, where the outside is polished, removing the fiber-rich outer bran coating and leaving relatively few nutrients.

The whole grains listed in this book are a vital part of an optimal diet, and along with legumes, for centuries they have been a staple food for long-lived, healthy people throughout the world. Grains can be cooked, soaked, sprouted, or ground into flour and baked.

Don't be surprised if your grocery store doesn't yet stock some of the grains mentioned in this chapter. At the moment they are sold mostly at natural food, gourmet, ethnic, or progressive grocery stores, or by mail order (see "Resources" section at the back of the book). Be sure to store grains in tightly covered containers in a cool, dry place.

COOKING GRAINS FOR MAIN COURSE ENTREES AND SIDE DISHES

When cooking grains, begin by bringing the required amount of water* to a boil in a saucepan. Then slowly add the grain and bring to a boil again. Reduce heat to low, cover, and simmer for the recommended amount of time,* or until all the water is absorbed. The grains should be chewy, not pasty, tough, crunchy, or hard. Remove the grains from the heat and let the pan sit, covered, for five to ten minutes. This produces a lighter, less sticky texture. Gently fluff with a fork and serve.

◆ Rinse grains only if they look dirty or are mixed with pieces of debris.
◆ Don't stir grains during cooking. This makes them sticky and gummy instead of fluffy.
◆ Vegetable or chicken broth and/or some dry white wine may be used along with or instead of cooking water.
◆ Herbs, spices, chopped vegetables, and so on can be added to the cooking water along with the grains.
◆ As a general guideline, use ½ cup of raw grain per person. Use more or less, depending on the meal, grain, and personal preferences.

COOKING HOT WHOLE-GRAIN CEREALS

Add the required amount of water* in a saucepan. Bring the water to a boil and stir in the grain. Bring to a boil again while stirring. Reduce heat to low and cook for the recommended time.* Stir occasionally to form a smooth, creamy consistency. Remove cereal from heat. Serve the cereal plain or add your choice of natural sweetener, skim milk, nonfat or low-fat plain yogurt, dried fruits, spices, ground nuts, or fresh fruit during the last few minutes of cooking. For additional hot cereal ideas, see the "Breakfast" section.

COOKING WITH WHOLE-GRAIN FLOURS

Although darker and heavier, whole-wheat flour can be used in traditional recipes calling for white all-purpose flour. Gluten, a

---

* See the "Whole-Grain Cooking" chart for required amounts and times.

component of both white and whole-wheat flour, reacts with active yeast and helps it to rise. Other whole-grain flours have either very little or no gluten, so they are rarely used alone in yeast breads. They can, however, be mixed with whole-wheat flour to produce delicious multigrain breads. Whole-wheat and other whole-grain flours may be used very successfully in making quick breads.

The "Whole-Grain Cooking" chart that follows gives information about the specific qualities and uses of each flour. By mixing these flours together in a recipe, you can create a nice balance of texture and flavor. Here is my favorite whole-grain flour mix, the one I use for most of my quick breads, cookies, and cakes. Try using it when a recipe calls for whole-grain flour: equal amounts of barley flour, oat flour, brown rice flour, and millet flour.

How to Cook Legumes

Legumes, by definition, are the edible mature seeds that grow inside the pods of leguminous plants. This important food group includes beans, peas, and lentils. Known for centuries as a "poor man's food," legumes are a staple for many of the world's healthiest and longest-lived people.

There are hundreds of varieties of legumes grown all over the world, and they are inexpensive, easy-to-use, nutrient-rich foods. Like grains, dry legumes need to be cooked to make them digestible. Some legumes may also be eaten fresh — the most common examples are peas, green (string) beans, and lima beans. Dry legumes are a convenient, economical, and practical food. Store them in tightly covered containers, and in a cool, dark, dry place, they will last for many months.

SELECTING LEGUMES

Legumes are usually sold in clear plastic bags, making it easy for the consumer to see the quality prior to buying them. Here are some tips for selecting the best dried legumes:

◆ Choose *bright, uniformly colored* legumes rather than those with a dull look. The more faded the color, the longer they have usually been stored and the longer they may take to cook.
◆ Look for *consistent size* among individual legumes. This is important to prevent some legumes from being undercooked while others are overcooked in a recipe.

GRAIN (1 cup raw)	Main Course/Side Dish Grains			Hot	
	WATER (cups)	COOKING TIME	YIELD (cups)	WATER (cups)	COOKING TIME
Amaranth	2	15–25 min	2–2½	3	15–25 min
Barley, hulled	2–2½	45–50 min	2–3	3	20–25 min
Brown rice	2	35–45 min	2–3	4	5–10 min
Buckwheat, hulled	2	15–20 min	2½–4	5	10–12 min
Cornmeal	3–4	25 min	3–4	4	5–10 min
Millet	2	20–25 min	2–3	3–4	20–30 min
Oats	2	45 min	2–2½	2	10–15 min
Quinoa	2	10–15 min	3	—	—
Rye	3–4	1½ hr	2⅔	3	10 min
Sorghum	2–3	45 min	3½	—	—
Triticale	4	1 hr	2½	—	—
Wheat	4	2–3 hr	2½	4	15 min
Wild rice	2–3	35–45 min	3	4	45–1 hr

* Indicates unavailable data at the time of publication

Cereal YIELD (cups)	Flour	Additional Comments
2½	May be used as a thickener similar to cornstarch or arrowroot. Good for sauces.	May be popped like popcorn. Use a skillet without oil.
3	Similar texture and flavor to wheat. Little gluten. A good substitute for wheat if eliminating gluten is desired.	Use barley flakes for hot cereal. The outer bran coating is polished off pearl barley; use only if hulled isn't available.
4	Granular, crumbly texture. Short-grain rice is best. Good combined with oat, millet, and barley flour.	Use rice ground into grits for hot cereal. Rice flakes also work well for hot cereal.
4	Dark, heavy, distinctive flavor. Good in buckwheat pancakes. Use unhulled buckwheat for flour.	White buckwheat is hulled and unroasted — the best choice. Use flakes for hot cereal. Whole-grain also works well.
4	Best used in corn or mixed whole-grain breads. High lysine cornmeal is a good choice.	Use cornmeal grits for hot grain cereal. Use cornmeal or flour as a main course grain — polenta.
4	Cakey texture. Good in sauces. Best mixed with rice, oat, and barley flours.	Whole-grain is used as a main course grain and for hot cereal.
1¾	Moist texture. Unhulled oats are ground into flour. Rolled oats may be ground in blender to make flour.	Use rolled oats for hot cereal. Grits, groats, and quick oats may also be used for hot cereal.
—	Whole grain may be ground into flour and used mixed with other whole-grain flours.	Just recently available in the U.S. Used mostly as a main course grain.
3	Dark rye flour is best. Light rye has the outer bran coating removed.	Use quick-cooking flakes for hot cereal. Groats and regular flakes may also be used.
—	Sorghum flour is also known as milo flour. Best used with other whole-grain flours.	May be roasted whole and eaten like popcorn. Difficult to find in the U.S.
—	Has a small amount of gluten. It's very sensitive and must be handled gently in yeast breads.	A hybrid cross between wheat and rye.
4	Significant gluten content. Best flour for yeast breads.	Use quick-cooking flakes for hot cereal. Use whole-wheat pastry flour for quick breads.
4	Moist texture. Best used with other whole-grain flours.	Use whole-grain for cooking hot cereal.

◆ Avoid packages that have a lot of legumes that are *cracked, shriveled, or have pinholes* (this may indicate insect damage).

COOKING LEGUMES

One common reason given for not eating legumes is that they produce intèstinal "gas." But soaking legumes in water before cooking will remove most of the indigestible carbohydrates called alpha-galactosides or trisaccharides — the gas makers. Some legumes don't need to be presoaked before cooking. These include baby lima beans, split peas, and lentils. Here are simple preparation steps to create great-tasting, easily digestible legumes:

1. Measure out the amount of legumes you will be using.
2. Sort through the legumes and remove any pebbles, dirt, grit, cracked, shriveled, discolored, or unusual ones.
3. Place legumes in a strainer or colander and rinse under running water. Then pour them into a large pot and fill to the top with boiling water.
4. Cover the pot and let legumes soak overnight, in the refrigerator if possible (see next page for the quick-cooking method.)
5. In the morning, pour off the soaking water and refill with fresh water. Let legumes soak again until you're ready to cook them. Although some water-soluble vitamins may be lost by discarding the soaking water, the now more easily digestible legumes are still nutrient-rich, high-quality foods.
6. When you're ready to cook the legumes, pour off the soaking water and refill the pot to three-quarters full with fresh water. Place the pot on the stove and bring the water and legumes to a boil. Reduce the heat to low and partially cover with a lid. Some beans (garbanzo and soy especially) will produce a foam on top of the water. You can remove it easily with a large spoon.
7. Cook legumes according to the times listed on the "Dry Legume Cooking" chart that follows. Check them regularly to make certain they don't overcook. Test to see if they're done by lifting out one legume with a spoon. Let it cool slightly and pinch it between your fingers or teeth. If the inside is soft and easy to press, with a texture similar to a well-cooked baked potato, then remove the legumes from the heat. Drain, and they are ready to use. When cooking legumes for use in salads, make sure they are firm but tender by keeping a careful watch on the pot and remove them at the appropriate time.

QUICK-COOK METHOD

If you forget to soak legumes, or plan a meal too late for overnight soaking, here's a quick alternative: Sort and rinse legumes as directed in the seven-step method. Put the legumes into boiling water in a large pot, or begin with cool water and legumes in the pot and bring to a rapid boil. Boil legumes for two to five minutes. Turn the heat off, cover, and let sit at least one hour. Pour off soaking water and replace with fresh water. Then go ahead with the final cooking. Legumes soaked using this quick method may require a slightly longer cooking time.

Unless indicated in a specific recipe, make sure you wait until the legumes are almost finished cooking before you add other ingredients. Fat, salt, broth, wine, and acids (tomatoes, vinegar, lemon, or molasses) will all toughen the legumes' skins and create longer cooking times. Exceptions to this principle are garlic, onions, herbs, and spices.

MAKING LEGUMES EASY TO USE

Since soaking and relatively long cooking times are needed to prepare many legumes, one alternative is buying cooked legumes in cans or jars. This is a convenient way to include these nutritious foods more often in your diet. Some companies now sell legumes packed in just water. Others have added salt. If you would like to reduce the sodium content in the salted legumes, rinse them under running water before using. Because some companies add preservatives, sugar, fats, or artificial colors to their canned legumes, read labels carefully and try to avoid these. Even a can or jar stating "all natural" on the front label may contain sugar, fat, and other undesirable ingredients.

One alternative to commercial legumes from cans or jars is making a large batch each time you cook legumes and saving the extra quantity. They keep in the refrigerator for up to a week and can be frozen for up to six months. To freeze legumes, drain well in a colander or strainer after cooking. Let the legumes dry slightly and then put them into a tightly covered container. Prior to freezing, label and date the container.

Cooking time is determined by the type of legume. Check the "Dry Legume Cooking" chart for approximate times. Your actual cooking time may vary according to where the legumes were grown, how long they have been stored, the altitude at which you are cooking (higher altitudes usually take longer), whether you have hard or soft

◆ DRY LEGUME COOKING ◆

The cooking times given are for presoaked beans with the exception of lentil, lima, and split pea.

The use of a pressure cooker can greatly reduce cooking times, but this method is not recommended for fava beans, lima beans, split peas, and most grains.

Dry Legume (1 cup)	Water (minimum, in cups)	Cooking Time (approximate)	Yield Cooked (approximate, in cups)
Adzuki beans*	4	45 – 1½ hr	2½
Black beans (turtle)	4	1½ – 2 hr	2 – 2½
Black-eyed peas	3 – 4	1 hr	2
Fava beans	3 – 4	1 – 1½ hr	2½
Garbanzo beans (chickpeas)	4	2½ – 3 hr	3¼ – 4
Great northern beans	3 – 4	1 hr	2
Kidney beans	3	1½ – 2½ hr	2 – 2½
Lentils	3	45 – 1 hr	2 – 2¼
Lima beans, baby	2	1½ hr	1¾
Lima beans, large	2	1½ hr	1¼
Mung beans	3 – 4	3 hr	2½
Navy beans (or pea beans)	2 – 3	1 hr	2
Peas, split	3	45 – 1 hr	2
Peas, whole	2 – 3	1 – 1½ hr	2 – 2½
Pinto beans	3	1½ – 2½ hr	2
Small red or pink beans	3	1½ – 2½ hr	2
Soybeans	3 – 4	3 or more hr	2

* *Adzuki* beans are also spelled *aduki* and *azuki*.

water (hard water takes longer), the soaking method, and other variables. Use the chart as a starting point for general guidance. As you cook different legumes, write in your own cooking times for future reference.

Many recipes list the quantity of legumes needed in either dry (raw) or cooked amounts, but not both. The following list gives the approximate equivalencies of dry to cooked legumes, so you can substitute if you have cooked legumes on hand and a recipe calls for dry amounts, or vice versa.

Cooked Legumes	Dry or Raw Legumes
1 cup	⅓ cup
1¼ cups	½ cup
1¾ cups	¾ cup
2½ cups	1 cup
3½ cups	1⅓ cups
4 cups	1⅔ cups

How to Bake Homemade Bread
BAKING YEAST BREADS

The sight and scent of freshly baked bread has a timeless romantic appeal. More and more Americans are reclaiming the lost art of baking homemade bread. With our busy schedules and heavy reliance on convenience foods, many of us never learned to bake bread. And we believed that bread baking meant spending all day in the kitchen. But that's a fallacy. To bake homemade bread, the most time you'll need at one stretch is twenty minutes, although you need to be at home over a period of several hours. Once you're organized, you generally need only two to five minutes of attention each hour. By baking a double recipe, which doesn't take any longer than a single one, you can freeze a loaf for future use.

The whole-grain bread you bake at home will be more nutritious and taste much better than store-bought varieties. You can eat it with breakfast, lunch, snacks, and dinners, and your family will appreciate the special personal touch and taste. This weekend, read the information below and try baking one of the whole-grain bread recipes in this book.

BASIC INGREDIENTS

Have ingredients at room temperature before you begin.

1. *Active dry yeast* must be refrigerated. Compressed or cake yeast may also be used.
2. *Water* (skim milk, potato water, etc.) must be warmed to 100 to 115°F. Yeast exposed to a heat much higher than 115°F will die, and temperatures much cooler than 100°F may take longer to create a reaction. For compressed yeast, have liquid temperature between 80 and 95°F.
3. *Flour* for yeast bread needs to have a significant gluten content. Wheat is the grain highest in gluten. Choose whole-wheat flour. The gluten in the flour traps the carbon dioxide bubbles given off by the yeast and stretches as the bubbles expand, holding the dough together as it rises. Rye, corn, oat, millet, buckwheat, barley, rice, soy, potato, triticale, amaranth, quinoa, and sorghum have either little or no gluten content. The less gluten the flour has, the more dense the loaf of bread.
4. *Sweeteners* are not essential in yeast bread. Very small amounts may be used for flavor and act as a natural preservative. Sweeteners may also be used to start the action of the yeast at the beginning of a recipe.
5. *Salt* is not a necessary ingredient in baking bread. You can successfully decrease or eliminate it from a recipe. However, salt does help control the rate at which the dough rises. A dough made without salt needs careful timing to prevent over-rising.
6. *Fats* flavor and help to create a moist loaf that resists drying out during storage. Very small amounts of fat can be used with great results. Fats are needed to "grease" baking utensils; small amounts of unsalted butter or margarine are generally the best choice, although olive oil, extra-light olive oil, other monounsaturated or polyunsaturated oils, and nonstick cooking sprays will also work.

BAKING METHODS

There are several popular methods for making yeast breads. All depend on the live action of the yeast shown by "proofing." This process tests the activity of the yeast. If the yeast is not active, the dough will not rise. A warm liquid added to the yeast will begin a reaction. After five to ten minutes, the yeast mixture should be foaming and frothy. If it isn't, chances are:

- the water was too hot, and it killed the yeast. Or,
- the water was too cold, and thus did not provide an environment warm enough for the yeast to grow quickly. Or,
- the yeast was too old. Look for an expiration date on the package or buy in quantities you know you will use in time.

If the yeast mixture does not activate after five to ten minutes, try adding a teaspoon of natural sweetener. Let proof for another five minutes. If the yeast mixture still does not react, pour out the mixture and begin again.

All the following baking methods work well. Choose your favorite.

Method A: The Fast and Simple Method

1. Heat water or liquid between 100 and 115°F. Pour liquid into a very large bowl. Add sweetener if desired and sprinkle yeast on top. Let proof for ten minutes.
2. Add the remaining ingredients slowly, adding only enough flour to form a stiff dough. Proceed with step 4.

Method B: The Sponge Method

1. Heat the required amount of liquid between 110 and 115°F. Pour the liquid into a very large bowl. Add sweetener if desired. Sprinkle yeast on top of the water and let proof for ten minutes.
2. To the proofed yeast, slowly add approximately one-quarter of the total flour called for in the recipe. Mix with an electric beater on low speed. Once everything is mixed, increase mixer speed to high and beat for three minutes. Or use a wooden spoon instead (three hundred strokes). This mixture is now called a "sponge."
3a. By hand, stir in half of the remaining flour and the other ingredients. Proceed with step 4. *Or*
3b. Cover the sponge (with a damp cloth, wax paper, or plastic wrap) and put in a warm (80°F) place to rise approximately one hour. This extra step may improve the texture of the loaf and is sometimes well worth the extra time required. Stir in half the flour and the other remaining ingredients. Then proceed with step 4.

Method C: The Wet and Dry Method

1. Mix one-fourth of the flour with the salt (optional), yeast, and any other dry ingredients in a large bowl. Heat all the wet ingredients between 100 and 110°F in a saucepan.

2. Pour the wet ingredients into the dry and beat with an electric mixer (or by hand vigorously) for three minutes.
3. Slowly add half the remaining flour, mixing by hand. Then proceed with step 4.

Kneading the Dough

4. Turn the dough out onto a floured counter or surface. It will be crumbly, lumpy, and sticky at this point. Begin kneading by the rhythmic action of pulling the top of the dough toward you with your right hand and then pushing the heel of this hand into the center of the dough. With your left hand, push the dough in a clockwise direction. Repeat with your right hand, then the left again. Knead in enough flour as you go to form a soft yet firm dough. Do this by sprinkling flour on the counter and kneading the dough on top of it. This is not an exact art. As long as you can work out some type of rhythmic movement, similar to the one I've described here, you will succeed. If the dough is still sticky, knead in more flour. Be careful not to add too much flour, since this will result in a heavier, more dense loaf. But don't worry; it will still turn out fine. Learning how much flour to knead in will take practice. The amount of flour needed for yeast breads varies. The temperature and humidity inside and outside your home, the age and type of flour used, and several other factors will be variables in the exact quantity of flour you used.

Knead the dough for approximately ten minutes. When it has been kneaded enough, it will have a smooth, elastic texture and a cool feeling. Whole-grain flours, other than wheat, will tend to stay slightly sticky.

Lightly oil the inside of a very large bowl. Place the dough in the bowl and then turn the dough over once to coat the top and bottom with oil. Lightly cover the dough with wax paper, plastic wrap, or a damp cloth. Let the dough rise in a warm, draft-free place (80 to 85°F) for about forty-five minutes to one hour, or until the dough has doubled in size. A gas oven with a pilot light will be about the right temperature. Try heating your electric oven slightly — for just a minute. Turn the heat off and place the bread inside the oven to rise. Have a thermometer available to check the temperature periodically. If the temperature is too high, the yeast will die. If it is too cool, the bread will take longer to rise.

Punching Down the Dough

5. Remove the dough from the bowl and "punch down" (literally hit the dough to flatten it), redistributing the gluten and air bubbles. Proceed with step 6 or, for a finer-textured bread, you may knead the dough for two minutes and put it aside to rise again for about forty-five minutes more. This extra rise is not necessary for most breads, but may be recommended in a few recipes.

Shaping the Dough

6. Bread dough can be shaped almost any way you can imagine. Here are instructions for making three common shapes. For others, see specific recipes in this book or refer to other bread cookbooks.

   a. *The traditional pan loaf:* Divide the dough into the number of loaves indicated in your recipe. Flatten each piece into a rectangle (approximately 7 × 10 inches). On the shorter side of each rectangle, begin tightly rolling up the dough until each piece is a long log shape. Pinch all the seams and ends with your thumb and forefinger. Gently roll the loaves on the counter to smooth over the seams. Place in a lightly greased loaf pan. Cover again and set in a warm place (80 to 85°F) to rise for about forty-five minutes (or until doubled in size).

   b. *The round loaf:* Divide the dough into the number of loaves indicated in your recipe. With your hands, shape each piece of dough into a smooth round circle. Lightly oil a baking sheet and sprinkle cornmeal or flour on it. Place the loaves on the baking sheet far enough apart so that when they rise and spread they will not touch. Cover and let the loaves rise in a warm place (80 to 85°F) for about forty-five minutes (or until doubled in size).

   c. *Rolls:* Divide the dough into the number of rolls desired. Rolls can be made many different ways. Here are a few of my favorites:

      ◆ Shape each piece of dough into a small round loaf for individual round buns.
      ◆ Roll each piece of dough into a six-inch strand and tie into a knot.
      ◆ Shape the pieces of dough into rounds and place in a baking dish so they rise and touch each other when baked.
      ◆ Divide each piece of dough into three pieces. For each roll, place all three pieces in one muffin cup.

Baking the Dough

7. Many breads are baked at 350°F. In each recipe, follow the directions given for oven temperature and cooking time. Test the bread to make sure it is done. This is another imprecise art. Sometimes, because of your oven, baking pan, or other variables, the bread might not be fully cooked in the length of time the recipe states. Here is a tip: Remove bread from the oven, lift the bread out of the pan, and tap the bottom. If it is done, it will sound hollow and have a light brown crust. If you think it needs to cook longer, just put it back in the oven for a few more minutes.

When the bread is finished baking, remove it from the pan and cool on a rack. The bread should cool slightly before you cut and eat it (although it's hard to keep my family from sneaking a piece right away). Finally, take a moment to admire your creation.

After years of bread baking, I have developed a few favorite techniques. I personally prefer using "Method B" for mixing most bread dough. I let my dough rise in an unheated oven. I place a quart measuring cup filled with hot water in the oven with the dough to provide a warm, moist environment that works very well.

HIGH-ALTITUDE BAKING

Baking at high altitudes calls for special considerations. Yeast doughs rise more rapidly at high altitudes, so less yeast will help slow the rising time. Also, flour has a tendency to dry out at higher altitudes so your recipe may require more liquid. Increased baking times and temperatures are also necessary. For making quick breads at high altitudes, you may need to decrease slightly the amount of baking powder and sweetener and increase slightly the liquid called for in recipes.

BAKING QUICK BREADS

Quick breads are made from a batter that is poured into pans and baked immediately. Quick breads tend to have a cakey texture. The rising action comes from baking powder and/or baking soda instead of yeast. Quick breads are usually relatively sweet and somewhat higher in fat than the more time-consuming yeast breads. Quick breads don't require wheat flour, as yeast breads do, since the baking powder or soda doesn't need gluten to help create the rise. Any whole-grain flour will do. I find that whole-wheat pastry flour gives the best overall texture, although a combination of flours also works very well. Some of the most popular quick breads are muffins and biscuits.

Here are several tips for making quick breads successfully. First, work quickly and do not overmix the batter. Use a large bowl for the dry ingredients: flour, baking powder, baking soda, spices, dry sweetener, and so on. Use a smaller bowl for the wet ingredients, such as butter, margarine, or oil, liquid sweeteners, extracts, and eggs. This method keeps the wet separate from the dry until immediately before you are ready to pour the batter into the pan and pop it into the oven. Once your pans are buttered or oiled, your oven is preheated, and all the ingredients are mixed in their separate bowls, you are then ready to combine the wet and dry ingredients.

Quickly pour the wet ingredients into the dry. Now, with a rubber spatula, mix *only* until a smooth batter is formed and all the wet and dry ingredients are incorporated. Pour the batter into the prepared pan and put it in the oven. Set the timer for the required amount of time and clean up while you wait.

When you think the bread is ready, or when the timer rings, test the center of the loaf, muffin, or cake with a toothpick. If it comes out dry or with a small bit of crumb on it, the bread is finished. If the toothpick comes out moist or wet, the loaf needs to bake longer. Once the loaf is finished, remove it from the oven and let it cool for a few minutes. Then take the loaf out of the pan and cool it on a rack. The bread should be cool to the touch before you cut it.

Many quick bread recipes make two loaves. You can double recipes to make four loaves, as quick breads freeze well. I like to make large batches that yield twice the amount of bread for the same amount of work — one loaf for immediate snacking, one to keep in the refrigerator, and two that can be frozen for future snacks, gifts, or last-minute entertaining. Try slicing the bread before freezing if thawing only one piece at a time is more convenient.

◆◆◆◆◆

8

◆◆◆◆◆

Meal Planning: Your Key to Delicious Eating and Good Health

MOST OF US don't spend much time planning our meals. We decide on an entree and let the rest of the meal fall into place with whatever's available. Too often the "fill-in" doesn't create a balanced meal — falling short on nutritional requirements or exceeding the recommended amount of fat or cholesterol.

Many of us have the desire to fix a wide variety of health-promoting meals and snacks for ourselves and our families but don't know how. Sometimes we have dozens of cookbooks on our shelves but find it very difficult to design a varied and exciting meal plan, what to serve with what. Even if you have managed to use healthful ingredients in your recipes, you may be uncertain about the actual content of fat, protein, fiber, cholesterol, and other nutrients when recipes are combined into meals.

This cookbook is different. The recipes are arranged into menus, taking the guesswork out of designing your own meal plan. The nutritional analysis at the end of each recipe and meal will help you focus on important nutritional factors like fat, cholesterol, protein, and sodium. With this information you can design your own meal plans and choose snacks that meet your individual needs.

Having a Plan

How many times have you come home from work, school, or picking up the kids and had to come up with a meal at the last minute? Unless you are exceptionally creative in the kitchen and have a fully stocked pantry and good grasp of today's nutritional requirements, the meal you put on the table will rarely be well balanced. But planning ahead helps. The menus in this cookbook provide you with a set sample schedule. The meals have been nutritionally analyzed and combined to give your diet variety and flavor, and to meet the necessary average dietary requirements.

"America's New Low-Fat Cuisine 28-Day Meal Plan," which follows, has been designed to give you both a suggested schedule and options. You can choose breakfast and snacks according to your own lifestyle and tastes. It may be helpful to total the full day's nutritional analyses when planning your meals and snacks. You may be very surprised to see that a slice of Hot Apple Crumb Pie fits nicely into your diet as a light evening snack.

Hot Soup for Cool Days, Cool Soup for Warm Days

The reason for warm weather and cool weather menus? For many of us, certain recipes sound most appealing in a particular season. Chilled Fresh Peach Soup or Fresh Fruit and Whole-Grain Ambrosia with Red Raspberry Yogurt Sauce are much more popular in the summer than winter — and the fresh fruit ingredients are most readily available during warm weather months. Many of us have a hard time even thinking about Thick and Hearty Vegetable Chili when the temperature is soaring and the hot and humid summer air is leaving us weary. With fourteen days of warm-weather menus and fourteen days of cool-weather menus, this cookbook provides two full weeks of meals in each season, not including the menus you can design yourself.

Five to Six Small Meals and Light Snacks a Day

One of the fastest ways to eliminate midmorning and midafternoon slumps is to eat small, nutritious between-meal snacks. This helps the body's digestion, absorption, and metabolism function more efficiently, contributing to a steady supply of energy. Large meals swamp our digestive system and interfere with absorption of nutrients. It's easier for the body to absorb nutrients from small amounts of food every two to three hours during the day. Of course, this doesn't mean a candy bar, or snacks in addition to *huge* main meals. The key is learning to eat three moderate, high-quality main meals and then adding two or three light and nutritious between-meal snacks. This cookbook provides a wide range of snack recipes.

Enough or Too Much?

As you will see, the meals in this cookbook are substantial. Although they are hearty, they're also designed to be slimming. Individuals who want or require a higher-calorie diet may enjoy larger servings or second helpings. Eating larger snacks can also help you increase calories, if necessary. The meals and snacks in this cookbook have been designed to help all of us committed to weight control. By keeping meals and snacks low in fat, as recommended throughout this book, you've taken a major dietary step toward reducing or controlling body fat. Add a regular aerobic exercise program, and you've covered both parts of the body fat control picture.

Lighten Up

This book offers guidelines and options instead of rigid rules. Take your time and make a smooth, gradual transition into the new era of healthful eating. Be patient with yourself and others who accompany you on this journey. Begin with the planned meals or by picking a few dishes that sound best to you. Remember, slow change tends to be lasting change.

America's New Low-Fat Cuisine 28-Day Meal Plan

Here's a sample 28-day meal plan. You can follow this format or use it as a guideline to create your own meal plans for warm and cool seasonal dining.

14-DAY COOL WEATHER MENU

◆ **DAY 1**
Breakfast: See "Breakfast Ideas and Options," p. 73.
Midmorning Snack: See "Snack Ideas and Options," p. 315.
Lunch: Autumn's Acorn Cheddar Soup
      Colorful Corn Salad
      Gingerbread Muffins
Midafternoon Snack: See "Snack Ideas and Options," p. 315.
Dinner: Saffron Bouillabaisse
      Fresh Spinach and Garlic Sauté
      Whole-Wheat French Bread
Light Evening Snack: See "Snack Ideas and Options," p. 315.

◆ DAY 2
Breakfast
Midmorning Snack
Lunch: Garden-Fresh Nachos
      Mexican Jicama Salad
Midafternoon Snack
Dinner: Pasta Rustica
      Red, White, and Green Salad with Creamy Garlic Dressing
Light Evening Snack

◆ DAY 3
Breakfast
Midmorning Snack

Lunch: Cutlet Parmesan Hero
　　　　Tossed Salad with Creamy Buttermilk Dressing
Midafternoon Snack
Dinner: Risotto Vino Blanco
　　　　Warm Spinach Salad
　　　　Crostini
Light Evening Snack

◆ DAY 4
Breakfast
Midmorning Snack
Lunch: Caribbean Black Bean Soup
　　　　Citrus Season Salad with Ginger Horseradish Dressing
　　　　Lemon Honey Muffins
Midafternoon Snack
Dinner: Baked Potatoes with Tuna Tomato Sauce
　　　　Tossed Greens with Balsamic Splash
　　　　Country Farmhouse Bread
Light Evening Snack

◆ DAY 5
Breakfast
Midmorning Snack
Lunch: Spaghetti Squash with Peperonata Sauce
　　　　Whole-Grain Garlic Bread
Midafternoon Snack
Dinner: Savory Soybeans au Gratin
　　　　Crunchy Tossed Salad with Blackberry-Pecan Vinaigrette
　　　　Sprouted Wheat-Berry Bread
Light Evening Snack

◆ DAY 6
Breakfast
Midmorning Snack
Lunch: Minestrone Soup
　　　　Whole-Grain Soda Biscuits
Midafternoon Snack
Dinner: Squash and Cheese Casserole
　　　　Mixed Greens with Poppy Seed–Tahini Dressing
　　　　Honey–Cracked Wheat Bread
Light Evening Snack

◆ DAY 7
Breakfast
Midmorning Snack
Lunch: Oriental Hot and Sour Ramen
      Tamari Rice
Midafternoon Snack
Dinner: Mexican Bean and Cheese Enchiladas
        Grated Mixed Vegetable Salad with Spicy Tomato Dressing
Light Evening Snack

◆ DAY 8
Breakfast
Midmorning Snack
Lunch: German Cabbage Caraway Soup
      Burgundy Beet Salad
      Onion Rye Flat Bread
Midafternoon Snack
Dinner: Portuguese Potato and Artichoke Pie
      Spanish Rice
      Fresh Green Bean Salad
Light Evening Snack

◆ DAY 9
Breakfast
Midmorning Snack
Lunch: Thick and Hearty Vegetable Chili
      Melt-in-Your-Mouth Corn Bread
Midafternoon Snack
Dinner: Simple Salmon Loaf with Lemon Mustard Sauce
      Brussels Sprouts in White Wine
      Honey Dinner Rolls
Light Evening Snack

◆ DAY 10
Breakfast
Midmorning Snack
Lunch: Herbal Tomato Rice Soup
      Carrot, Cheddar, and Chickpea Slaw with Fresh Parsley
        Parmesan Dressing
Midafternoon Snack

Dinner: Lasagna Rolls with Two Sauces
       Festive Italian Salad with Creamy Lemon Mustard
         Vinaigrette
Light Evening Snack

◆ DAY 11
Breakfast
Midmorning Snack
Lunch: Brazilian Black Beans and Brown Rice
       Winter Vegetable Salad with Sweet Red Pepper Vinaigrette
Midafternoon Snack
Dinner: American Tuna Noodle Casserole
       Crunchy Tossed Salad with Tangy Tomato Dressing
       Whole-Wheat Monkey Bread
Light Evening Snack

◆ DAY 12
Breakfast
Midmorning Snack
Lunch: Split Pea and Wild Rice Soup
       Winter's Fresh Vegetable Marinade
Midafternoon Snack
Dinner: Pasta with Marinara Sauce
       Spinach and Mushroom Salad with Pignoli Dressing
Light Evening Snack

◆ DAY 13
Breakfast
Midmorning Snack
Lunch: Fettuccine with Winter Garden Sauce
       Mushroom Salad with Radishes
Midafternoon Snack
Dinner: Picante Seafood Veracruz
       Baked Sweet Potatoes with Nutmeg Cream
       Seasonal Steamed Vegetables
       Whole-Wheat and Honey Challah
Light Evening Snack

◆ DAY 14
Breakfast
Midmorning Snack

Lunch: Creamy Corn Chowder
　　　　Whole-Grain Irish Soda Bread
Midafternoon Snack
Dinner: Pasta with Turkey Tomato Sauce
　　　　Vegetable Antipasto with Low-Fat Blue Cheese Dressing
Light Evening Snack

14-DAY WARM WEATHER MENU

◆ DAY 1
Breakfast
Midmorning Snack
Lunch: Middle Eastern Baked Falafel
　　　　Dilled Cucumber Salad
Midafternoon Snack
Dinner: California Cutlets
　　　　Lemon Linguine Parmesan
　　　　Salad Nouveau with Creamy Watercress Dressing
Light Evening Snack

◆ DAY 2
Breakfast
Midmorning Snack
Lunch: Mexican Ensalada
　　　　Whole-Grain Pita Chips with Salsa
Midafternoon Snack
Dinner: Village Paella
　　　　Crisp Cos, Tomato, and Onion Salad
　　　　Spanish Country Bread
Light Evening Snack

◆ DAY 3
Breakfast
Midmorning Snack
Lunch: Ratatouille
　　　　Cucumber and Red Grape Salad
　　　　Corn and Rye Bread
Midafternoon Snack
Dinner: Angel Hair Pasta with Fresh Tomato Sauce
　　　　Mixed Greens Salad with Creamy Fresh Basil Dressing
Light Evening Snack

◆ DAY 4
Breakfast
Midmorning Snack
Lunch: White Bean Pâté with Lettuce, Tomato, and Onion
        Chilled Sweet Pea Soup
        Quick Onion Pumpernickel Bread
Midafternoon Snack
Dinner: Turkey Burgers or Zucchini–Oat Bran Burgers
        Spicy French Potatoes
Light Evening Snack

◆ DAY 5
Breakfast
Midmorning Snack
Lunch: Rigatoni with Ricotta Pecan Pesto
        Raspberry-Marinated Tomatoes and Onions
Midafternoon Snack
Dinner: Garden Tostadas with Beans and Brown Rice
Light Evening Snack

◆ DAY 6
Breakfast
Midmorning Snack
Lunch: Thick and Zesty Gazpacho
        Potato Salad Dijon
        Multigrain Black Bread
Midafternoon Snack
Dinner: Linguine with Salmon Sauce
        Crudités with Dijon Dip
        Bruschetta
Light Evening Snack

◆ DAY 7
Breakfast
Midmorning Snack
Lunch: Greek Salad
        Olive Bread
Midafternoon Snack
Dinner: Cutlets or Filets with Fresh Tomato Relish
        Fan Potatoes

Honey-Glazed Carrots
Whole-Grain Buttermilk Biscuits
Light Evening Snack

◆ DAY 8
Breakfast
Midmorning Snack
Lunch: Fresh Fruit and Whole-Grain Ambrosia with Red Raspberry
      Yogurt Sauce
      Cinnamon-Raisin Swirl Bread
Midafternoon Snack
Dinner: Variety Kebabs
      Brown Rice and Barley Pilaf
      European Mixed Vegetable Salad with Artichoke
        Vinaigrette
Light Evening Snack

◆ DAY 9
Breakfast
Midmorning Snack
Lunch: Tuna Niçoise
      French Breadstick Twists
Midafternoon Snack
Dinner: Pasta with Sweet Pea and Pimiento Sauce
      Saladier with Vinaigrette Fines Herbes
Light Evening Snack

◆ DAY 10
Breakfast
Midmorning Snack
Lunch: Creamy Vegetable Tofu Spread Sandwiches
      Cool Magenta Borscht
      Brown Rice and Artichoke Salad
Midafternoon Snack
Dinner: Grilled Cutlets with Country Mustard Marinade
      Grilled Vegetables
      Baked Potatoes with Cucumber Dill Sauce
Light Evening Snack

◆ DAY 11
Breakfast
Midmorning Snack

Lunch: Fruity Pasta Salad
    Whole-Grain Bagels
Midafternoon Snack
Dinner: Chilled Tomato Cucumber Soup
    White Bean and Red Onion Salad
    Oatmeal Soda Bread
Light Evening Snack

◆ DAY 12
Breakfast
Midmorning Snack
Lunch: Hummus-in-Pita Sandwiches
    Israeli Salad
Midafternoon Snack
Dinner: Pasta Pizza
    Stuffed Artichokes
Light Evening Snack

◆ DAY 13
Breakfast
Midmorning Snack
Lunch: Greek Pasta Salad
    Whole-Wheat French Bread
Midafternoon Snack
Dinner: Seafood Filets or Steaks with Red Pepper Coulis
    Specialty Green Beans
    Mashed Potatoes with a Difference
Light Evening Snack

◆ DAY 14
Breakfast
Midmorning Snack
Lunch: Chilled Fresh Peach Soup
    Bibb Lettuce with Apricot Yogurt Dressing
    Banana – Poppy Seed Muffins
Midafternoon Snack
Dinner: Low-Fat Deep-Dish Pizza or Veggie-Rich Pita Pizza
    Tossed Greens Salad
Light Evening Snack

Breakfast Recipes

Breakfast Ideas
and Options

Breakfast is steadily regaining popularity as health researchers tout its importance to our health, fitness, and performance. Even when morning minutes are limited, a well-balanced and satisfying breakfast can be had. Variety in your choices from day to day and week to week is important too. Many of us find we get into a breakfast rut, eating the same thing morning after morning. I've included a selection of breakfast recipes from light to hearty.

Even if cold cereal and milk is your daily choice, try buying an assortment of cereals and combining different ones each day. Slice a little fruit on top — one day banana, the next peaches, then raspberries, strawberries, blueberries, and so on. And if fresh, warm bread entices you into eating breakfast, an assortment of bread baking machines can bake bread while you sleep. It's as easy as placing the ingredients in the machine at night and setting the timer according to your rising hour, and you'll wake up to the aroma of freshly baked bread. These machines are available at many department stores and in some cooking catalogues (see "Resources").

Here's a quick guide to some breakfast options.

Fast Breakfasts That Take Only Minutes:
- Cold cereal and skim milk, with or without fruit
  Look for cereals that have no added fat. Natural foods stores and some grocery stores sell cereals unsweetened or lightly sweetened with fruit juices or natural sweeteners. Cereal and milk is a fast, easy breakfast. Choose from cereals with oats, oat bran, wheat, brown rice, barley, or other whole grains.
- Hot cereal with or without sliced fruit on top*
- Leftover muffins, reheated*
- Fruit shakes*
- Whole-grain toast with fruit spreads or jam

---

* Recipes are in this cookbook.

- Nonfat yogurt or low-fat cottage cheese with or without fruit and toast
- Nonfat plain or fruit-flavored yogurt with dry cereal (Grape-Nuts are good)

Breakfasts That Are Fast in the Morning with Advance Preparation:
- Homemade granola with skim milk or nonfat yogurt*
- Muesli*
- Cottage, Fruits, and Nuts*
- Bagel or whole-grain bread with low-fat cream cheese – style spreads*
- Stewed fruit with hot cereal, nonfat yogurt, low-fat cottage cheese, or toast*

Special Breakfasts for Mornings That Are Less Rushed:
- Whole-grain pancakes and waffles*
- French toast*
- Homemade muffins and quick breads*
- Warm stewed fruit with hot cereal*

Best Breakfast Choices When Dining Out:
- Cold cereal with skim milk
- Fresh fruit with nonfat or low-fat yogurt or cottage cheese
- Oatmeal with skim milk and fruit
- Whole-grain toast with fruit spread or jam
- Pancakes without butter

Muesli

This unique cereal originated in Switzerland. It is easy to make and very satisfying. Rolled oats are soaked overnight, instead of being cooked and served with seasonal fruit. In cool weather, use more oats than fruit. In warm weather, add extra fruit. Although advance planning is needed for soaking the oats, this meal is fast and easy to make. Muesli can be made with a variety of different ingredients. It quickly becomes a favorite.

Mix the following ingredients according to your personal preferences.

½ cup rolled oats (more or less, as
    you desire) per person

---

* Recipes are in this cookbook.

◆§ Put the oats in a bowl. Pour just enough water over the oats to cover them. Cover the bowl, place in the refrigerator, and let the oats soak overnight.

◆§ In the morning, add any or all of these options:
  ◆ Nonfat yogurt
  ◆ Natural sweetener (a small amount of date sugar, maple syrup, honey, fructose, or other)
  ◆ Fresh fruits (or canned, unsweetened fruit), chopped
  ◆ Nuts, finely ground (a small amount; almonds are quite good)
  ◆ Dried, unsweetened fruits (raisins, chopped dates, currants, diced papaya, or others)
  ◆ Spices and flavorings (cinnamon, nutmeg, vanilla, or other flavored extracts)

NORTHERN SUMMERS MUESLI

This is one of our favorite warm weather muesli recipes. The portions are large.

2 cups rolled oats
¼ cup currants or raisins
2 tablespoons nonfat plain
  yogurt
2 tablespoons finely ground
  almonds
2 tablespoons maple syrup or
  honey
1 cup raspberries
1 cup blueberries
1 cup strawberries
1 cup seedless grapes
Dash of nutmeg

Serves 4
Prep: 5 minutes
Soak: Overnight

◆§ Put the oats in a bowl and pour just enough water over the oats to cover them. Cover the bowl, place it in the refrigerator, and soak the oats overnight.

◆§ In the morning, stir in the currants, yogurt, almonds, and sweetener.

◆§ Gently fold in the fruit and serve topped with nutmeg.

Nutritional Analysis: 1 serving
cal 298; chol 0; fat-total 5.7 g; fat-mono 1.5 g+; fat-poly 0.8 g+;
fat-sat 0.3 g+; protein 8.88 g; carbo 57 g; fiber 7.41 g; calcium
82 mg; sodium 12 mg; fat 16%; protein 11%; carbo 73%

APPLE CINNAMON MUESLI

This muesli is perfect for the autumn and winter months when
apples are abundant.

2 cups rolled oats
3 apples, chopped
½ cup raisins or currants
2 tablespoons nonfat plain yogurt
2 tablespoons maple syrup or
  honey, or to taste
2 tablespoons finely ground
  almonds or walnuts
½ teaspoon cinnamon
Dash of nutmeg

Serves 4
Prep: 5 minutes
Soak: Overnight

≈§ Put the oats in a bowl and pour just enough water over the oats to
    cover them. Cover the bowl, place it in the refrigerator, and soak
    the oats overnight.
≈§ In the morning, stir in the remaining ingredients.

Nutritional Analysis: 1 serving
cal 321; chol 0; fat-total 4.8 g; fat-mono 1.2 g+; fat-poly 0.5 g+;
fat-sat 0.4 g+; protein 8.29 g; carbo 65.2 g; fiber 6.18 g; calcium
75 mg; sodium 11 mg; fat 13%; protein 10%; carbo 77%

TROPICAL FRUIT MUESLI

This recipe is delicious any time of year. Make it with fresh, canned,
or dried fruits.

2 cups rolled oats

1 ripe banana, sliced

½ cup chopped fresh pineapple, or ½ cup unsweetened crushed pineapple

½ cup chopped fresh papaya, or ¼ cup diced, dried, unsweetened papaya

½ cup chopped fresh mango, or ¼ cup diced, dried, unsweetened mango

¼ cup chopped dates

2 tablespoons finely ground almonds or macadamia nuts

2 tablespoons nonfat plain yogurt

2 tablespoons date sugar or honey, or to taste

Serves 4

Prep: 5 minutes

Soak: Overnight

◄§ Put the oats in a bowl and pour just enough water over the oats to cover them. Cover the bowl, place it in the refrigerator, and soak the oats overnight.

◄§ In the morning, stir in the remaining ingredients.

Nutritional Analysis: 1 serving
cal 308; chol 0; fat-total 5 g; fat-mono 1.3 g +; fat-poly 0.4 g +; fat-sat 0.3 g +; protein 8.53 g; carbo 60.7 g; fiber 5.17 g; calcium 57 mg +; sodium 10 mg; fat 14%; protein 11%; carbo 75%

◆ Analysis is based on fresh fruits.

WINTER FRUIT MUESLI

Use unsweetened, canned pineapple, peaches, and pears if fresh fruit isn't available where you live.

2 cups rolled oats

1 ripe banana, sliced

1 apple, chopped

2 kiwifruits, peeled and sliced

¼ cup crushed pineapple

¼ cup peach slices

¼ cup pear slices

¼ cup raisins, currants, and/or chopped dates

2 tablespoons finely ground almonds

2 tablespoons nonfat plain yogurt

2 tablespoons honey or maple syrup, or to taste

Serves 4

Prep: 5 minutes

Soak: Overnight

◆§ Pour the oats in a bowl and pour just enough water over the oats to cover them. Cover the bowl, place it in the refrigerator, and soak the oats overnight.

◆§ In the morning, stir in the remaining ingredients.

Nutritional Analysis: 1 serving
cal 337; chol 0; fat-total 4.9 g+; fat-mono 1.3 g+; fat-poly 0.5 g+; fat-sat 0.3 g+; protein 8.97 g; carbo 67.8 g; fiber 5.66 g; calcium 66 mg+; sodium 13 mg; fat 13%; protein 10%; carbo 77%

Hot Cereals

On a cold winter morning, hot cereal is a warm and comforting way to start the day. There are as many hot cereal options as there are whole grains. In general, 1 cup of grain cooked with 3 to 4 cups of water will make a good cereal. For more information, refer to the "Whole-Grain Cooking" chart in Chapter 7. Many grains are now available ground and packaged for hot cereal. Some of my family's favorites are oat bran; corn grits; cream of rye, rice, wheat, or buckwheat; and millet. You can also mix a variety of cereals together to create your own multigrain hot cereal. Any of the following ingredients can be added when making hot cereal:

◆ Raisins, currants, chopped dates, or other dried fruits
◆ Honey, maple syrup, fructose, or other sweeteners
◆ Nonfat plain yogurt, skim milk, nonfat dry milk, evaporated skim milk
◆ Seeds or ground nuts in small amounts
◆ Fresh, frozen, or unsweetened canned fruits
◆ Spices like cinnamon, nutmeg, or chili powder (in corn grits)

CREAMY HOT OAT BRAN CEREAL

Oat bran has become popular because of its water-soluble fiber, thought to help decrease blood cholesterol levels. Oat bran has a smooth, creamy texture and a mild, pleasant taste. Creamy Hot Oat Bran Cereal takes only minutes to make. Try topping the hot cereal with sliced peaches and an extra dash of nutmeg.

2 cups water   *Serves 2*
⅔ cup oat bran   *Cook: 5 minutes*
¼ cup or more skim milk

1 tablespoon maple syrup or
   honey, or to taste
¼ cup raisins or currants
Dash of cinnamon
Dash of nutmeg

◆§ Bring the water to a boil in a saucepan. Slowly stir in the oat bran and lower the heat to simmer.
◆§ Add the remaining ingredients and cook for 1 to 2 minutes while stirring.
◆§ Add more milk or sweetener if desired.

Nutritional Analysis: 1 serving
cal 228; chol 1 mg; fat-total 2.7 g; fat-mono 0+; fat-poly 0+; fat-sat 0.1 g+; protein 9.13 g; carbo 42.4 g; fiber 1.29 g; calcium 84 mg; sodium 31 mg; fat 11%; protein 16%; carbo 73%

CINNAMON RAISIN OATMEAL

Mix oatmeal with a variety of ingredients to create a new recipe each morning of the week. This recipe is quite traditional — cinnamon, raisins, and maple syrup. Try adding currants, chopped dates, or other dried fruits, ground nuts, fresh fruit, honey, or evaporated skim milk.

1 cup water   *Serves 1*
½ cup rolled oats   *Cook: 10 minutes*
1 tablespoon raisins
1–2 teaspoons maple syrup or
   honey, or to taste
⅛ teaspoon cinnamon
Dash of nutmeg
2 tablespoons skim milk, or more

◆§ Bring the water to a boil in a small saucepan.
◆§ Stir in the oats and lower the heat to simmer. Cook for approximately 10 minutes, stirring occasionally.
◆§ During the last few minutes of cooking, stir in the raisins, sweetener, and spices. Cook until thick.
◆§ Mix in enough milk to reach a desired consistency and serve.

Nutritional Analysis: 1 serving
cal 200; chol 0; fat-total 2.7 g; fat-mono 0+; fat-poly 0+; fat-sat 0.1 g+; protein 6.82 g; carbo 38.8 g; fiber 2.95 g; calcium 36 mg; sodium 3 mg; fat 12%; protein 13%; carbo 75%

HOMEMADE MULTIGRAIN GRANOLA

Traditional granola can be very high in fat. I've created this low-fat granola recipe using a variety of grains, although you may substitute oats for the barley and rye flakes. Pineapple juice concentrate and honey are the secret to its sweet flavor. Serve with skim milk or mix into nonfat plain yogurt. Store granola for several weeks in a tightly covered container.

3 cups rolled oats
1½ cups barley flakes*
1½ cups rye flakes*
½ cup oat bran
3 tablespoons unsalted butter or
   margarine, melted
3 ounces pineapple juice
   concentrate, thawed
¾ cup honey
2 tablespoons boiling water
1 tablespoon vanilla
½ cup raisins
½ cup chopped dates

Serves 20
Prep: 10 minutes
Bake: 40 minutes

⋄§ Preheat oven to 350°F.
⋄§ Mix the oats, barley, rye, and oat bran in a large bowl. Toss the grains with the butter and the undiluted pineapple juice concentrate.
⋄§ Spread out the grains in a very large baking pan. Bake for 15 minutes.
⋄§ Mix the remaining ingredients, except the raisins and dates, in a separate bowl.
⋄§ Pour the cooked grains back into a large bowl. Add the liquid ingredients and toss very well. Spread out the mixture in the pan

* Available at natural foods stores

and bake for 15 minutes. Stir the granola and cook for another 10 minutes.

◆§ Remove the pan from oven and let the granola cool *completely*. It will harden as it cools.

◆§ Add the raisins and dates and store in a covered jar.

Nutritional Analysis: 1 serving (½ cup)
cal 168; chol 5 mg; fat-total 3.1 g; fat-mono 0.5 g+; fat-poly 0.1 g+; fat-sat 1.1 g+; protein 3.86 g; carbo 33 g; fiber 1.75 g; calcium 19 mg; sodium 3 mg; fat 16%; protein 9%; carbo 75%
◆ Analysis is based on 6 cups rolled oats instead of barley and rye flakes.
◆ With margarine instead of butter: chol 0; fat-mono 0.8 g+; fat-poly 0.6 g+; fat-sat 0.3 g+

Fruit Shakes
Fruit shakes are a quick, wonderful taste treat. Using fruits, juices, and skim milk, you can create a variety of nonfat and low-fat shakes in your blender. Here are some ingredient ideas and a basic recipe for Frosty Strawberry Shakes. Fruit shakes make for a fresh and satisfying breakfast when combined with a whole-grain muffin, bagel, or toast. Add any of the following ingredients:
◆ Skim milk
◆ Nonfat or low-fat plain yogurt
◆ Fruit juice
◆ Fresh, frozen, or dried fruit
◆ Cinnamon, nutmeg, vanilla
◆ Sweeteners
◆ Carob powder
To make a thicker shake, add a ripe banana. To make it frosty, add frozen fruit. To make it slushy, add crushed ice.

FROSTY STRAWBERRY SHAKES

½ ripe banana   *Serves 2*
½ cup frozen strawberries   *Prep: 5 minutes*
1 cup or more skim milk

◆§ Combine all the ingredients in a blender. Mix until very smooth. Add additional milk if necessary.
◆§ Serve immediately.

Nutritional Analysis: 1 serving
cal 134; chol 2 mg; fat-total 0.5 g; fat-mono 0.1 g+; fat-poly 0.1 g+; fat-sat 0.2 g+; protein 4.5 g; carbo 29.3 g; fiber 1.38 g; calcium 158 mg+; sodium 65 mg; fat 3%; protein 13%; carbo 84%

Pancakes and French Toast

Pancakes and French toast are delicious treats for weekend breakfasts or any time. These recipes are as easy as opening a box of mix, and they are superior in both taste and nutritional value. And homemade pancakes and French toast can be low in fat and high in complex carbohydrates. A good-quality griddle is the key to perfect results. You have a number of options. Some griddles are coated with a nonstick finish that allows you to cook without added fat. Nonstick sprays are also available and add only a very small amount of fat to a recipe. Some brands contain only natural ingredients. Even cast iron or stainless steel skillets work well, but they need added fat to prevent sticking. If you enjoy pancakes and French toast (and even a variety of low-fat burgers), a good griddle may be worth the investment.

Another interesting option is an old-fashioned soapstone griddle. Soapstone is an amazing granitelike rock, which has a naturally smooth and greasy surface — hence its nonstick quality. It has excellent heat-absorbing properties and is easy to clean. Soapstone has been quarried since the 1850s as an excellent cooking material known for its even heating. Traditionally, it has been used on wood cookstoves, but it also works well on electric or gas. This is a natural way to cook low-fat without the use of synthetic nonstick pans and sprays. Soapstone griddles are available from the Vermont Soapstone Company, Perkinsville, Vermont 05151; (802) 263-5404.

WHOLE-GRAIN PANCAKES

These hearty whole-grain cakes rise high and are quite filling. I've included several variations on the basic recipe. My son's favorite is strawberry buttermilk, and my husband likes the batter made with 3 teaspoons of vanilla and a few drops of lemon extract. You can serve these pancakes topped with Fruit Syrup (page 85), Fruit Coulis (page 312), fresh fruit, unsweetened jams, or pure maple syrup. And this batter makes good waffles, too.

2½ cups whole-grain flour
4 teaspoons baking powder
2 cups skim milk
4 tablespoons honey or maple
  syrup
1 egg or 2 egg whites or egg
  replacer, beaten
1 tablespoon oil (canola, corn,
  safflower, or other mild-
  flavored oil)
1 – 3 teaspoons vanilla

Makes 14 large
pancakes
Prep: 5 minutes
Cook: Varies

- ∙§ Heat a griddle or skillet.
- ∙§ Mix the dry ingredients in a large bowl.
- ∙§ Combine the wet ingredients in a separate bowl.
- ∙§ Add the wet ingredients to the dry and stir until blended but still slightly lumpy.
- ∙§ Spoon the batter onto the hot griddle. Let cook several minutes until the pancake bottoms brown lightly and bubbles begin to appear on the top of the cakes.
- ∙§ Gently flip the cakes with a spatula and cook several minutes more.
- ∙§ Repeat with the rest of the batter.

Buttermilk Pancakes
- ∙§ Prepare pancake batter as in the basic recipe but reduce baking powder to 2 teaspoons and add 1 teaspoon of baking soda. Substitute 2½ cups cultured nonfat buttermilk for the skim milk.

Buckwheat Pancakes
- ∙§ Prepare pancake batter as in the basic recipe but use 1 cup buckwheat flour and 1½ cups whole-grain flour. Add extra skim milk to thin the batter.

Oat Bran or Oatmeal Pancakes
- ∙§ Prepare pancake batter as in the basic recipe but substitute ¼ cup oat bran or oatmeal for ¼ cup of the flour.

Fruit-Filled Pancakes
- ∙§ Prepare any of the suggested pancake batters. Fold in 1 cup fruit. You can use any type. Chop the fruit into small pieces if necessary. Some favorites in our house are blueberries, raspberries, blackberries, strawberries, pineapple, bananas, and peaches.

Nutritional Analysis: 1 pancake, basic recipe
cal 118; chol 20 mg; fat-total 1.8 g; fat-mono 0.3 g; fat-poly 1 g; fat-sat 0.3 g; protein 4.43 g; carbo 22.1 g; fiber 2.08 g; calcium 122 mg; sodium 113 mg; fat 14%; protein 14%; carbo 72%
◆ With egg whites instead of a whole egg: chol 1 mg; fat-mono 0.2 g; fat-poly 0.9 g; fat-sat 0.2 g
◆ Analysis is figured using a nonstick griddle. No added fat is used in cooking.

CINNAMON WHOLE-GRAIN FRENCH TOAST

I love making French toast. And homemade bread, of course, tastes the best. Bread that is several days old works very well. As a teenager, I had incredible homemade bread every Friday night. Even with the large quantities of fresh bread we all ate the night it was baked, come Sunday there was usually enough left over to make French toast. What a treat and a wonderful way to use old bread. Leftover challah (page 224) is my favorite. There's something very special about the taste and the task. And it seems to get the whole house off to a pleasant start in the morning.

3 eggs
1½ cups skim milk or evaporated
  skim milk
1 tablespoon vanilla
1 tablespoon honey or maple
  syrup
1½ teaspoons cinnamon
½ teaspoon nutmeg
10 thick slices whole-grain bread

Serves 10
Prep: 5 minutes
Cook: Varies

◆§ Beat the eggs in a bowl. Add the remaining ingredients, except the bread. Beat well with a fork.
◆§ Heat a griddle.
◆§ Soak the bread in the egg mixture. You may need to soak a few at a time. Make sure the bread fully absorbs the mixture. Be careful: the bread falls apart easily.
◆§ Remove one piece of bread at a time and hold it over the dish to let the excess liquid drip off. Place the bread on the griddle and

cook until the bottom browns. Turn the bread over with a spatula. Cook until lightly browned.

◄§ Repeat this process with the rest of the bread. To save time, soak a new piece of bread in the egg mixture each time you remove one. You may need to use more or less bread (to soak up all the egg), depending on the type you use.

Options

◄§ For a real taste treat, stir 2 tablespoons Grand Marnier liqueur into the egg and milk mixture.

◄§ Mix some cinnamon and fructose and sprinkle on the toast as it cooks.

◄§ For a richer flavor, substitute evaporated skim milk for the skim milk.

◄§ For a lower-cholesterol French toast, use 1 whole egg and 4 egg whites or egg replacer as a substitute for the whole eggs.

Nutritional Analysis: 1 serving
cal 123; chol 110 mg; fat-total 3.5 g; fat-mono 1.3 g; fat-poly 0.6 g; fat-sat 1.2 g; protein 6.61 g; carbo 17.3 g; fiber 1.57 g; calcium 81 mg; sodium 227 mg; fat 25%; protein 21%; carbo 54%

◆ With a whole egg and 4 whites instead of 3 whole eggs: chol 28 mg; fat-mono 0.6 g; fat-poly 0.4 g, fat-sat 0.6 g

◆ Analysis is figured using a nonstick griddle. No added fat is used in cooking.

FRUIT SYRUP

Fresh, frozen, or canned fruit is cooked with a little sweetener to make a wonderful syrup for pancakes, French toast, waffles, or frozen yogurt.

1 pound fruit, such as
strawberries, pineapple,
peaches, blueberries,
raspberries, or blackberries
1 – 3 tablespoons maple syrup,
honey, or fructose
1 – 2 teaspoons arrowroot
Dash of nutmeg

Serves 4
Cook: 5 – 15 minutes

◆§ Bring all the ingredients to a boil in a saucepan. Lower the heat and simmer several minutes until the syrup is slightly thickened. Some fruit may need a little extra sweetener, arrowroot for thickening, or cooking time. Adjust the recipe accordingly.

◆§ Serve hot, warm, or chilled.

Nutritional Analysis: 1 serving
cal 118; chol 0; fat-total 0.2 g; fat-mono 0; fat-poly 0.1 g+; fat-sat 0; protein 0.42 g; carbo 31.4 g; fiber 0.71 g+; calcium 7 mg; sodium 2 mg; fat 1%; protein 1%; carbo 98%
◆ Analysis is based on frozen blueberries.

COTTAGE, FRUITS, AND NUTS

This refreshing treat is delicious for breakfast or lunch. You may use any fruit instead of, or in addition to, those I've listed.

2 cups low-fat cottage cheese

2 tablespoons honey

2 – 3 tablespoons lemon juice

½ teaspoons nutmeg

¼ cup raisins or currants

¼ cup chopped almonds

3 tablespoons pumpkin seeds

1 tablespoon poppy seeds

2 apples, chopped

30 seedless grapes

½ small cantaloupe, cubed

¼ honeydew melon, cubed

Serves 6
Prep: 15 minutes

◆§ Mix the cottage cheese in a large bowl with the honey, lemon juice, and nutmeg.

◆§ Gently toss in the remaining ingredients. Refrigerate until well chilled before serving.

Nutritional Analysis: 1 serving
cal 260; chol 6 mg; fat-total 7.6 g; fat-mono 3.1 g; fat-poly 2.3 g; fat-sat 1.9 g; protein 13.96 g; carbo 37.2 g; fiber 3.47 g+; calcium 109 mg; sodium 320 mg; fat 25%; protein 20%; carbo 55%

STEWED FRUIT

Almost any dried fruit, or variety of fruits, can be cooked into a sweet-tasting breakfast treat. Stewed Fruit is very versatile. It tastes great hot or cold, on top of cooked cereal, nonfat yogurt, low-fat cottage cheese; with toast or pancakes; or even as a dessert, served alone or on top of frozen yogurt. I prefer a combination of dried fruits cooked with a cinnamon stick for a sweet, rich flavor.

3 cups mixed dried fruits, such as
   peaches, pears, apricots,
   apples, pitted prunes
1 cinnamon stick
3 cups water

Makes 4 cups
Cook: 20 minutes

- Place the dried fruits and cinnamon in a large saucepan and fill with water.
- Bring to a boil. Lower the heat to simmer and cook for 20 minutes or until the fruits are rehydrated and the remaining water is syrupy. Remove the cinnamon stick before serving.

Nutritional Analysis: 1 serving (½ cup)
cal 111; chol 0; fat-total 0.3 g; fat-mono 0.1 g; fat-poly 0.1 g; fat-sat 0 g; protein 1.38 g; carbo 29.3 g; fiber 6.08 g; calcium 19 mg; sodium 10 mg; fat 2%; protein 4%; carbo 94%

Cool Weather Lunch
Menus and Recipes

◆◆◆◆◆◆◆◆◆◆◆◆◆◆◆◆◆◆◆◆◆◆◆◆◆◆◆◆◆◆◆◆◆◆◆◆◆◆

⊸§ Autumn's Acorn Cheddar Soup
Colorful Corn Salad
Gingerbread Muffins

This is a perfect meal for the cool days of autumn when squash is at its best. The entire meal makes wonderful leftovers — the soup is easily reheated, the salad improves in flavor as it marinates, and the muffins are great snacks.

AUTUMN'S ACORN CHEDDAR SOUP

This soup has a subtle yet hearty flavor and conjures up images of crisp fall days. The creamy orange color is very appealing to the eye and the texture is smooth, rich, and thick. You can cook the squash in a microwave oven to quicken the cooking time. Or precook the squash in a regular oven and then prepare the soup in just 10 minutes!

2 medium acorn squash
1 tablespoon unsalted butter or
   margarine
3 cups vegetable broth
¼ teaspoon sage
1 teaspoon garlic powder
1 teaspoon freshly ground black
   pepper
1½ cups evaporated skim milk
6 ounces part–skim milk
   Cheddar cheese, grated
Nutmeg

Serves 6
Bake: 45 minutes
Prep: 10 minutes

◆§ Preheat oven to 475°F. Cut each squash in half with a sharp knife, scoop out the seeds with a spoon, and place cut side down on a baking sheet (one with edges that will prevent the juice from dripping into your oven). Bake for 45 minutes or until soft.

◆§ Remove the squash from the oven and spoon the pulp into a food processor. Purée until smooth. (If you don't have a food processor, scoop the squash pulp into a soup pot and whisk until smooth.) Add the next four ingredients. Mix well.

◆§ Transfer the purée from the processor to a soup pot. Heat on low for several minutes.

◆§ Slowly add the cheese and milk while stirring. Once the cheese has melted, keep the soup warm on the lowest heat until ready to serve. Thin with additional milk if necessary.

◆§ Serve in bowls with a sprinkle of nutmeg on top.

Nutritional Analysis: 1 serving
cal 302; chol 22 mg; fat-total 7.5 g; fat-mono 2 g; fat-poly 0.3 g; fat-sat 4.5 g; protein 15.8 g; carbo 48.6 g; fiber 3.44 g; calcium 514 mg; sodium 236 mg; fat 21%; protein 19%; carbo 60%
◆ With margarine instead of butter: chol 17 mg; fat-mono 2.3 g; fat-poly 0.8 g; fat-sat 3.7 g

COLORFUL CORN SALAD

As the name suggests, this salad makes an appealing presentation. It's fast and easy to prepare. The longer it marinates, the more the flavor is enhanced.

4 cups frozen corn, thawed
1 cup frozen peas, thawed
¼ cup finely chopped red onion
1 small green pepper, finely chopped
1 can (14 ounces) artichoke hearts packed in water, drained, sliced
4 ounces pimientos, diced
¼ cup minced fresh parsley
2 tablespoons olive oil
2 tablespoons white wine vinegar

Serves 6
Prep: 5 minutes
Chill: 15 minutes

½ teaspoon garlic powder
½ teaspoon basil
Lots of freshly ground black pepper
Salt to taste (optional)

◆§ Combine all the ingredients in a bowl. Toss well. Chill until ready to serve. Taste to adjust seasoning. (Leftovers keep well in refrigerator several days.)

Nutritional Analysis: 1 serving
cal 189; chol 0; fat-total 5.1 g; fat-mono 3.4 g+; fat-poly 0.5 g+; fat-sat 0.7 g+; protein 6.4 g; carbo 33.3 g; fiber 7 g+; calcium 28 mg; sodium 56 mg; fat 23%; protein 12%; carbo 65%

GINGERBREAD MUFFINS

A moist and aromatic muffin with an old-fashioned flavor. Always a favorite.

2 cups whole-grain flour
½ cup nonfat dry milk powder
1 tablespoon ginger
1½ teaspoons cinnamon
1 teaspoon baking soda
1 teaspoon baking powder
½ teaspoon nutmeg
½ teaspoon cloves
1 cup skim milk
½ cup molasses
6 tablespoons maple syrup

Makes 16 muffins
Prep: 10 minutes
Bake: 20 minutes

3 tablespoons unsalted butter or margarine, melted
1 egg or 2 egg whites or egg replacer, beaten

◆§ Preheat oven to 350°F. Line 16 muffin tins with paper cups.
◆§ Mix all the dry ingredients in a large bowl.
◆§ Mix all the wet ingredients in a small bowl.
◆§ Add the wet ingredients to the dry and mix just to incorporate. Quickly spoon the batter into the tins.
◆§ Bake for approximately 15 to 20 minutes or until a toothpick inserted in the center of a muffin comes out dry.
◆§ Remove the muffins from the pan and cool them on a rack. (Store leftovers in the refrigerator.)

Nutritional Analysis: 1 muffin
cal 129; chol 24 mg; fat-total 2.8 g; fat-mono 0.8 g; fat-poly 0.3 g; fat-sat 1.5 g; protein 3.67 g; carbo 23.3 g; fiber 1.45 g+; calcium 148 mg; sodium 107 mg; fat 19%; protein 11%; carbo 70%

◆ With margarine and egg whites instead of butter and a whole egg: chol 1 mg; fat-sat 0.5 g; fat-mono 1 g; fat-poly 0.8 g

Nutritional Analysis for Lunch Meal: 1 serving
cal 620; chol 46 mg; fat-total 15.4 g; fat-mono 6.2 g+; fat-poly 1.1 g+; fat-sat 6.7 g+; protein 25.87 g; carbo 105.3 g; fiber 11.89 g+; calcium 690 mg; sodium 399 mg; fat 21%; protein 16%; carbo 63%
◆ With margarine and egg whites instead of butter and a whole egg: chol 18 mg; fat-sat 4.8 g; fat-mono 6.7 g; fat-poly 2.2 g

~§ Garden-Fresh Nachos
Mexican Jicama Salad

GARDEN-FRESH NACHOS

Here's another traditional dish turned low-fat delight. Pita chips are substituted for fried tortilla chips, and part–skim milk Cheddar cheese replaces regular high-fat cheese. Cottage Cream replaces regular sour cream, and a lower-fat version of guacamole is offered. You may use canned refried beans instead of homemade, but be sure to choose some made with unsaturated vegetable oil instead of lard.

Whole-Grain Pita Chips (recipe
  follows)
4 cups Mexican Refried Beans
  (recipe follows)
1 cup grated part–skim milk
  Cheddar cheese
2 cups chopped romaine lettuce
6 scallions, chopped
2 tomatoes, chopped
1 cucumber, chopped
12 black olives, sliced (optional)
1 can (4 ounces) mild green
  chilis, chopped (optional)

Serves 4
Prep: 25 minutes

Picante sauce or salsa to taste
  (optional)
Cottage Cream (optional, page
  319)
Guacamole (optional, page 321)

~§ Place the Whole-Grain Pita Chips in an 8 × 12-inch baking dish, piling them high. Preheat broiler. Spread warm Mexican Refried Beans evenly over the chips. Sprinkle with cheese and place the dish under the broiler until the cheese melts.

~§ Remove the nachos from the oven and top them with the vegetables. Serve immediately (if the nachos sit too long they will become soggy), using a spatula. You can use the chips on the bottom to scoop the beans. Pass the toppings.

Nutritional Analysis: 1 serving
cal 556; chol 15 mg; fat-total 10.3 g; fat-mono 2.8 g; fat poly 2.2 g; fat-sat 4.3; protein 34.61 g; carbo 83.9 g; fiber 3.99 g; calcium 378 mg; sodium 1795 mg; fat 16%; protein 24%; carbo 60%

WHOLE-GRAIN PITA CHIPS

These chips are made from whole-wheat pita pockets, a popular Middle Eastern flat bread. It's generally made with wheat, water, yeast, and salt. That's all! The dough is rolled flat in the shape of a circle and baked quickly in a very hot oven. This creates an air space, and when the bread is cut in half it becomes a pocket for fillings. To make these chips, the pita is cut into triangles, then baked until crisp. Eat them as a snack, with or without spreads, serve with soups or salads, use them for nachos, and in every other way you would use fried corn or tortilla chips.

4 pieces whole-wheat pita bread

Prep: 5 minutes
Bake: 10 minutes

- ✑ Preheat oven to 350°F. With a sharp knife, cut each pita bread in half to form two pockets. Then cut each half into 3 triangles. Cut each triangle piece at the bottom to form 2 single-layer triangles.
- ✑ Place the bread on an unoiled baking sheet. Do not let the triangles overlap. Bake for 8 to 10 minutes or until the chips are crisp and begin to brown slightly.

Nutritional Analysis: 1 serving (12 chips)
cal 75; chol 0; fat-total 1 g; fat-mono 0.4 g; fat-poly 0.3 g; fat-sat 0.4 g; protein 3.5 g; carbo 13 g; fiber 1.4 g; calcium 0; sodium 204 mg; fat 12%; protein 19%; carbo 69%

MEXICAN REFRIED BEANS

To prepare this recipe, soak and cook the beans, then cook them again in a skillet to make them "refried." Pinto beans are most commonly used, but black, kidney, red, or other beans work just as well. Refried beans are used in a variety of Mexican dishes, such as tostados, burritos, and tacos, as well as in Mexican salads or with rice.

4 cups cooked kidney, pinto,
   adzuki, black, or red beans (1⅔
   cups raw)
1 tablespoon olive oil
1 teaspoon onion powder

Makes 4 cups
Prep: 25 minutes
Soak: Overnight

1 teaspoon garlic powder
1 teaspoon chili powder
Cayenne or black pepper to taste
Salt to taste (optional)
1 teaspoon white wine vinegar

❧ Drain the beans, saving the liquid in a separate bowl.
❧ Heat the oil in a large skillet and add all the ingredients, except the reserved bean liquid.
❧ Simmer while crushing the beans with a potato masher, the back of a fork, or a wooden spoon to create a pasty consistency, adding a little reserved bean liquid as needed. (If the beans get too thin, cook them, uncovered, on medium heat to thicken.)
❧ Keep the beans on a very low heat and stir them often until ready to use. (They freeze well and are easy to reheat in a skillet.)

Nutritional Analysis: 1 serving (1 cup)
cal 304; chol 0; fat-total 4.6 g; fat-mono 2.7 g; fat-poly 0.9 g; fat-sat 0.6 g; protein 15 g; carbo 50.6 g; fiber 11.36 g; calcium 93 mg; sodium 10 mg; fat 14%; protein 20%; carbo 66%

MEXICAN JICAMA SALAD

Jicama (pronounced hee-ka-ma) is a root vegetable popular in Mexico and sometimes called the Mexican potato. In Mexico, it's common to eat jicama with a squirt of lime and a dash of chili powder. In this recipe, its mild flavor and crisp texture are enhanced in a salad.

1 small jicama, peeled and cut
  into julienne
1 cucumber, peeled if waxed, and
  cubed
½ green pepper, sliced
Juice of 1 lime
Freshly ground black pepper to
  taste
Chili powder to taste
Salt to taste (optional)

Serves 4
Prep: 5 – 10 minutes

ᴥᙠ Toss all the ingredients in a bowl and refrigerate until ready to serve.

Nutritional Analysis: 1 serving
cal 44; chol 0; fat-total 0.3 g; fat-mono 0; fat-poly 0.1 g+; fat-sat 0; protein 1.43 g; carbo 9.6 g; fiber 1.1 g; calcium 23 mg; sodium 9 mg; fat 5%; protein 12%; carbo 83%

Nutritional Analysis for Lunch Meal: 1 serving
cal 600; chol 15 mg; fat-total 10.5 g; fat-mono 2.8 g+; fat-poly 2.3 g+; fat-sat 4.4 g+; protein 36.04 g; carbo 93.5 g; fiber 5.09 g; calcium 401 mg; sodium 1804 mg; fat 15%; protein 24%; carbo 61%

৵ Cutlet Parmesan Heros
Tossed Salad with Creamy Buttermilk Dressing

This sandwich is something special. It's very quick and easy to make. Because we always have the ingredients available, it has become a popular fast-food option in our house. The original inspiration for this recipe comes from a tiny southern Italian restaurant I loved as a child. Heros were made with veal, fried eggplant, or meatballs. This recipe is more healthful but retains the traditional feeling.

CUTLET PARMESAN HEROS

Although this recipe is made with chicken breasts, tempeh is a favorite substitute in our house. Even tofu slices work very well. One chicken serving is half a skinless, boneless breast. A package of tempeh will make 2 large heros (cut lengthwise) or 4 small ones. Slice tofu as desired.

1 chicken breast, skinned, boned,
  and halved
1 cup tomato sauce
1 ounce part–skim milk
  mozzarella cheese, grated
Oregano
¼ loaf Whole-Wheat French
  Bread (page 181), sliced in half,
  or 2 whole-wheat hero rolls

Serves 2
Prep: 15 minutes
Bake: 15 minutes

- ৵ Preheat broiler.
- ৵ Pound both pieces of chicken to flatten slightly. Broil until cooked through.
- ৵ Set oven at 375°F.
- ৵ Pour ½ cup of tomato sauce on the bottom of a baking dish just big enough to fit the chicken breasts without overlapping. Pour the remaining sauce over the chicken.
- ৵ Sprinkle cheese on the chicken and crush a bit of oregano on each half breast.
- ৵ Bake for 15 minutes or until bubbling.

✧§ Cut the bread in half lengthwise. Place each piece of chicken on one half of the bread. Spoon any tomato sauce left in the dish onto the bread. Close the sandwich and serve hot.

Nutritional Analysis: 1 serving
cal 688; chol 76 mg; fat-total 7.4 g; fat-mono 1.9 g; fat-poly 1.7 g; fat-sat 2.4 g; protein 52.43 g; carbo 109.8 g; fiber 15.35; calcium 200 mg; sodium 1256 mg; fat 9%; protein 29%; carbo 62%

TOSSED SALAD

Make this salad with these vegetables or with any number of others — whatever's available in your market or refrigerator.

2 cups leaf lettuce   *Serves 2*
1 carrot, sliced or grated   *Prep: 5 minutes*
½ green pepper, sliced or
  chopped
½ cup thinly sliced red cabbage
¼ red onion, thinly sliced
2 radishes, sliced

Nutritional Analysis: 1 serving
cal 4; chol 0; fat-total 0.3 g; fat-mono 0; fat-poly 0.2 g; fat-sat 0; protein 2.13 g; carbo 8.8 g; fiber 3.89 g; calcium 62 mg; sodium 21 mg; fat 5%; protein 19%; carbo 76%

CREAMY BUTTERMILK DRESSING

¼ cup cultured nonfat buttermilk   *Serves 2*
2 tablespoons tomato sauce or   *Prep: 5 minutes*
  juice
2 tablespoons low-fat cottage
  cheese
½ small clove garlic, minced
⅛ teaspoon basil
⅛ teaspoon dry mustard powder
Dash of paprika
Dash of celery seed
Freshly ground black pepper to
  taste

◄§ Mix dressing ingredients in a blender until very smooth. Refrigerate until ready to use.

Nutritional Analysis: 1 serving
cal 29; chol 2 mg; fat-total 0.3 g; fat-mono 0.1 g; fat-poly 0; fat-sat 0.2 g; protein 3.18 g; carbo 3.3 g; fiber 0.09 g; calcium 54 mg; sodium 75 mg; fat 10%; protein 44%; carbo 46%

Nutritional Analysis for Lunch Meal: 1 serving
cal 758; chol 77 mg; fat-total 7.9 g; fat-mono 2 g; fat-poly 2 g; fat-sat 2.6 g; protein 57.73 g; carbo 121.8 g; fiber 19.32 g; calcium 316 mg; sodium 1352 mg; fat 9%; protein 29%; carbo 62%

◆§ Caribbean Black Bean Soup
Citrus Season Salad with Ginger
Horseradish Dressing
Lemon Honey Muffins

This meal takes some advance planning, as the beans soak overnight and take a while to cook. You can soak the beans in the morning and prepare the soup in the evening. A pressure cooker will greatly reduce the cooking time. The entire meal is actually quite simple to make and requires very little time in the kitchen.

CARIBBEAN BLACK BEAN SOUP

This rich and hearty soup is one of my favorites. The garnishes — tangy yogurt, picante sauce, chives — make a striking contrast to the creamy black soup. Chopping the vegetables in a food processor will quicken the preparation. With recipes that require a significant amount of cooking time I always consider making a double batch and freezing half for a future meal. Don't let the number of ingredients or the cooking time discourage you from preparing this tasty soup.

3 cups dry black beans
8 cups vegetable broth
1 bay leaf
1 tablespoon olive oil
1 onion, finely chopped
1 green pepper, finely chopped
1 carrot, finely chopped
1 celery, finely chopped
4 cloves garlic, minced
1 tablespoon dry sherry or red
  wine
2 teaspoons cumin
2 teaspoons coriander
2 teaspoons lemon juice
1 teaspoon oregano
1 teaspoon chili powder

Serves 6
Soak: Overnight
Prep: 20 minutes
Cook: 2¹/₂ hours

2 tablespoons white wine vinegar
2 teaspoons fresh cilantro
  (optional)
Lots of freshly ground black
  pepper
Tabasco sauce or red pepper
  flakes to taste

Salt or soy sauce to taste
   (optional)
¾ cup nonfat plain yogurt

6 tablespoons picante sauce or
   salsa
6 teaspoons chives

~§ Sort through the beans and discard any foreign matter. Rinse the beans and put them in a soup pot filled with water. Soak overnight.

~§ Drain the water, return the beans to the pot, and add the broth and bay leaf.

~§ Bring the beans to a rapid boil, reduce the heat to medium-low, cover with lid ajar, and cook for 30 minutes.

~§ Meanwhile, heat the oil in a large skillet and sauté the vegetables and the garlic for 10 minutes. Stir the sherry, cumin, coriander, lemon juice, oregano, and chili powder into the sauté. After the beans have cooked for a ½ hour, add the sauté to the pot, cover, and cook for 2 hours more. Stir occasionally.

~§ Mix in the vinegar and cilantro. Season to taste with black pepper, Tabasco, and a dash of salt. Crush the beans slightly with a potato masher, fork, or spoon to thicken the soup.

~§ Remove the bay leaf and serve, topping each bowl with 2 tablespoons yogurt, 1 tablespoon picante sauce, and 1 teaspoon chives.

Nutritional Analysis: 1 serving
cal 400; chol 0; fat-total 4.3 g; fat-mono 2 g+; fat poly 1.4 g+; fat-sat 0.6 g+; protein 24.13 g; carbo 69.1 g; fiber 12.71 g+; calcium 196 mg; sodium 67 mg; fat 9%; protein 23%; carbo 68%

CITRUS SEASON SALAD

Most of the fat in this salad comes from the avocado. Because the remainder of the meal is low in fat, the avocado is a real taste treat that fits in well.

6 cups lettuce, such as Bibb,
   romaine, red leaf, and green
   leaf
2 tangerines, peeled and
   sectioned
1 cup sliced mushrooms

Serves 6
Prep: 10 minutes

6 radishes, thinly sliced
1 avocado, sliced
Alfalfa sprouts (optional)

◦§ Wash, dry, and tear the lettuce into pieces. Divide among 6 salad bowls and top with remaining ingredients.

Nutritional Analysis: 1 serving
cal 77; chol 0; fat-total 5.2 g; fat-mono 3.2 g; fat-poly 0.6 g; fat-sat 0.8 g; protein 2.12 g; carbo 7.4 g; fiber 2.35 g; calcium 38 mg; sodium 10 mg; fat 55%; protein 10%; carbo 35%

GINGER HORSERADISH DRESSING

A creamy, slightly sweet, mildly tangy dressing that's the perfect topping for the Citrus Season Salad.

¼ cup nonfat plain yogurt
¼ cup low-fat cottage cheese
¼ cup orange or tangerine juice
2 teaspoons prepared horseradish
1 teaspoon ginger
¼ teaspoon honey

Serves 6
Prep: 5 minutes

◦§ Combine all the ingredients in a blender and mix until smooth. Store the dressing in the refrigerator until you're ready to serve.

Nutritional Analysis: 1 serving
cal 21; chol 1 mg; fat-total 0.2 g; fat-mono 0.1 g +; fat-poly 0; fat-sat 0.1 g +; protein 1.95 g; carbo 2.7 g; fiber 0.03 g +; calcium 27 mg; sodium 46 g; fat 9%; protein 38%; carbo 53%

LEMON HONEY MUFFINS

These muffins are nice and light, with a sweet lemony flavor.

2¼ cups whole-grain flour
1½ teaspoons baking soda
⅛ teaspoon nutmeg
3 tablespoons unsalted butter or
    margarine, softened
¾ cup honey

Makes 14 muffins
Prep: 10 minutes
Bake: 20 minutes

1 egg or 2 egg whites or egg
  replacer
Juice and grated rind of 1 lemon

ఆ§ Preheat oven to 375°F. Line muffin tins with paper cups.
ఆ§ Mix the dry ingredients in a small bowl.
ఆ§ Cream the butter in a separate bowl. Add the honey, egg, and
  lemon juice and rind, beating after each addition.
ఆ§ Add the dry ingredients to the wet and stir just to incorporate.
  Immediately spoon the batter into muffin tins.
ఆ§ Bake for 20 minutes or until a toothpick inserted into the center
  of a muffin comes out dry. Remove the muffins from the tins and
  cool them on a rack.

Nutritional Analysis: 1 serving
cal 149; chol 26 mg; fat-total 3.1 g; fat-mono 0.9 g; fat-poly 0.3 g;
fat-sat 1.7 g; protein 3.09 g; carbo 29.3 g; fiber 1.88 g; calcium
39 mg; sodium 130 mg; fat 18%; protein 8%; carbo 74%
◆ With margarine and egg whites instead of butter and a whole egg:
  chol 0; fat-mono 1.1 g; fat-poly 0.9 g; fat-sat 0.5 g

Nutritional Analysis for Lunch Meal: 1 serving
cal 646; chol 27 mg; fat-total 12.8 g; fat-mono 6.2 g+; fat-poly
2.4 g+; fat-sat 3.1 g+; protein 31.29 g; carbo 108.6 g; fiber
16.97 g+; calcium 299 mg; sodium 253 mg; fat 17%; protein 19%;
carbo 64%
◆ With margarine and egg whites instead of butter and a whole egg:
  chol 1 mg; fat-mono 6.4 g+; fat-poly 3 g+; fat-sat 2 g+

◄§ Spaghetti Squash with Peperonata Sauce
Whole-Grain Garlic Bread

This light yet satisfying meal is quick and easy to prepare. Leftovers can be conveniently refrigerated and reheated in a microwave oven. The versatile Peperonata Sauce is also delicious over pasta, rice, baked potatoes, or as an appetizer with crusty hunks of French or Italian bread.

SPAGHETTI SQUASH WITH PEPERONATA SAUCE

Spaghetti squash is great fun. When it's cooked, the inside forms yellow strands that actually look like spaghetti. Take a fork and scrape the strands out, and you have a low-cal, high-fiber vegetable ready for sauce. In this recipe, it's topped with a variety of peppers that are stewed in a tomato sauce. The surprise ingredients are the little chunks of potatoes. And peperonata is wonderful when made spicy with the addition of hot peppers (optional in this recipe). For a fast meal, use a microwave oven to cook the squash — it takes half the time of a regular oven.*

1 small spaghetti squash
2 tablespoons olive oil
1 onion, sliced
8 cloves garlic, sliced
3 green peppers, cut into thick
   strips
1 red pepper or 5 ounces
   pimientos, cut into thick strips
Jalapeño or green chili peppers to
   taste (optional)
1 teaspoon basil
2 potatoes, cubed

Serves 4
Prep and Cook: 45
minutes

½ – 1 teaspoon freshly ground
   black pepper
6 ounces tomato paste
¼ cup chopped fresh parsley
1½ cups water

---

* To cook squash in a microwave oven: cut and clean the squash as directed in the recipe, place it in a microwave-safe dish, and cover tightly with plastic wrap. Cook in the microwave on high power for approximately 15 to 20 minutes. Let cool slightly before handling.

☙ Preheat oven to 450°F. Cut the squash in half lengthwise with a sharp knife. Scoop out the seeds and discard. Place the squash face down on a lightly oiled baking sheet. Bake for 45 minutes or until the squash is soft.

☙ Heat the olive oil in a medium saucepan. Sauté the onion and garlic for 3 minutes. Add all three kinds of peppers and the basil. Cook for 10 minutes, stirring occasionally.

☙ Meanwhile, wash the potatoes and cut into cubes. Boil or steam them for 10 to 15 minutes, or just until tender. Drain and set aside.

☙ When the peppers are cooked, add the black pepper, tomato paste, parsley, water, and potatoes. Cover and simmer gently for 10 to 15 minutes.

☙ Remove the squash from the oven and use a fork to scrape out the cooked flesh. Divide among 4 bowls. Top with sauce and serve.

Nutritional Analysis: 1 serving
cal 345; chol 0; fat-total 8.6 g; fat-mono 5.2 g+; fat-poly 1.4 g+; fat-sat 1.3 g+; protein 8.16 g; carbo 63.3 g; fiber 13.14 g; calcium 127 mg; sodium 101 mg; fat 21%; protein 9%; carbo 70%

WHOLE-GRAIN GARLIC BREAD

A unique twist turns the familiar high-fat garlic bread into a delicious whole-grain option. I vividly remember one particular restaurant my father took me to as a child. In my young mind, it seemed as though we went to this restaurant just for the fabulous, garlicky bread. Because of the whole-grain heartiness of the bread in this recipe, it too can handle lots of garlic. Add more if you like.

¼ loaf Whole-Wheat French or
   Italian Bread (page 181)
1½ tablespoons unsalted butter
   or margarine, softened
2 cloves garlic, minced, or ½
   teaspoon garlic powder
1 tablespoon parsley
1 tablespoon grated Parmesan
   cheese
Freshly ground black pepper to
   taste

Serves 4
Prep: 5 minutes
Bake: 15 minutes

◄§ Preheat oven to 400°F. Cut the bread in half lengthwise and spread the butter evenly on the inside of both pieces.

◄§ Use a knife to spread the garlic on top of the butter.

◄§ Sprinkle the parsley, Parmesan cheese, and pepper on top of the garlic. Close the loaf and wrap it in aluminum foil.

◄§ Bake for 15 to 20 minutes, or until ready to serve. Remove the foil and cut the bread into 4 slices, serving each person a top and bottom piece.

Nutritional Analysis: 1 serving
cal 166; chol 13 mg; fat-total 5.4 g; fat-mono 1.5 g; fat-poly 0.5 g; fat-sat 3 g; protein 5.52 g; carbo 25.6 g; fiber 3.42 g; calcium 37 mg; sodium 116 mg; fat 28%; protein 13%; carbo 59%

◆ With margarine instead of butter: chol 1 mg; fat-mono 2.2 g; fat-poly 1.6 g; fat-sat 1.2 g

Nutritional Analysis for Lunch Meal: 1 serving
cal 511; chol 13 mg; fat-total 14 g; fat-mono 6.8 g +; fat-poly 1.9 g +; fat-sat 4.3 g +; protein 13.68 g; carbo 88.9 g; fiber 16.56 g; calcium 163 mg; sodium 217 mg; fat 23%; protein 10%; carbo 67%

◆ With margarine instead of butter: chol 1 mg; fat-mono 7.4 g +; fat-poly 3.1 g +; fat-sat 2.5 g +

◄§ *Minestrone Soup*
Whole-Grain Soda Biscuits

MINESTRONE SOUP

This recipe is so full of vegetables, it's more like a stew than a soup. In fact, many Europeans think that minestrone should be so thick with vegetables that a spoon can stand upright in it. For a little extra touch of flavor, try adding a few spoonfuls of Pesto Sauce, Red Pepper Coulis, or tomato paste as the soup finishes cooking.

4 tablespoons olive oil*
1 onion, chopped
3 large cloves garlic, chopped
2 stalks celery, chopped
1 green pepper, chopped
2 small potatoes, cubed
1 carrot, sliced
1 can (28 ounces) Italian-style
  tomatoes, with liquid
¼ cup dry red wine
4 cups vegetable or chicken broth
1 cup uncooked whole-grain
  macaroni
4 cups cooked kidney, pinto,
  navy, and/or garbanzo beans
  (1⅔ cups raw)
¼ cup chopped fresh parsley
2 teaspoons basil

Serves 8
Prep: 15 minutes
Cook: 40–45 minutes

2 teaspoons oregano
Freshly ground black pepper to
  taste
½ teaspoon sage
Salt to taste (optional)
10 ounces frozen spinach
1 cup frozen peas
Grated Parmesan cheese
  (optional)

◄§ Heat the oil in a large soup pot. Saute the onion, garlic, celery, and pepper for 5 minutes.

◄§ Stir in the potatoes and carrot. Cook for 3 minutes more.

◄§ Cut the tomatoes in quarters and add them to the pot along with the tomato liquid, wine, and broth.

◄§ Bring the soup to a boil, reduce the heat to simmer, cover, and cook for 20 minutes, or until the potatoes are tender.

◄§ Meanwhile, cook the pasta until al dente, 8 to 10 minutes.

---

* You may reduce the olive oil to as little as 1 tablespoon.

◆§ Add the remaining ingredients to the soup. Stir and simmer until the spinach is thawed and the soup is hot, about 20 minutes. (This soup freezes well and reheats easily.)

◆§ Sprinkle each serving with a little Parmesan cheese.

Nutritional Analysis: 1 serving
cal 306; chol 0; fat-total 8.8 g; fat-mono 5.4 g; fat-poly 1.4 g; fat-sat 1.1 g; protein 12.54 g; carbo 46.3 g; fiber 9.04 g; calcium 146 mg; sodium 196 mg; fat 25%; protein 16%; carbo 59%

WHOLE-GRAIN SODA BISCUITS

These little breads are fast to make and taste good with a variety of entrees. Try eating them with Black Olive and Pimiento Spread or Vegetable Cream Spread. They are also delicious with a little honey.

2½ cups whole-grain flour   *Makes 12 biscuits*
½ teaspoon baking soda   *Prep: 5 minutes*
½ teaspoon salt   *Bake: 20–30 minutes*
2 cups cultured nonfat buttermilk

◆§ Preheat oven to 400°F. Lightly oil 12 muffin tins.

◆§ Mix the flour, baking soda, and salt in a large bowl.

◆§ Stir the buttermilk into the flour with a fork. Mix just well enough to incorporate all the ingredients.

◆§ Spoon the batter into the prepared pan and bake for 20 to 30 minutes. Remove the biscuits from the pan and cool slightly on a rack. Serve warm.

Nutritional Analysis: 1 serving
cal 98; chol 1 mg; fat-total 0.5 g; fat-mono 0.1 g; fat-poly 0.2 g; fat-sat 0.1 g; protein 4.67 g; carbo 19.7 g; fiber 2.42 g; calcium 61 mg; sodium 146 mg; fat 4%; protein 18%; carbo 78%

Nutritional Analysis for Lunch Meal: 1 serving
cal 404; chol 1 mg; fat-total 9.2 g; fat-mono 5.4 g; fat-poly 1.6 g; fat-sat 1.2 g; protein 17.20 g; carbo 66 g; fiber 11.46 g; calcium 207 mg; sodium 342 mg; fat 20%; protein 17%; carbo 63%

⊷ら Oriental Hot and Sour Ramen
Tamari Rice

This oriental meal originated from Chinese hot and sour soup and fried rice. The soup doesn't contain the traditional pork, but it has an abundance of vegetables — and you have the option of adding tofu, chicken, or whatever else suits you. The Tamari Rice is much lighter, lower in fat, than traditional fried rice and again you can vary it according to your personal taste. As with many oriental-style dishes, soy sauce increases the sodium content. If you or a family member are sodium-sensitive, or if you're on a sodium-restricted diet, use only reduced-sodium soy sauce or decrease the amount of soy sauce in this meal.

ORIENTAL HOT AND SOUR RAMEN

The addition of noodles makes this broth soup into *ramen*. Chinese noodles are especially delicious, but cooked spaghetti will also taste fine. The "hot and sour" refers to a slightly spicy, sweet and sour flavor. My family likes the soup filled with lots of vegetables and noodles, leaving little broth unaccompanied at the bottom of the bowl. You can find unique ingredients like chili purée with garlic, rice wine, rice vinegar, and Chinese noodles in the oriental foods section in most progressive grocery or specialty stores.

1 tablespoon sesame oil, peanut
   oil, or mild-flavored oil
1 clove garlic, minced
¼ pound mushrooms
4 cups vegetable or chicken broth
3 tablespoons Chinese rice wine
2 tablespoons Chinese rice
   vinegar
2 tablespoons reduced-sodium
   soy sauce
½ – 1 teaspoon chili purée with
   garlic
1 carrot, grated

Serves 4
Prep: 10 minutes
Cook: 15 minutes

2 cups chopped bok choy or
   spinach
2 cups broccoli florets
6 ounces Chinese noodles,
   broken into bite-size pieces

◆§ Heat the oil in a large saucepan and sauté the garlic and mushrooms until soft.

◆§ Stir in the remaining ingredients and bring the soup to a boil. Lower the heat to simmer and cook, stirring occasionally to break up the noodles. When the noodles are cooked, taste to adjust seasoning, adding more wine, vinegar, soy sauce, or chili purée.

Nutritional Analysis: 1 serving
cal 185; chol 25 mg; fat-total 4.8 g; fat-mono 1.9 g; fat-poly 1.6 g; fat-sat 0.9 g; protein 9.18 g; carbo 29.1 g; fiber 7.06 g; calcium 185 mg; sodium 561 mg; fat 22%; protein 19%; carbo 59%

TAMARI RICE

Brown rice is cooked with sautéed vegetables to create a tasty dish that is similar to both pilaf and fried rice. Add any other vegetables you like.

1 tablespoon sesame oil, peanut oil, or mild-flavored oil
1 small onion, chopped
1 clove garlic, minced
1 red or green pepper, chopped
½ carrot, finely chopped or grated
1½ cups long-grain brown rice
3 cups water or vegetable broth
3 tablespoons reduced-sodium soy sauce
1½ teaspoons ginger
1 cup frozen peas, thawed

Serves 4
Prep: 10 minutes
Cook: 45–50 minutes

◆§ Heat the oil in a large saucepan and sauté the onion, garlic, pepper, and carrot until soft. Stir in the rice. Cook, stirring several minutes, until the rice browns slightly.

◆§ Add the remaining ingredients, except the peas, and bring to a boil. Lower the heat to simmer and cook, covered, for about 45 minutes or until all the water has been absorbed.

◆§ Remove the rice from the heat and gently toss in the peas.

◆§ Let the rice sit, covered, for 5 to 10 minutes before serving. (Leftovers reheat well.)

Nutritional Analysis: 1 serving
cal 339; chol 0; fat-total 5 g; fat-mono 2.3 g+; fat-poly 1.7 g+; fat-sat 0.9 g+; protein 9.46 g; carbo 65.1 g; fiber 6.77 g+; calcium 44 mg; sodium 818 mg; fat 13%; protein 11%; carbo 76%

Nutritional Analysis for Lunch Meal: 1 serving
cal 523; chol 25 mg; fat-total 9.8 g; fat-mono 4.2 g+; fat-poly 3.3 g+; fat-sat 1.8 g+; protein 18.64 g; carbo 65.1 g; fiber 6.77 g+; calcium 44 mg; sodium 1379 mg; fat 16%; protein 14%; carbo 70%

⊷ *German Cabbage Caraway Soup*
Burgundy Beet Salad
Onion Rye Flat Bread

The soup is light, the salad bright, and the bread is a taste treat all its own.

GERMAN CABBAGE CARAWAY SOUP

This light yet hearty cabbage soup has a creamy texture, with caraway adding an extra bite.

1 tablespoon olive oil
2 large onions, chopped
2 large cloves garlic, minced
2 teaspoons caraway seeds
2 teaspoons basil
2 teaspoons dill weed
Salt to taste (optional)
Freshly ground black pepper to
   taste
1 medium green cabbage,
   shredded
6 cups vegetable broth

3 medium potatoes, cubed
½ cup skim milk
½ cup nonfat plain yogurt

Serves 6
Prep: 15 minutes
Cook: 40 – 45 minutes

- ⊷ Heat the oil in a large soup pot and sauté the onions and garlic for 5 minutes.
- ⊷ Stir in the caraway seeds, herbs, salt, and pepper. Sauté for 5 minutes more.
- ⊷ Add the cabbage and vegetable broth. Cover the pot and simmer for 25 to 30 minutes, stirring occasionally.
- ⊷ Meanwhile, steam or boil the potatoes until tender.
- ⊷ Purée the cooked potatoes with milk and yogurt in a food processor or blender.
- ⊷ Add the purée to the soup and simmer for 15 minutes more. Taste to adjust seasonings.

Nutritional Analysis: 1 serving
cal 116; chol 1 mg; fat-total 3 g; fat-mono 1.9 g; fat-poly 0.5 g; fat-sat
0.4 g; protein 5.85 g; carbo 17.1 g; fiber 3.06 g+; calcium 175 mg;
sodium 58 mg; fat 23%; protein 20%; carbo 57%

BURGUNDY BEET SALAD

Canned beets help speed this dish along, eliminating the cooking
time.

2 pounds small beets*
¼ cup apple cider vinegar
1 clove garlic, minced
1 tablespoon honey
1 onion, thinly sliced
1 green pepper, thinly sliced
1 cup low-fat cottage cheese
1 cup nonfat plain yogurt
2 tablespoons chives
1 teaspoon dill weed

Serves 6
Prep: 10 minutes
Cook: 30 minutes
Marinate: 30 minutes

◄§ Wash the beets and boil or steam them for 25 minutes. Rinse
them in cool water and rub off the skins.
◄§ Cut the beets into cubes or slices.
◄§ Marinate the beets in a bowl with the vinegar, garlic, honey,
onion, and pepper for 30 minutes.
◄§ Cream the cottage cheese in a blender or food processor until
smooth. Mix the cottage cream, yogurt, chives, and dill. Toss
with the marinated beet mixture. This salad is good both warm or
well chilled.

Nutritional Analysis: 1 serving
cal 97; chol 4 mg; fat-total 0.8 g; fat-mono 0.2 g; fat-poly 0.1 g; fat-sat
0.5 g; protein 8.41 g; carbo 14.6 g; fiber 2.57 g+; calcium 120 mg;
sodium 216 mg; fat 7%; protein 34%; carbo 59%

---

*If you're using canned beets, choose small whole beets packed in water, with
nothing else added.

ONION RYE FLAT BREAD

I've had this recipe in my files since I was about eleven years old. Its traditional name is *pletzel,* and because I have changed the ingredients to fit today's health guidelines, I have also changed the name. It is fast and simple to make, yet with its crunchy edges and onion-rye flavor it always gets rave reviews.

2½ cups rye flour
2½ teaspoons baking powder
2 teaspoons poppy seeds
3 tablespoons olive oil
2 small onions, grated or finely
  chopped
1 clove garlic, minced
Salt to taste (optional)
Water

Serves 6
Prep: 15–20 minutes
Bake: 20 minutes

◆§ Preheat oven to 400°F. Lightly oil a baking sheet.
◆§ Combine the flour, baking powder, and poppy seeds.
◆§ Add the remaining ingredients to the flour mixture, including enough water (added slowly) to make a stiff and not too sticky dough. Mix with your hands to form a ball.
◆§ Place the dough on the baking sheet and roll it out to a ¼-inch thickness. Use a little extra flour to prevent the rolling pin from sticking to the dough.
◆§ Bake for 20 minutes or until the edges of the bread turn golden brown.
◆§ Cool on the baking sheet and cut into 12 pieces.

Nutritional Analysis: 1 serving (2 pieces)
cal 219; chol 0; fat-total 8.2 g; fat-mono 5.2 g+; fat-poly 0.9 g+; fat-sat 1 g+; protein 5.59 g; carbo 33.4 g; fiber 0.88 g+; calcium 137 mg; sodium 131 mg; fat 32%; protein 10%; carbo 58%

Nutritional Analysis for Lunch Meal: 1 serving
cal 432; chol 5 mg; fat-total 12 g; fat-mono 7.3 g+; fat-poly 1.5 g+; fat-sat 2 g; protein 19.85 g; carbo 65.2 g; fiber 6.51 g+; calcium 431 mg; sodium 405 mg; fat 24%; protein 18%; carbo 58%

ఆ Thick and Hearty Vegetable Chili
Melt-in-Your-Mouth Corn Bread

There are so many variations of chili — with beans or without, hot or not, meat or vegetables — each with its own special qualities. And what better to make a bowl of chili complete than a thick chunk of corn bread. If you have a favorite chili recipe, look at the note that follows this recipe on how to make healthful substitutions.* To quicken the cooking time for the chili, you can cook it in a microwave or pressure cooker.

THICK AND HEARTY VEGETABLE CHILI

For many of us, a steaming bowl of chili brings back memories of cold, snowy days. I've created a new version of this old favorite, with vegetables replacing the beef. And you can even create another complete meal by serving the chili over brown rice or other whole grains, a baked potato, a pizza crust, or in lasagna — use your imagination.

1 tablespoon olive oil
1 onion, chopped
4 large cloves garlic, minced
1 carrot, thinly sliced
1 green pepper, chopped
½ pound mushrooms, sliced
1 small zucchini, sliced
12 black olives (optional)
(Ingredients continued on page 118)

Serves 6
Prep: 25 minutes
Cook: 30 minutes or
more

---

* To make your favorite chili recipe more healthful, substitute ground turkey breast (all fat and skin removed before grinding) for the beef. If oil or fat is called for, use only 1 to 3 tablespoons of olive oil. Cut back on or eliminate salt — add some of the seasonings called for in this recipe, and use a tomato sauce that has no added fat. Be sure to serve with a salad if vegetables are not included in your chili.

Here's a traditional chili con carne recipe, using ground turkey breast instead of beef: sauté a chopped onion, green pepper, and garlic clove with 1 pound of ground turkey breast in 1 to 2 tablespoons of olive oil until the turkey is browned. Add a 16-ounce can of tomatoes, 16 ounces kidney beans, 1 cup tomato sauce, 2 teaspoons chili powder, and ½ teaspoon basil. Bring to a boil, then reduce heat to simmer. Cook, covered, at least 20 to 30 minutes.

1 can (28 ounces) tomatoes, with liquid, chopped
2 cups tomato sauce
⅓ cup diced mild green chilis
4 cups cooked kidney, pinto, *adzuki*, or black beans (1⅔ cups raw)
3 tablespoons chili powder
1 tablespoon oregano
2 teaspoons cumin
2 teaspoons paprika
Crushed red pepper to taste (optional)

Cayenne pepper to taste (optional)
1 tablespoon white wine vinegar
Chopped cilantro to taste (optional)

Optional toppings: grated Parmesan cheese, grated part–skim milk cheese, a drop of nonfat yogurt, Guacamole (page 321), or Cottage Cream (page 319)

◆§ Heat the oil in a soup pot and sauté the onion, garlic, carrot, green pepper, mushrooms, zucchini, and olives for 20 minutes.

◆§ Add the remaining ingredients, except the vinegar and cilantro, and simmer for at least 30 minutes. Stir often to prevent burning. Add the vinegar and cilantro, and simmer until ready to serve. Garnish with one of the toppings. (This chili freezes well and reheats easily.)

Nutritional Analysis: 1 serving
cal 296; chol 0; fat-total 4.8 g; fat-mono 2 g +; fat-poly 1.3 g +; fat-sat 0.6 g +; protein 13.79 g; carbo 51.8 g; fiber 13.90 g; calcium 150 mg; sodium 883 mg; fat 14%; protein 18%; carbo 68%

◆ To lower the sodium level, use unsalted canned tomatoes and tomato sauce.

MELT-IN-YOUR-MOUTH CORN BREAD

A subtly sweet, soft, and cakey multigrain corn bread. This is not the dry, crumbly kind. The addition of corn kernels adds a unique twist. This recipe also makes great muffins.

1¼ cups cornmeal
1¼ cups whole-grain flour
1 teaspoon baking powder
1 teaspoon baking soda
1 teaspoon chili powder

12 squares or muffins
Prep: 10 minutes
Bake: 20–30 minutes

Dash of cinnamon
Salt to taste (optional)
1½ cups skim milk
1 egg or 2 egg whites or egg
  replacer, beaten

3 tablespoons unsalted butter or
  margarine, melted
2 tablespoons molasses
1 cup frozen corn, thawed

◆§ Preheat oven to 400°F. Very lightly oil an 8 × 8-inch baking dish or line muffin tins with paper cups.

◆§ Mix the dry ingredients in a large bowl. Mix the remaining ingredients, except the corn, in a small bowl.

◆§ Add the wet ingredients to the dry and mix just well enough to incorporate. Fold in the corn kernels.

◆§ Spoon the batter into the prepared pan. Bake for 20 minutes for muffins, 30 minutes for bread, or until a toothpick inserted in the center comes out dry.

◆§ Cool on a rack. Serve the corn bread directly from the pan, or remove muffins from the pan. (Leftovers are excellent snacks, cold or warm.)

Nutritional Analysis: 1 serving
cal 149; chol 31 mg; fat-total 4.1 g; fat-mono 1.2 g; fat-poly 0.6 g; fat-sat 2 g; protein 4.73 g; carbo 24.7 g; fiber 3.74 g; calcium 92 mg; sodium 124 mg; fat 24%; protein 12%; carbo 64%
◆ With margarine and egg whites instead of butter and a whole egg: chol 1 mg; fat-mono 1.4 g; fat-poly 1.3 g; fat-sat 0.7 g

Nutritional Analysis for Lunch Meal: 1 serving
cal 445; chol 31 mg; fat-total 8.9 g; fat-mono 3.2 g+; fat-poly 1.9 g+; fat-sat 2.7 g+; protein 18.52 g; carbo 76.4 g; fiber 17.64 g; calcium 242 mg; sodium 1007 mg; fat 17%; protein 16%; carbo 67%
◆ With margarine and egg whites instead of butter and a whole egg: chol 1 mg; fat-mono 3.5 g; fat-poly 2.6 g; fat-sat 1.3 g

◢§ Herbal Tomato Rice Soup
Carrot, Cheddar, and Chickpea
Slaw with Fresh Parsley
Parmesan Dressing

HERBAL TOMATO RICE SOUP

My favorite soup as a child was tomato and rice. Here I've created a soup that brings back the memory but with a more healthful flair. The true tomato taste combines with the heartiness of brown rice and a perfect blend of seasonings.

2 cups water
1 cup brown rice
1½ tablespoons olive oil
1 large onion, chopped
3 cloves garlic, minced
2 cans (28 ounces) tomatoes,
 drained (save liquid for
 another purpose)
1 teaspoon fructose or honey
1 cup dry white wine
½ teaspoon dried oregano, or ¾
 tablespoon chopped fresh
½ teaspoon dried basil, or ¾
 tablespoon chopped fresh

Serves 4
Prep: 10 minutes
Cook: 45 minutes

½ teaspoon dried thyme, or ¾
 tablespoon chopped fresh
½ teaspoon dried marjoram, or ¾
 tablespoon chopped fresh
Freshly ground black pepper to
 taste

◢§ Bring the water to a boil in a small saucepan. Add the rice and bring to a boil again. Reduce the heat to simmer, cover, and cook for 35 minutes or until all the water has been absorbed and the rice is cooked.

◢§ Meanwhile, heat the oil in a soup pot and sauté the onion for 5 to 10 minutes. Add the remaining ingredients, cover, and simmer for 30 minutes. Stir occasionally to break up the tomatoes.

◢§ Pour the soup into a food processor or blender and purée until smooth. Pour the soup back into the pot and stir in the cooked rice. Continue heating gently until ready to serve.

Nutritional Analysis: 1 serving
cal 288; chol 0; fat-total 7.3 g; fat-mono 4.4 g; fat-poly 1 g; fat-sat 1 g; protein 6.16 g; carbo 51.6 g; fiber 5.3 g; calcium 103 mg; sodium 37 mg; fat 22%; protein 8%; carbo 70%

CARROT, CHEDDAR, AND CHICKPEA SLAW

The ingredients in this salad are basic, but the combination is both interesting and very tasty.

3 cups grated carrots   *Serves 4*
2 cups cooked garbanzo beans   *Prep: 5 minutes*
  (⅞ cup raw)
4 ounces part–skim milk
  Cheddar cheese, grated

◈ Combine the ingredients in a large bowl and toss to mix well. Chill until ready to serve.

Nutritional Analysis: 1 serving
cal 260; chol 15 mg; fat-total 7 g; fat-mono 1.4 g+; fat-poly 0.2 g+; fat-sat 3.1 g+; protein 17.05 g; carbo 34 g; fiber 8.89 g; calcium 290 mg; sodium 185 mg; fat 24%; protein 26%; carbo 50%

FRESH PARSLEY PARMESAN DRESSING

This is a creamy dressing similar to Green Goddess but without all the fat.

3 tablespoons nonfat plain yogurt   *Serves 4*
3 tablespoons low-fat cottage   *Prep: 5 minutes*
  cheese
3 tablespoons grated Parmesan ·
  cheese
2 tablespoons fresh parsley,
  packed
1 tablespoon skim milk
1 tablespoon lemon juice   ¼ teaspoon oregano
½ tablespoon white wine vinegar   ¼ teaspoon tarragon
¼ teaspoon chives   Freshly ground black pepper to
¼ teaspoon basil   taste

◆§ Combine all the ingredients in a blender or food processor and mix until very smooth.

◆§ Refrigerate until ready to serve.

Nutritional Analysis: 1 serving
cal 40; chol 4 mg; fat-total 1.8 g; fat-mono 0.4 g+; fat-poly 0; fat-sat 0.9 g+; protein 3.77 g; carbo 2.4 g; fiber 0.02 g+; calcium 98 mg; sodium 124 mg; fat 39%; protein 37%; carbo 24%

Nutritional Analysis for Lunch Meal: 1 serving
cal 588; chol 19 mg; fat-total 16 g; fat-mono 6.2 g+; fat-poly 1.2 g+; fat-sat 5 g+; protein 26.98 g; carbo 87.9 g; fiber 14.21 g+; calcium 490 mg; sodium 346 mg; fat 24%; protein 18%; carbo 58%

ᴤ Brazilian Black Beans and Brown Rice
Winter Vegetable Salad with Sweet Red Pepper Vinaigrette

This is a warm and hearty winter meal. Advance planning is needed, as with most legume dishes, for bean soaking and cooking. A pressure cooker can shorten the cooking time significantly, and chopping the vegetables in a food processor will cut down on the preparation time. Although the beans need to cook a while, the actual amount of time you'll need to spend in the kitchen is minimal.

BRAZILIAN BLACK BEANS AND BROWN RICE

Beans and rice are a staple in many countries around the world. This recipe combines black beans (one of my favorites) with both sweet and spicy ingredients to create a wonderful blend of flavors, enhanced even more by the nutty taste of brown rice.

2 cups dry black beans
4 cups vegetable broth
1 tablespoon olive oil
1 onion, chopped
1 carrot, finely chopped
1 green pepper, chopped
1 stalk celery, chopped
4 cloves garlic, minced
2 bay leaves
½ teaspoon oregano
½ teaspoon thyme
½ – 1 teaspoon ginger
1 teaspoon cumin
1 teaspoon coriander
½ cup orange juice
2 cups water

Serves 6
Soak: Overnight
Prep: 30 minutes
Cook: 1½ – 2 hours

1 cup brown rice
2 tablespoons white wine vinegar
Red pepper flakes to taste
Freshly ground black pepper to taste
Salt or soy sauce to taste (optional)

ᴤ Sort through the beans and remove any foreign matter. Rinse the beans and put them in a soup pot filled with water. Soak overnight.

◄§ Drain the water, return the beans to the soup pot, and add the broth.

◄§ Bring the beans to a rapid boil, reduce the heat to medium-low, cover partially, and cook for 30 minutes.

◄§ Meanwhile, heat the oil in a large skillet and sauté the vegetables and garlic for 10 minutes. Stir the herbs into the sauté.

◄§ After the beans have cooked for 30 minutes, add the sauté and the orange juice. Continue cooking for 1½ to 2 hours, or until the beans are soft and the sauce is thick.

◄§ Boil 2 cups of water in a saucepan and add the rice. Bring to a boil again, reduce the heat to simmer, cover, and cook for 35 to 45 minutes, or until all the water has been absorbed. Keep covered and set aside until ready to serve.

◄§ When the beans are cooked, season them with vinegar, red and black pepper, and salt. Cook for 10 minutes more. Remove the bay leaves.

◄§ Serve the beans on top of or beside the rice. (This meal freezes and reheats very well.)

Nutritional Analysis: 1 serving
cal 395; chol 0; fat-total 4.1 g; fat-mono 2 g+; fat-poly 1.2 g+; fat-sat 0.6 g+; protein 18.45 g; carbo 73.6 g; fiber 11.34 g+; calcium 129 mg; sodium 29 mg; fat 9%; protein 18%; carbo 73%

WINTER VEGETABLE SALAD

This salad is made with fresh vegetables that are readily available during the winter season. They are lightly cooked to bring out their best color and flavor. Add or omit any vegetables according to your own tastes.

2 cups Brussels sprouts	*Serves 6*
2 cups sliced carrots	*Prep: 10 minutes*
2 cups cauliflower florets	*Cook: 30 minutes*
2 cups sliced parsnips	
2 cups cubed turnips	
2 cups broccoli florets	

◄§ Place the Brussels sprouts in a large steamer pot and steam for 15 minutes.

◆§ Add the remaining vegetables, except the broccoli, to the pot and cook for 10 minutes more.

◆§ Add the broccoli and cook for another 5 minutes, or until the broccoli is bright green. Remove the pot from the heat and quickly rinse in cold water. Drain the vegetables and place in a serving bowl. Serve this salad hot, warm, or chilled.

Nutritional Analysis: 1 serving
cal 120; chol 0; fat-total 0.7 g; fat-mono 0.1 g; fat-poly 0.3 g; fat-sat 0.2 g; protein 5.33 g; carbo 27.3 g; fiber 9.62 g; calcium 136 mg; sodium 85 mg; fat 5%; protein 16%; carbo 79%

SWEET RED PEPPER VINAIGRETTE

Sweet red peppers or pimientos are puréed with olive oil and vinegar to create a rich and brightly flavored dressing.

3 tablespoons olive oil
1 tablespoon sherry vinegar or
   red wine vinegar
1 clove garlic, minced
8 ounces pimientos or roasted red
   peppers
½ teaspoon tarragon
Freshly ground black pepper to
   taste
Salt to taste (optional)

Serves 6
Prep: 5 minutes

◆§ Combine all the ingredients in a blender or food processor and mix until very smooth.

◆§ Chill until ready to serve.

Nutritional Analysis: 1 serving
cal 74; chol 0; fat-total 7.2 g; fat-mono 5.2 g+; fat-poly 0.6 g+; fat-sat 0.9 g+; protein 0.4 g; carbo 2.8 g; fiber 0.01 g+; calcium 7 mg; sodium 10 mg; fat 84%; protein 2%; carbo 14%

Nutritional Analysis for Lunch Meal: 1 serving
cal 590; chol 0; fat-total 12 g; fat-mono 7.3 g+; fat-poly 2.1 g+; fat-sat 1.8 g; protein 24.18 g; carbo 103.7 g; fiber 20.97 g+; calcium 271 mg; sodium 123 mg; fat 17%; protein 16%; carbo 67%

⋐ Split Pea and Wild Rice Soup
Winter's Fresh Vegetable Marinade

The soup is so low in fat it allows for a salad in which the fat content by itself is high. They combine to make a meal that's just right.

SPLIT PEA AND WILD RICE SOUP

This is a thick and hearty split pea soup with a twist — wild rice. The recipe is both fast and easy. Chop the vegetables in a food processor to quicken the preparation time.

2½ cups water
1 cup wild rice
1 tablespoon olive oil
4 carrots, finely chopped
4 cloves garlic, minced
4 stalks celery with leaves,
  chopped
2 onions, chopped
3 cups split peas
10 cups vegetable broth
1 bay leaf
1 teaspoon thyme
1 teaspoon dry mustard powder
⅛ teaspoon sage

Serves 8
Prep: 15 minutes
Cook: 45 minutes

Lots of freshly ground black
  pepper
Salt to taste (optional)
2 tablespoons lemon juice or
  white wine vinegar

⋐ Bring the water to a boil in a saucepan. Add the rice, lower the heat to simmer, cover, and cook for 35 to 45 minutes, or until the water has been absorbed.

⋐ While the rice is cooking, heat the oil in a large soup pot and sauté the carrots, garlic, celery, and onion for 10 minutes.

⋐ Stir the split peas into the sauté. Add all but the last 3 ingredients and bring to a boil.

⋐ Cover the pot and lower the heat to medium-low. Cook for 45 minutes.

⋖§ Add the cooked rice to the soup and stir well. Add pepper, salt, and lemon juice. Simmer until the soup is thick and the peas are fully cooked. Remove the bay leaf and serve.

Nutritional Analysis: 1 serving
cal 438; chol 0; fat-total 3.2 g; fat-mono 1.6 g+; fat-poly 0.6 g+; fat-sat 0.4 g+; protein 24.71 g; carbo 81.3 g; fiber 5.63 g+; calcium 84 mg; sodium 45 mg; fat 6%; protein 22%; carbo 72%

WINTER'S FRESH VEGETABLE MARINADE

In this recipe, some of winter's most plentiful vegetables are lightly steamed and marinated, producing a crunchy, flavorful salad. The longer the salad marinates, the more the flavor is enhanced.

3 cups cauliflower florets
3 cups carrots, cut into julienne
3 cups broccoli florets
1 red onion, thinly sliced
1 clove garlic, minced
1 large shallot, minced
4 tablespoons olive oil
2–3 tablespoons white wine
   vinegar
2 teaspoons Dijon-style mustard
½ teaspoon tarragon
2 tablespoons chives
4 ounces pimientos, sliced
¼ cup pine nuts
2 tablespoons minced fresh
   parsley
Freshly ground black pepper to
   taste

Serves 6
Prep and Cook: 20
   minutes
Marinate: 1 hour or
   more

⋖§ Steam the cauliflower and carrots for 10 minutes. Add the broccoli and steam until bright green.
⋖§ Toss the steamed vegetables and onion in a large shallow bowl. Mix the next 7 ingredients in a separate bowl to make a marinade.
⋖§ Pour the marinade over the steamed vegetables and mix well. Toss in the remaining ingredients and chill for at least 1 hour. Stir several times while marinating.

Nutritional Analysis: 1 serving
cal 199; chol 0; fat-total 12.7 g; fat-mono 8 g+; fat-poly 2.2 g+;
fat-sat 1.8 g+; protein 5.48 g; carbo 19.7 g; fiber 6.91 g+; calcium
143 mg; sodium 94 mg; fat 53%; protein 10%; carbo 37%

Nutritional Analysis for Lunch Meal: 1 serving
cal 637; chol 0; fat-total 15.9 g; fat-mono 9.6 g+; fat-poly 2.9 g+;
fat-sat 2.2 g+; protein 30.19 g; carbo 101.1 g; fiber 12.54 g; calcium
227 mg; sodium 140 mg; fat 21%; protein 18%; carbo 61%

❧ Fettuccine with Winter Garden Sauce
Mushroom Salad with Radishes

FETTUCCINE WITH WINTER GARDEN SAUCE

A bright green sauce is made from vegetables that are easy to find in the winter. This light and fresh-tasting lunch is fast and easy to make.

1 cup broccoli florets
1 cup frozen peas, thawed
3 tablespoons olive oil
1 onion, chopped
1 green pepper, chopped
1 clove garlic, minced
1 cup spinach, lightly packed
1 pound whole-grain fettuccine
½ teaspoon fructose or sugar
Lots of freshly ground black pepper to taste

Serves 6
Prep and Cook: 25 minutes

Salt to taste (optional)
10 tablespoons grated Parmesan cheese

❧ Steam the broccoli and peas until bright green and tender. Be careful not to overcook them.

❧ Heat the oil in a large skillet and sauté the onion, green pepper, and garlic for 10 minutes. Add the spinach and cook until wilted.

❧ Cook the fettuccine until al dente, about 8 to 10 minutes. Drain.

❧ Combine all the vegetables in a food processor or blender and purée until very smooth. Return the purée to the skillet and add the fructose, pepper, and salt to taste. Stir in 4 tablespoons of the Parmesan cheese and simmer until ready to serve.

❧ Toss the fettuccine with the sauce and sprinkle the remaining Parmesan cheese on each serving.

Nutritional Analysis: 1 serving
cal 416; chol 7 mg; fat-total 10.6 g; fat-mono 5.8 g; fat-poly 0.8 g; fat-sat 2.7 g; protein 15.7 g; carbo 62.3 g; fiber 3.49 g+; calcium 196 mg; sodium 189 mg; fat 23%; protein 15%; carbo 62%

MUSHROOM SALAD WITH RADISHES

Thinly sliced mushrooms are tossed with spicy radishes and cool yogurt to make a nice luncheon salad.

18 leaves Bibb lettuce
¾ pound mushrooms
¾ cup thinly sliced radishes
½ cup nonfat plain yogurt
2¼ teaspoons lemon juice
2 teaspoons chives
Freshly ground black pepper to
    taste

Serves 6
Prep: 15 minutes

◆§ Wash and dry the lettuce. Place 3 lettuce leaves on each plate.
◆§ Rub dirt off the mushrooms with a paper towel (don't wash with water or mushrooms will become brown and soft). Cut off the bottom of the stems, discard, and slice the mushrooms very thin.
◆§ Toss the mushrooms with the radishes, yogurt, and lemon juice.
◆§ Spoon equal amounts of mushroom salad on top of the lettuce leaves and sprinkle each with chives and pepper.

Nutritional Analysis: 1 serving
cal 30; chol 0; fat-total 0.2 g; fat-mono 0; fat-poly 0.1 g+; fat-sat 0; protein 1.94 g; carbo 4.4 g; fiber 2.13 g+; calcium 59 mg; sodium 23 mg; fat 6%; protein 29%; carbo 65%

Nutritional Analysis for Lunch Meal: 1 serving
cal 446; chol 7 mg; fat-total 10.7 g; fat-mono 5.8 g; fat-poly 0.8 g+; fat-sat 2.7 g; protein 17.64 g; carbo 66.7 g; fiber 5.61 g+; calcium 256 mg; sodium 213 mg; fat 22%; protein 16%; carbo 62%

⋘ Creamy Corn Chowder
Whole-Grain Irish Soda Bread

This meal is light yet filling and is also delicious for a quick, informal dinner.

CREAMY CORN CHOWDER

Traditional corn chowder is made with whole milk or cream. In this recipe I substitute evaporated skim milk and a few cups of puréed corn to give the soup a thick, creamy texture. Cilantro is a highly flavorful herb that looks similar to parsley. In fact, it is often referred to as Chinese or Mexican parsley because of its use in those two cuisines. (Cilantro leaves and coriander seeds are from the same plant, yet their flavors are completely different.) Cilantro has a unique taste that complements legumes and is well suited to soups and stews. It can be strong, so use it in small amounts at first. Cilantro is sometimes difficult to find in the produce market, so I like to dry a bunch when it is available. This allows me to use the herb whenever I need it. A bit of cilantro adds a special touch to Creamy Corn Chowder.

1 tablespoon olive oil or corn oil
1 onion, chopped
1 carrot, chopped
1 stalk celery, chopped
1 green pepper, chopped
4 cloves garlic, minced
3 medium potatoes, cubed
2½ cups vegetable broth
3 cups evaporated skim milk
2 pounds frozen corn, thawed
¼ cup chopped fresh parsley
1–3 teaspoons chopped fresh
 cilantro

Serves 6
Prep: 20 minutes
Cook: 35–45 minutes

Freshly ground black pepper to
 taste
Salt to taste (optional)
1 tablespoon Worcestershire
 sauce (optional)

⋘ Heat the oil in a soup pot and sauté the onion, carrot, celery, green pepper, and garlic for 10 minutes.

⋘ Stir the potatoes into the sauté, add the broth and milk and bring to a boil. Lower the heat to simmer and cook, covered, for 20 to 25 minutes, or until the potatoes are tender.

◆§ Purée 3 cups of the corn kernels in a food processor or blender until creamy.

◆§ Slowly stir the purée and remaining ingredients into the soup. Simmer for 10 minutes.

◆§ Season to taste before serving.

Nutritional Analysis: 1 serving
cal 336; chol 5 mg; fat-total 3.1 g; fat-mono 1.8 g; fat-poly 0.4 g; fat-sat 0.5 g; protein 16.35 g; carbo 67 g; fiber 9.29 g; calcium 398 mg; sodium 171 mg; fat 8%; protein 18%; carbo 74%

WHOLE-GRAIN IRISH SODA BREAD

This traditional daily bread from Ireland is fast to make and full of low-fat, whole-grain goodness. Because soda bread doesn't use yeast for rising, you can use any whole-grain flour (whole-wheat pastry, rye, oat, barley, corn, etc.) or combination of flours. When serving this bread with Creamy Corn Chowder, I like to make it with cornmeal and whole-wheat pastry flour. Try spreading a slice of bread with a little honey or one of the creamy spreads in the "Additional Recipes" section.

2½ cups whole-grain flour
½ teaspoon baking soda
½ teaspoon salt
1 – 1¼ cups cultured nonfat
   buttermilk

Serves 6
Prep: 5 minutes
Bake: 35 – 45 minutes

◆§ Preheat oven to 400°F. Lightly oil a baking sheet and sprinkle it with cornmeal or flour.

◆§ Mix the flour, baking soda, and salt. Make a well in the flour and pour the 1 cup buttermilk into the center.

◆§ Quickly and gently knead the dough to form a ball. It will be soft and sticky (add more buttermilk if necessary). Place the dough on the baking sheet and flatten slightly. Cut an X into the top and bake for 35 – 45 minutes.

Nutritional Analysis: 1 serving
cal 181; chol 1 mg; fat-total 0.9 g; fat-mono 0.1 g; fat-poly 0.5 g; fat-sat 0.2 g; protein 8.01 g; carbo 37.6 g; fiber 4.84 g+; calcium 72 mg; sodium 270 mg; fat 4%; protein 17%; carbo 79%

Nutritional Analysis for Lunch Meal: 1 serving
cal 518; chol 5 mg; fat-total 4 g; fat-mono 2 g+; fat-poly 0.9 g+; fat-sat 0.7 g+; protein 24.36 g; carbo 104.6 g; fiber 14.13 g+; calcium 470 mg; sodium 441 mg; fat 7%; protein 18%; carbo 75%

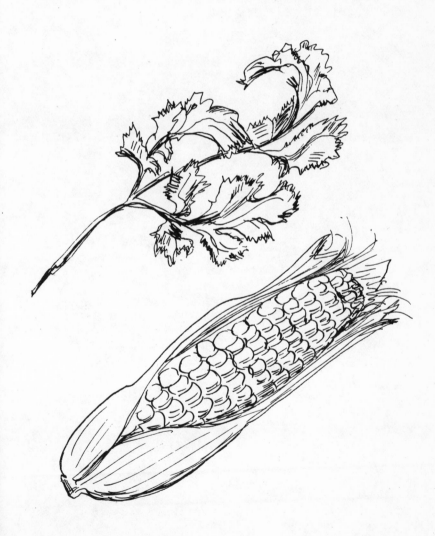

Warm Weather Lunch
Menus and Recipes

◆◆◆

◆◆◆

❧ Middle Eastern Baked Falafel
Dilled Cucumber Salad

MIDDLE EASTERN BAKED FALAFEL

In Israel, *falafel* is sold at fast-food stands, much as pizza is sold in America. Traditional *falafel* balls are deep-fried and then covered with a heavy tahini (ground sesame seeds) sauce. I have created a low-fat variation: baked *falafel* with a light Yogurt-Tahini Dressing.

6 pieces whole-wheat pita bread

Falafel
2½ cups cooked garbanzo beans
   (1 cup raw)
2 large cloves garlic, minced
2 tablespoons fresh parsley
1 tablespoon soy sauce (optional)
2 teaspoons coriander
2 teaspoons cumin
½ teaspoon chili powder
Cayenne or freshly ground black
   pepper to taste

Topping
2 tomatoes, chopped
½ cup minced onion
3 cups chopped romaine lettuce

Serves 6
Prep: 15 minutes
Bake: 20 minutes

Yogurt-Tahini Dressing
2 tablespoons nonfat plain yogurt
2 tablespoons tahini
1 tablespoon lemon juice
1 small clove garlic, minced
1 teaspoon minced fresh parsley
Water for thinning (about ½ cup)
Cayenne pepper or Tabasco sauce
   to taste

137

◆§ Drain the garbanzo beans well. Combine all the *falafel* ingredients (including enough cayenne pepper to make this mixture relatively spicy) in a food processor or blender and mix thoroughly into a thick paste.

◆§ Combine all the dressing ingredients in a food processor or blender, adding enough water to make a thin dressing and enough cayenne to make it spicy. Refrigerate until ready to use. This thickens as it chills. Thin again with water before serving if necessary.

◆§ Preheat oven to 400°F. Lightly oil a baking sheet. Roll the *falafel* into small 1-inch balls and place on the sheet. Bake for 20 minutes or until lightly browned.

◆§ Mix tomatoes and onions in a bowl and serve as a topping, buffet-style, along with separate bowls of lettuce, Yogurt-Tahini Dressing, *falafel* balls, and the pita bread.

◆§ To eat, slice the pita in half to form two pockets. Fill each pocket with lettuce, *falafel* balls, dressing, and top with the tomato-onion mixture and more dressing. (*Falafel* balls and dressing can be made ahead of time. Leftovers store well in the refrigerator.)

Nutritional Analysis: 1 serving
cal 321; chol 0; fat-total 6.7 g; fat-mono 2.2 g+; fat-poly 2.6 g+; fat-sat 1.4 g+; protein 15.79 g; carbo 50.9 g; fiber 6.15 g+; calcium 79 mg; sodium 427 mg; fat 19%; protein 19%; carbo 62%

DILLED CUCUMBER SALAD

A cool, crisp, low-fat salad that takes advantage of the summer's abundance of fresh cucumbers. Peel the cucumbers if the skin is bitter or waxed.

2 large cucumbers, thinly sliced
    or cubed
2 scallions, thinly sliced
1 tablespoon white wine vinegar
    or lemon juice
¼ cup nonfat plain yogurt
½ teaspoon dill weed
⅛ teaspoon garlic powder

Serves 4
Prep: 10 minutes

**Freshly ground black pepper to
 taste**
Salt to taste (optional)

⋅⧼ᵇ Toss all the ingredients in a medium bowl until mixed well.
⋅⧼ᵇ Cover and refrigerate until ready to serve.

Nutritional Analysis: 1 serving
cal 34; chol 0; fat-total 0.2 g; fat-mono 0; fat-poly 0.1 g; fat-sat 0.1 g;
protein 1.75 g; carbo 6.2 g; fiber 0.92 g+; calcium 55 mg; sodium
14 mg; fat 6%; protein 21%; carbo 73%

Nutritional Analysis for Lunch Meal: 1 serving
cal 355; chol 0; fat-total 7 g; fat-mono 2.2 g+; fat-poly 2.7 g+; fat-sat
1.4 g+; protein 17.54 g; carbo 57.1 g; fiber 7.07 g+; calcium
133 mg; sodium 441 mg; fat 17%; protein 19%; carbo 64%

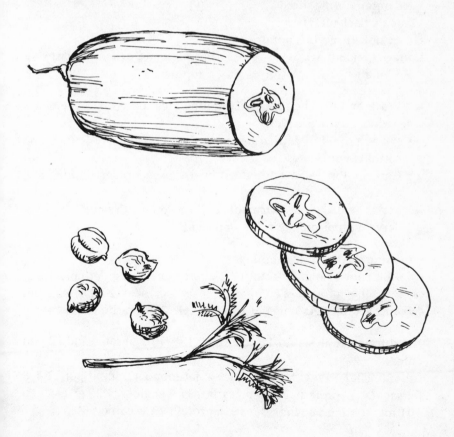

◆§ Mexican Ensalada
Whole-Grain Pita Chips with Salsa

MEXICAN ENSALADA

This Mexican-style salad is a meal in itself. The combination of beans, cheese, and vegetables is light yet very satisfying. Serve with whole-grain pita chips (page 96) and salsa.

12 leaves leaf lettuce	*Serves 4*
4 cups Mexican Refried Beans	*Prep: 15 minutes*
(page 96)	
1 cup grated part–skim milk	
Cheddar cheese	
2 tomatoes, chopped or sliced	
1 cucumber, thinly sliced	
1 red onion, thinly sliced	
12 small black olives	
Guacamole (page 321, optional)	
Cottage Cream (page 319,	Picante sauce or salsa to taste
optional)	(optional)

◆§ Wash and dry the lettuce. Line individual bowls or large plates with the lettuce leaves.

◆§ Put a mound of refried beans in the center of the lettuce and sprinkle with cheese.

◆§ Garnish the salad with the tomatoes, cucumber, onion, and olives.

◆§ Top the salad with Guacamole and/or Cottage Cream.

◆§ Serve with picante or salsa on the side.

Nutritional Analysis: 1 serving
cal 430; chol 15 mg; fat-total 10.2 g; fat-mono 3.3 g; fat-poly 1.8 g; fat-sat 3.9 g; protein 27.55 g; carbo 59.9 g; fiber 2.49 g; calcium 401 mg; sodium 1456 mg; fat 21%; protein 25%; carbo 54%

Nutritional Analysis for Lunch Meal: 1 serving of salad and 12 pita chips
cal 580; chol 15 mg; fat-total 12.2 g; fat-mono 4.1 g; fat-poly 2.4 g; fat-sat 4.7 g; protein 34.55 g; carbo 85.9 g; fiber 5.29 g; calcium 401 mg; sodium 1864 mg; fat 19%; protein 23%; carbo 58%

◄§ Ratatouille
Cucumber and Red Grape Salad
Corn and Rye Bread

RATATOUILLE

Ratatouille is a French dish in which the ingredients largely depend on the summer's abundance of garden-fresh vegetables. With the excellent produce and farmer's markets across America today you won't need your own garden's harvest to dictate which vegetables go into your recipe. You can serve Ratatouille in many ways: warm or cold on top of cooked whole grains, pasta, baked potatoes, pizza, mashed potatoes, in crepes, in pita bread, stuffed in vegetables, in lasagna, and so on.

2 tablespoons olive oil
1 large onion, chopped
6 large cloves garlic, minced
1 green pepper, cut into strips
1 red pepper, cut into strips
1 medium eggplant, cubed
2 cups mushrooms, thickly sliced
12 small black olives, cut into
  quarters
3 small zucchini, thickly sliced
4 tomatoes, cubed
1 cup tomato purée
¼ cup dry red wine or sherry
1 teaspoon thyme

Serves 6
Prep: 15–20 minutes
Cook: 30 minutes

1 teaspoon basil
Lots of freshly ground black
  pepper to taste
Dash of cumin
Salt to taste (optional)
¼ cup chopped fresh parsley

◄§ Heat the oil in a very large skillet or medium pot and sauté the onion for 5 minutes. Add the remaining ingredients, except the parsley, and stir well. Cover and cook on medium-low heat for about 30 minutes. Gently stir occasionally. Add the parsley during the last 10 minutes of cooking.

◄§ Serve hot, at room temperature, or refrigerate until well chilled.

Nutritional Analysis: 1 serving
cal 124; chol 0; fat-total 6.3 g; fat-mono 4.3 g+; fat-poly 0.7 g+; fat-sat 0.9 g+; protein 3.08 g; carbo 15.2 g; fiber 4.90 g; calcium 58 mg; sodium 66 mg; fat 44%; protein 9%; carbo 47%

CUCUMBER AND RED GRAPE SALAD

This simple salad is full of flavors and textures — sweet, tangy, cool, and crunchy.

3 cucumbers, thinly sliced
2 cups seedless red grapes
2 stalks celery, chopped
½ cup nonfat plain yogurt
1 tablespoon apple cider vinegar
1 teaspoon dill weed
1 teaspoon chives
1 teaspoon Dijon-style mustard
1 teaspoon honey
Freshly ground black pepper to
    taste

Serves 4
Prep: 10 minutes

⋈ Combine cucumbers, grapes, and celery in a large bowl.
⋈ Mix the remaining ingredients in a cup.
⋈ Pour the dressing over the salad. Toss gently and chill until ready to serve.

Nutritional Analysis: 1 serving
cal 78; chol 1 mg; fat-total 0.5 g; fat-mono 0.1 g; fat-poly 0.2 g; fat-sat 0.2 g; protein 2.9 g; carbo 15.7 g; fiber 2 g+; calcium 105 mg; sodium 61 mg; fat 6%; protein 15%; carbo 79%

CORN AND RYE BREAD

This bread has a nice flavor and whole-grain texture. It is easy to slice and makes a good sandwich bread.*

2½ cups warm water
    (110–115°F)
1½ tablespoons molasses
1 tablespoon honey

Serves 16
Bake: 45 minutes

---

* See Chapter 7 for added tips and information on baking bread.

1 tablespoon active dry yeast
4½ – 6 cups whole-wheat flour
¾ cup cornmeal
¾ cup rye flour

4 tablespoons poppy seeds
2 tablespoons caraway seeds
1½ tablespoons olive oil
½ teaspoon salt

- ᴥ§ Mix the water, molasses, and honey in a large bowl. Sprinkle yeast on top and let proof for 10 minutes.
- ᴥ§ Add 2 cups of the whole-wheat flour to the yeast mixture. Beat for 3 minutes with an electric beater or vigorously by hand.
- ᴥ§ Add the rest of the ingredients, except the remaining whole-wheat flour. Beat well.
- ᴥ§ Slowly stir in enough whole-wheat flour (2½ to 4 cups) to form a firm dough. Turn out the dough on a floured surface and knead for 10 minutes, adding more flour as needed to form a smooth, elastic dough.
- ᴥ§ Very lightly coat a large bowl with oil. Put the dough in the bowl and turn to coat with oil. Cover the bowl and let the dough rise in a warm place for about 1 hour or until the dough is doubled in size.
- ᴥ§ Very lightly oil 2 loaf (9 × 5 inches) pans.
- ᴥ§ Punch down the dough and divide it into 2 equal pieces. Knead a few minutes and shape into loaves.
- ᴥ§ Place the dough in the loaf pans, cover, and let rise in a warm spot for 45 minutes.
- ᴥ§ Preheat oven to 350°F. Bake the bread for 45 minutes. Remove the loaves from the pans and cool on a rack.

Nutritional Analysis: 1 serving
cal 196; chol 0; fat-total 3.3 g; fat-mono 1.3 g+; fat-poly 1.3 g+; fat-sat 0.4 g; protein 6.82 g; carbo 37.4 g; fiber 4.65 g+; calcium 69 mg; sodium 71 mg; fat 15%; protein 13%; carbo 72%

Nutritional Analysis for Lunch Meal: 1 serving
cal 398; chol 1 mg; fat-total 10.2 g; fat-mono 5.7 g+; fat-poly 2.2 g+; fat-sat 1.4 g+; protein 12.80 g; carbo 68.3 g; fiber 11.55 g+; calcium 232 mg; sodium 198 mg; fat 22%; protein 12%; carbo 66%

◄§ White Bean Pâté with Lettuce, Tomato, and Onion
Chilled Sweet Pea Soup
Quick Onion Pumpernickel Bread

The pâté needs to be made at least a day in advance to help blend the flavors and improve the texture. The soup is served well chilled and is easy to make in advance as well. The combination of flavors, colors, and textures creates a very festive lunch.

WHITE BEAN PÂTÉ

This is a meatless pâté, made with vegetables and white beans. It's baked and then chilled thoroughly before being cut into slices. Place the pâté on a slice of bread along with a lettuce leaf, slice of tomato, and onion. You may also add mustard.

1 tablespoon olive oil
1 onion, chopped
5 cloves garlic, minced
2 carrots, finely chopped
2 cups cooked navy, great northern, pea, or other white beans (1 cup raw)
2 eggs or 4 egg whites or egg replacer, beaten
½ cup bread crumbs
⅓ cup vegetable broth
3 tablespoons dry red wine
2 tablespoons lemon juice
1 teaspoon basil

1 teaspoon coriander
1 teaspoon thyme
Lots of freshly ground black pepper to taste
Salt to taste (optional)

Serves 6
Prep: 15 minutes
Bake: 50 minutes – 1 hour
Chill: Overnight

- ◄§ Preheat oven to 400°F. Oil the bottom and sides of a 9 × 5-inch loaf pan or pâté terrine *very* well.
- ◄§ Heat the olive oil in a small skillet and sauté the onion, garlic, and carrots for 5 minutes.
- ◄§ Combine the sauté with the remaining ingredients in a food processor or blender and mix until very smooth.

◄§ Pour the mixture into the prepared pan and cover. Bake for 50 minutes to 1 hour.

◄§ Remove the pâté from the oven and let it cool in the pan on a rack. Then refrigerate overnight.

◄§ To remove the pâté from the pan, turn it upside down onto a serving plate. Slice the pâté into 12 pieces and serve 2 to each person.

Nutritional Analysis: 1 serving (2 slices)
cal 176; chol 92 mg; fat-total 5.2 g; fat-mono 2.6 g; fat-poly 0.8 g; fat-sat 1.1 g; protein 8.65 g; carbo 25.1 g; fiber 4.05 g+; calcium 78 mg; sodium 99 mg; fat 26%; protein 19%; carbo 55%
◆ With egg whites instead of whole eggs: chol 0; fat-mono 1.9 g; fat-poly 0.6 g; fat-sat 0.5 g

CHILLED SWEET PEA SOUP

This simple soup has a delicious, fresh flavor and a bright green color that makes it an excellent choice for warm summer days. It's also good served hot.

2 tablespoons unsalted butter or
   margarine, melted
2 shallots, diced
4 cups fresh or frozen peas
3 cups vegetable or chicken broth
2 tablespoons sherry vinegar
1 cup nonfat plain yogurt
Salt to taste (optional)
Freshly ground black pepper
Cayenne pepper or Tabasco sauce
   to taste

Serves 6
Prep and Cook: 20
minutes
Chill: Several hours

3 tablespoons chopped fresh
   chives

◄§ Heat the butter in a pot and sauté the shallots for 1 minute. Add the peas and vegetable broth. Simmer for 5 minutes or until the peas are bright green and tender. Remove the pot from the heat and add the vinegar.

◄§ Purée the soup in a food processor or blender until smooth.

◆§ Return the soup to the pot, slowly stir or whisk in the yogurt, and season with salt, black pepper, and cayenne pepper to taste.

◆§ Chill for several hours and serve in bowls garnished with chives.

Nutritional Analysis: 1 serving

cal 142; chol 11 mg; fat-total 4 g; fat-mono 1.1 g +; fat-poly 0.3 g +; fat-sat 2.5 g +; protein 7.62 g; carbo 19.4 g; fiber 6.17 g; calcium 106 mg; sodium 123 mg; fat 25%; protein 21%; carbo 54%

◆ With margarine instead of butter: chol 1 mg; fat-mono 1.7 g +; fat-poly 1.3 g +; fat-sat 0.9 g +

QUICK ONION PUMPERNICKEL BREAD

This is an unusual yeast bread that doesn't require kneading. It has a mildly sweet flavor and a texture somewhere between a yeast bread and a quick bread. The hint of carob is an intriguing touch.

1 cup warm water (110–115°F)
½ cup warm skim milk
  (110–115°F)
¼ cup molasses
2 tablespoons active dry yeast
3 tablespoons unsalted butter or
  margarine
4 tablespoons carob powder
2¼ cups whole-wheat flour
1 small onion, finely chopped
1 cup dark rye flour

1 teaspoon salt
Skim milk for brushing dough
2 teaspoons caraway seeds

Serves 6
Prep: 20 minutes
Rise: 30 minutes
Bake: 30–35 minutes

◆§ Pour the warm water, warm milk, and molasses into a large bowl and sprinkle the yeast on top. Let proof for 10 minutes.

◆§ Melt the butter and carob in a small saucepan and cool. Very lightly oil a loaf pan.

◆§ Add the whole-wheat flour to the yeast mixture and beat with an electric mixer for 3 minutes. Beat in the carob mixture, onions, rye flour, and salt. Beat for 3 minutes more.

◆§ Pour the dough into the prepared loaf pan. Let the dough rise in a warm place for 30 minutes.

◆§ Preheat oven to 375°F. Brush the top of the dough with a little skim milk and sprinkle with caraway seeds.

෴ Bake for 30 to 35 minutes or until the loaf sounds hollow when tapped on the bottom. Remove from the pan and cool on a rack. Serve two slices per person.

Nutritional Analysis: 1 serving (2 slices)
cal 315; chol 16 mg; fat-total 6.7 g; fat-mono 1.9 g+; fat-poly 0.7 g+; fat-sat 3.7 g; protein 10.23 g; carbo 60.1 g; fiber 4.76 g+; calcium 170 mg; sodium 384 mg; fat 18%; protein 12%; carbo 70%
◆ With margarine instead of butter: chol 0; fat-mono 2.7 g+; fat-poly 2.3 g+; fat-sat 1.2 g

Nutritional Analysis for Lunch Meal: 1 serving
cal 648; chol 119 mg; fat-total 16 g; fat-mono 5.6 g+; fat-poly 1.8 g+; fat-sat 7.3 g+; protein 27.07 g; carbo 107.6 g; fiber 15.68 g+; calcium 360 mg; sodium 610 mg; fat 21%; protein 16%; carbo 63%
◆ With margarine and egg whites instead of butter and whole eggs: chol 1 mg; fat-mono 6.3 g+; fat-poly 4.2 g+; fat-sat 2.6 g+
◆ Analysis is based on half a tomato, 2 lettuce leaves, and a slice of onion for each serving of pâté.

↝ Rigatoni with Ricotta Pecan Pesto Raspberry-Marinated Tomatoes and Onions

The name *pesto* is derived from the method by which it was once prepared — with a mortar and pestle. In today's busy world, food processors do the trick in a few seconds. Pesto is traditionally made with fresh basil leaves, garlic, and olive oil, with additions such as pine nuts and Parmesan cheese, depending on the country and region in which it's served. Pesto is one of my favorite sauces. It's so versatile. Not only is it well suited to pasta, but it's great on pizza, lasagna, baked potatoes, bread, stirred into soup, or poured over cooked grains, fish, or vegetables. Because this sauce is so easy to make, I've included several pesto recipes in this cookbook, the most unique of which is made with low-fat ricotta cheese and pecans. See page 322 for a basic Pesto Sauce recipe.

RIGATONI WITH RICOTTA PECAN PESTO

The thick creamy sauce has a light garlic and pecan flavor that transcends the boundaries of traditional pesto. An easy, fast meal.

1 pound whole-grain rigatoni (or
   ziti, penne, or other pasta)
½ cup part–skim milk ricotta
   cheese
½ cup nonfat plain yogurt
½ cup pecans
¼ cup Parmesan cheese
1 large clove garlic
1 teaspoon dried basil or
   1 tablespoon fresh
½ cup fresh parsley
Lots of freshly ground black
   pepper

Serves 4
Prep: 15 minutes

↝ Cook the pasta until al dente, 8 to 10 minutes.
↝ Meanwhile, purée the next 6 ingredients in a food processor until smooth.

◄§ Add the parsley and purée just long enough to chop it coarsely into the sauce.

◄§ Drain the pasta, immediately toss it with the sauce, season with black pepper, and serve.

Nutritional Analysis: 1 serving
cal 583; chol 15 mg; fat-total 13.5 g; fat-mono 7 g; fat-poly 2.4 g; fat-sat 3.5 g; protein 23.01 g; carbo 87.8 g; fiber 1.08 g+; calcium 292 mg; sodium 180 mg; fat 21%; protein 16%; carbo 63%

RASPBERRY-MARINATED TOMATOES AND ONIONS

Raspberry vinegar gives the season's sweet and juicy red tomatoes the zip needed for a great salad. Try using a cold-pressed nut oil like hazelnut, walnut, or almond (available in natural foods stores and gourmet shops). Olive oil doesn't taste quite right in this recipe, but you may find that the taste of the extra-light variety of olive oil is better.

6 large ripe tomatoes, sliced *Serves 6*
1 red onion, thinly sliced *Prep: 10 minutes*
2 cups cooked navy, northern, or *Marinate: 2 hours or*
 other white beans (⅞ cup raw) *more*
2 tablespoons minced fresh
 parsley
1 teaspoon dried basil or 2
 tablespoons minced fresh
1 teaspoon garlic powder
1 teaspoon oregano
3 tablespoons raspberry vinegar Lots of freshly ground black
3 tablespoons nut oil, extra-light pepper
 olive oil, or canola oil Salt to taste (optional)

◄§ Gently toss all ingredients in a large shallow bowl. Cover and let marinate at room temperature or in the refrigerator for at least 2 hours. Gently stir occasionally.

Nutritional Analysis: 1 serving
cal 151; chol 0; fat-total 5.2 g; fat-mono 3.5 g+; fat-poly 0.7 g+;

fat-sat 0.7 g+; protein 5.98 g; carbo 20.9 g; fiber 3.91 g; calcium 59 mg; sodium 16 mg; fat 30%; protein 16%; carbo 54%
◆ Analysis is based on the amount of marinade absorbed by the salad.

Nutritional Analysis for Lunch Meal: 1 serving
cal 734; chol 15 mg; fat-total 18.7 g; fat-mono 10.4 g+; fat-poly 3.1 g+; fat-sat 4.2 g+; protein 28.99 g; carbo 108.7 g; fiber 4.99 g+; calcium 351 mg; sodium 196 mg; fat 23%; protein 16%; carbo 61%
◆ Analysis is based on the amount of marinade absorbed by the salad.

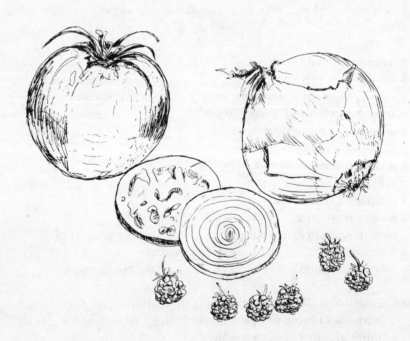

◆§ *Thick and Zesty Gazpacho*
Potato Salad Dijon
Multigrain Black Bread

This light summer meal has lots of flavor. You can make all the recipes ahead of time and refrigerate the soup and potato salad. For a quick meal, substitute a store-bought whole-grain bread for the Multigrain Black Bread.

THICK AND ZESTY GAZPACHO

Gazpacho is a delicious, chilled, tomato-based vegetable soup. As the name suggests, my interpretation is slightly spicy (you can increase or decrease the seasoning) and filled with chunks of vegetables. Even though the recipe has quite a few ingredients, it's very fast and easy to make.

4 cups tomato juice
1 tablespoon olive oil
1 large onion, finely chopped
2 large cloves garlic, minced
2 tablespoons red wine vinegar
1 green pepper, chopped
1 cucumber, chopped
2 tomatoes, chopped
1 tablespoon honey
1 teaspoon basil
1 teaspoon dill weed
½ teaspoon tarragon
½ teaspoon thyme
¼ teaspoon cumin
2 tablespoons minced fresh
   parsley

Serves 6
Prep: 15 – 20 minutes
Chill: 1 – 2 hours or
   more

1½ cups cooked garbanzo beans
   (⅔ cup raw)
Freshly ground black pepper to
   taste
Tabasco sauce to taste
6 tablespoons nonfat plain yogurt
Whole-wheat croutons (optional)
Chopped fresh chives (optional)

◆§ Combine all the ingredients, except the yogurt, croutons, and chives, in a large bowl. Mix well and chill for 1 to 2 hours or more.

◆§ Serve in 6 individual bowls and top each with a tablespoon of yogurt. Garnish with croutons and chives.

Nutritional Analysis: 1 serving
cal 171; chol 0; fat-total 3.7 g; fat-mono 2 g+; fat-poly 0.9 g+; fat-sat 0.5 g+; protein 7.31 g; carbo 29.9 g; fiber 4.21 g+; calcium 99 mg; sodium 36 mg; fat 18%; protein 16%; carbo 66%

POTATO SALAD DIJON

Dijon mustard, nonfat yogurt, olive oil, and vinegar take the place of mayonnaise in this European-style salad.

5 large potatoes, cubed

1 stalk celery, sliced

½ medium red onion, very thinly sliced

3 tablespoons olive oil

1 tablespoon white wine vinegar

1 tablespoon lemon juice

2 tablespoons nonfat plain yogurt

3 tablespoons Dijon-style mustard

2 teaspoons dill weed

1 teaspoon garlic powder

Freshly ground black pepper to taste

Serves 6
Prep: 30 minutes
Chill: 2 hours or more

Salt to taste (optional)
Chopped fresh chives (optional)
Pimientos (optional)

◄§ Steam or boil the potatoes just until tender. Gently toss them with the celery and onion in a large bowl.

◄§ Combine the remaining ingredients, except the chives and pimientos, in a separate bowl. Pour the dressing over the hot potato mixture. Toss gently.

◄§ Refrigerate the salad until well chilled. Garnish with chives and pimientos before serving.

Nutritional Analysis: 1 serving
cal 264; chol 0; fat-total 7.5 g; fat-mono 5.5 g; fat-poly 0.7 g; fat-sat 1 g; protein 4.60 g; carbo 44.8 g; fiber 4.54 g+; calcium 45 mg; sodium 118 mg; fat 25%; protein 7%, carbo 68%

MULTIGRAIN BLACK BREAD

This hearty bread has a combination of five whole grains that contribute to its dark color and fragrant aroma.*

2½ cups warm water
  (110 – 115°F)
4 tablespoons molasses
2 tablespoons honey
2 tablespoons active dry yeast
3 cups or more whole-wheat flour
¾ cup cornmeal
¾ cup rolled oats
¾ cup oat bran
½ cup rye flour
⅓ cup carob powder
3 tablespoons olive oil
½ teaspoon salt

Makes 2 loaves
Serves 16
Bake: 50 minutes – 1
hour

✑ Mix the warm water, molasses, and honey in a large bowl. Sprinkle the yeast on top and let proof for 10 minutes.

✑ Add the whole-wheat flour and beat for 3 to 5 minutes with an electric mixer or vigorously by hand. Cover and let rise in a warm place for 30 minutes.

✑ Stir in the remaining ingredients. Turn out the dough onto a heavily floured surface. Knead for 10 minutes, adding more whole-wheat flour as needed to form a moist but not too sticky dough. Don't add too much flour or the bread will be very heavy. This dough will be a bit sticky because of the large amount of nonwheat whole-grain flours.

✑ Very lightly oil a large bowl. Place the dough in the bowl and turn it to coat with oil. Cover and let rise in a warm place for 1 hour or until about doubled in size.

✑ Punch down the dough. Knead a few times and return to the bowl. Let the dough rise for another 30 to 45 minutes. Lightly oil a baking sheet and sprinkle with cornmeal.

✑ Punch down the dough again and divide it in half. Shape into 2 round loaves. Place the loaves on the baking sheet, cover, and let

---

* See Chapter 7 for added tips and information on bread baking.

them rise in a warm place for 15 to 30 minutes more. Preheat oven to 350°F.

- Bake for about 50 minutes to 1 hour, or until each loaf sounds hollow when tapped on the bottom.
- Remove the bread from the baking sheet and let cool on a rack.

Nutritional Analysis: 1 serving
cal 191; chol 0; fat-total 3.9 g; fat-mono 2.1 g+; fat-poly 0.6 g+; fat-sat 0.4 g+; protein 6.13 g; carbo 35.9 g; fiber 3.27 g+; calcium 61 mg; sodium 75 mg; fat 17%; protein 12%; carbo 71%

Nutritional Analysis for Lunch Meal: 1 serving
cal 627; chol 0; fat-total 15.1 g; fat-mono 9.5 g+; fat-poly 2.1 g+; fat-sat 2 g+; protein 18.04 g; carbo 110.6 g; fiber 12.02 g+; calcium 205 mg; sodium 229 mg; fat 21%; protein 11%; carbo 68%

∽§ *Greek Salad*
Olive Bread

GREEK SALAD

This simple salad has a rich blend of popular Greek ingredients. Usually served with olive oil and vinegar on the side, this salad can be extremely high in fat if you have a heavy hand with the oil. Fortunately, this recipe is filled with tasty morsels that need no adornment except a few sprinkles of a good-quality vinegar. I like to serve a salad like this with a variety of my favorite vinegars (balsamic, raspberry, champagne, sherry wine, herbed red and white wine) placed in the center of the table. Your guests can mix and match vinegars to add low-fat flavoring to their salad.

1 large head romaine lettuce, torn
   into pieces
2 large tomatoes, chopped
1 cucumber, chopped
1 red onion, thinly sliced
1 red pepper, thinly sliced
1 green pepper, thinly sliced
12 small black olives, cut in half
1 can (14 ounces) artichoke
   hearts packed in water,
   drained, quartered
4 ounces feta cheese,* crumbled
1½ cups cooked garbanzo beans
   (⅔ cup raw)

Serves 4
Prep: 20 minutes

Capers (optional)
Peperoncini (pickled Italian
   peppers, optional)
Several pinches of oregano

∽§ Place the lettuce on 4 large plates.
∽§ Add the remaining vegetables decoratively on the lettuce in the order listed.
∽§ Sprinkle the feta cheese, beans, capers, and *peperoncini* on top.
∽§ Finely crush several pinches of oregano with your fingers and sprinkle over each salad.

---

* To reduce sodium in the feta cheese, rinse under cool water and/or soak in water for 15 minutes to a ½ hour.

Nutritional Analysis: 1 serving
cal 288; chol 25 mg; fat-total 10.1 g; fat-mono 2.6 g+; fat-poly 0.7 g+; fat-sat 4.5 g+; protein 14.56 g; carbo 35.2 g; fiber 8.62 g; calcium 264 mg; sodium 433 mg; fat 31%; protein 20%; carbo 49%

OLIVE BREAD

Olives and whole-wheat flour pair up to create a delicious whole-grain bread speckled with black olives.*

1 cup warm water (110–115°F)   *Serves 6*
1 tablespoon active dry yeast   *Bake: 40 minutes*
3 – 3½ cups whole-wheat flour
1 teaspoon olive oil
1 onion, chopped
36 small black olives, chopped
1 teaspoon salt

- Pour the warm water into a large bowl and sprinkle the yeast on top. Let proof for 10 minutes.
- Add a cup of the flour to the yeast mixture and beat well for 3 minutes (I like to use an electric mixer).
- Heat the oil in a small skillet and sauté the onion until soft. Add the onions, olives, and salt to the dough.
- Slowly knead in enough of the remaining flour to form a soft, unsticky dough. Knead for 10 minutes.
- Place the dough in a large bowl that has been rubbed with a little oil and turn the dough in the bowl to coat with oil.
- Cover the dough and set aside in a warm place to rise for 1 hour, or until doubled in size.
- Punch down the dough, knead a few minutes more, and shape into a round loaf. Very lightly oil a baking sheet and sprinkle with flour. Set the loaf on the sheet, cover lightly, and let rise in a warm place for 40 minutes or until doubled in size.
- Preheat oven to 375°F. Dust the top of the loaf with flour. Bake for 40 minutes. Remove the bread from the baking sheet and cool on a rack.

---

* See Chapter 7 for added tips and information on baking bread.

Nutritional Analysis: 1 serving
cal 283; chol 0; fat-total 6 g; fat-mono 3.4 g; fat-poly 1.1 g; fat-sat 0.9 g; protein 10.17 g; carbo 52.1 g; fiber 8.51 g; calcium 58 mg; sodium 495 mg; fat 18%; protein 13%; carbo 69%

Nutritional Analysis for Lunch Meal: 1 serving
cal 571; chol 25 mg; fat-total 16.1 g; fat-mono 6 g+; fat-poly 1.8 g+; fat-sat 5.4 g+; protein 24.72 g; carbo 87.3 g; fiber 17.13 g; calcium 322 mg; sodium 928 mg; fat 24%; protein 17%; carbo 59%

✒ Fresh Fruit and Whole-Grain Ambrosia with Red Raspberry Yogurt Sauce
Cinnamon-Raisin Swirl Bread

This cool meal is light yet satisfying, using the season's abundance of fresh fruits — perfect for warm summer days. For a quick bread alternative, substitute Cinnamon Raisin Quick Bread (page 292) for the Cinnamon-Raisin Swirl Bread.

FRESH FRUIT AND WHOLE-GRAIN AMBROSIA WITH RED RASPBERRY YOGURT SAUCE

A bed of cooked grains is topped with juicy, fresh fruit and a creamy red raspberry sauce — a real summer treat. To quicken the cooking time, make the whole grain in a pressure cooker or microwave oven.

3 cups water
1½ cups whole grain (brown rice, hulled millet, and/or hulled barley)
½ cup low-fat cottage cheese
½ cup nonfat plain yogurt
1 cup raspberries
2 tablespoons honey
Dash of nutmeg
8 leaves Bibb lettuce
6 cups mixed fresh fruit, such as bananas, raspberries, blueberries, strawberries, cantaloupe, honeydew melon, watermelon, kiwifruit, grapes, and very ripe peaches and plums, cut into bite-size pieces
Fresh mint (optional)

Serves 4
Prep: 20–45 minutes
Chill: 30 minutes or more

✒ Bring the water to a boil in a medium saucepan. Add the grain and return to a boil. Lower the heat to simmer, cover, and cook for 20 to 45 minutes (depending on the type of grain used), until the water has been absorbed.

✒ Remove the pan from the heat and let it stand, covered, for 10 minutes. Pour the grain into a bowl and cool to room temperature or refrigerate.

◆§ Mix the next 5 ingredients in a blender or food processor and chill the sauce until ready to serve.

◆§ Line each plate or bowl with a couple of lettuce leaves. Divide the cooked grain among the bowls and top with fruits. Pour equal amounts of sauce over each serving. Garnish the bowls with a few mint leaves.

Nutritional Analysis: 1 serving
cal 432; chol 3 mg; fat-total 3.3 g; fat-mono 1 g; fat-poly 0.9 g; fat-sat 0.7 g; protein 12.48 g; carbo 90.8 g; fiber 11 g; calcium 141 mg; sodium 149 mg; fat 7%; protein 11%; carbo 82%
◆ Analysis is based on brown rice and 1 cup each of blueberries, strawberries, raspberries, watermelon, peaches, and grapes.

CINNAMON-RAISIN SWIRL BREAD

Raisins, cinnamon, honey, and fructose are rolled inside this yeast bread. It smells fabulous when baking, and when sliced it looks as good as it smells. This is an excellent snack, too. In fact, it's the favorite snack in my house, so I double the recipe and make four loaves at a time. I freeze two, put one in the refrigerator, and the fourth one is gone by the time it has cooled. Try it toasted — yum!*

1 cup warm skim milk
  (110–115°F)
1 cup warm water (110–115°F)
4 tablespoons maple syrup
1 tablespoon active dry yeast
4½–5½ cups whole-wheat flour
½ teaspoon salt
4 tablespoons unsalted butter or
  margarine, melted
3 tablespoons date sugar†
  (optional)
1 tablespoon vanilla
½ teaspoon lemon extract or
  grated lemon rind

Serves 16
Bake: 35–45 minutes

½ teaspoon + 1 tablespoon
  cinnamon
¾ teaspoon nutmeg
¼ cup fructose or sugar
2 tablespoons honey
¾ cup raisins

---

* See Chapter 7 for added tips and information on bread baking.
† Date sugar is made from ground dates and is available at many natural foods stores.

✥ Mix the warm milk, water, and maple syrup in a large bowl. Sprinkle yeast on top and let proof for 10 minutes.

✥ Add 1 to 2 cups of the whole-wheat flour and the salt and beat for 3 minutes with an electric mixer or vigorously by hand. Stir in 2 tablespoons of the butter, 2 tablespoons of the date sugar, the vanilla, lemon extract, ½ teaspoon of the cinnamon, and ¼ teaspoon of the nutmeg. Add enough of the remaining whole-wheat flour to form a workable dough, place on a floured surface, and knead for 10 minutes, adding more whole-wheat flour as needed to form a smooth, elastic dough.

✥ Very lightly oil a large bowl. Place the dough in the bowl and turn to coat with oil. Cover and let rise in a warm place for 1 hour or until about doubled in size.

✥ Very lightly oil 2 loaf pans. Combine the fructose with the remaining 1 tablespoon date sugar, 1 tablespoon cinnamon, and ½ teaspoon nutmeg in a cup.

✥ Punch down the dough, knead a few times, and divide in half. Shape each half into a rectangle (about 9 X 12 inches).

✥ Mix the honey with the remaining 2 tablespoons of melted butter. Brush each rectangle with the honey-butter mixture and sprinkle the fructose mixture and raisins on top. Roll the dough lengthwise, pinch the edges closed, and put into the prepared pans. Cover and let rise in a warm place for 30 minutes.

✥ Preheat oven to 350°F. Bake for 35 to 50 minutes, or until the tops are lightly browned. Remove the bread from the pans and cool on a rack.

Nutritional Analysis: 1 serving
cal 223; chol 8 mg; fat-total 3.6 g; fat-mono 0.9 g; fat-poly 0.5 g; fat-sat 1.9 g; protein 6.43 g; carbo 44.3 g; fiber 4.48 g; calcium 52 mg; sodium 78 mg; fat 14%; protein 11%; carbo 75%
◆ With margarine instead of butter: chol 0; fat-mono 1.4 g; fat-poly 1.3 g; fat-sat 0.7 g

Nutritional Analysis for Lunch Meal: 1 serving
cal 654; chol 11 mg; fat-total 6.9 g; fat-mono 1.9 g; fat-poly 1.4 g; fat-sat 2.7 g; protein 18.91 g; carbo 135.1 g; fiber 15.48 g; calcium 193 mg; sodium 227 mg; fat 9%; protein 11%; carbo 80%
◆ With margarine instead of butter: chol 3 mg; fat-mono 2.4 g; fat-poly 2.2 g; fat-sat 1.4 g

⋐ Tuna Niçoise
French Breadstick Twists

TUNA NIÇOISE

This salad from France has many different interpretations. Some say the salad should include only fresh, raw vegetables with tuna and possibly anchovies. I think we should choose from the ingredients we have available. For a vegetarian alternative, I suggest tempeh or tofu as a substitute for the tuna.

2 medium potatoes, cubed
2 cups fresh or frozen green
   beans
12 leaves leaf lettuce
1 can (6½ ounces) tuna fish
   packed in water, drained
8 artichoke hearts packed in
   water, drained, quartered
1 small red onion, thinly sliced
12 black olives
4 ounces pimientos, sliced
2 tomatoes, cut into wedges, or 16
   cherry tomatoes

Serves 4
Prep: 20 – 25 minutes

Olive oil (optional)
Assorted vinegars (optional)

⋐ Steam potatoes and beans, if fresh, until tender. Rinse them under cold water and drain well.

⋐ Line 4 plates or bowls with lettuce leaves. Gently flake the tuna with a fork and place a mound in the center of each plate of lettuce. Garnish with the remaining vegetables.

⋐ Place a bottle of olive oil and a variety of vinegars in the center of the table so each person can create a dressing. (Use a light hand with the oil, as every tablespoon has 14 grams of fat.)

Nutritional Analysis: 1 serving
cal 289; chol 26 mg; fat-total 3.3 g; fat-mono 1.4 g +; fat-poly 0.6 g +; fat-sat 0.6 g +; protein 23.01 g; carbo 43.3 g; fiber 7.11 g +; calcium 106 mg; sodium 379 mg; fat 10%; protein 31%; carbo 59%

FRENCH BREADSTICK TWISTS

These breadsticks are shaped into long twists. They are very moist and loaded with poppy and sesame seeds.*

1¼ cups warm water   *Serves 12*
  (110–115°F)   *Bake: 20–25 minutes*
2 tablespoons honey
1 tablespoon active dry yeast
3 cups whole-wheat flour
½ teaspoon salt
1 egg white
1 tablespoon olive oil
3 tablespoons poppy seeds
1 tablespoon sesame seeds
1 teaspoon garlic powder

◦§ Pour the warm water and honey into a large bowl and sprinkle the yeast on top. Let proof for 10 minutes.

◦§ Add a cup of the flour and the salt to the yeast mixture and beat well for 3 minutes (I like to use an electric mixer).

◦§ Slowly knead in enough of the remaining flour to form a smooth, elastic dough. Knead for 10 minutes.

◦§ Place the dough in a lightly oiled bowl and turn the dough to coat with oil.

◦§ Cover the dough and set in a warm place to rise for 1 hour or until the dough has doubled in size. Very lightly oil a baking sheet.

◦§ Punch down the dough and divide it into 12 pieces. Roll each piece into a long strand and twist the ends in opposite directions. (The dough will untwist a little.) Place the twists on the baking sheet, leaving room for them to expand. Cover them lightly and let rise in a warm place for 20 to 30 minutes. Mix the egg white and the oil. Preheat oven to 375°F.

◦§ Brush the twists with the egg white mixture and sprinkle each with a combination of poppy and sesame seeds and garlic powder.

◦§ Bake for 20 to 30 minutes or until the sticks are lightly browned. Cool slightly before serving.

---

* See Chapter 7 for added tips and information on baking bread.

Nutritional Analysis: 1 serving
cal 140; chol 0; fat-total 3 g; fat-mono 1.2 g; fat-poly 1.2 g; fat-sat 0.4 g; protein 5.06 g; carbo 25.1 g; fiber 3.14 g; calcium 46 mg; sodium 95 mg; fat 18%; protein 14%; carbo 68%

Nutritional Analysis for Lunch Meal: 1 serving
cal 429; chol 26 mg; fat-total 6.3 g; fat-mono 2.6 g +; fat-poly 1.8 g +; fat-sat 1 g; protein 28.08 g; carbo 68.4 g; fiber 10.25 g +; calcium 152 mg; sodium 474 mg; fat 13%; protein 25%; carbo 62%

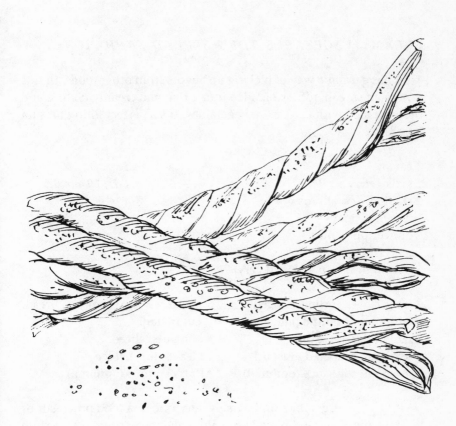

⌐§ Creamy Vegetable Tofu Spread Sandwiches
Cool Magenta Borscht
Brown Rice and Artichoke Salad

A variety of ingredients is combined to create a cool, light lunch. All the recipes can be made in advance and kept refrigerated until you're ready to serve. This is an excellent meal for a picnic. The spread is great on crackers, pita chips, toast, and fresh bread, or thinned with a little skim milk and used as a dip for raw vegetables, or as a sauce for steamed vegetables and baked potatoes.

CREAMY VEGETABLE TOFU SPREAD SANDWICHES

Tofu has a unique way of picking up flavors from other foods. In this sandwich spread, tofu is blended into a rich and creamy texture and then studded with cool, crisp vegetables. It's a perfect filling for pita bread.

1 carrot
1 stalk celery
2 shallots or scallions
½ green pepper
2 ounces pimientos
¼ cup fresh parsley
1 pound firm tofu, drained very well

Serves 6
Prep: 20 minutes

2 large cloves garlic,* minced
2 tablespoons nonfat plain yogurt
1 tablespoon olive oil
1 teaspoon prepared mustard
1 teaspoon soy sauce (optional)

6 pieces whole-wheat pita bread, cut in half
3 tomatoes, sliced
12 leaves leaf lettuce
Alfalfa sprouts (optional)

⌐§ Chop the vegetables and parsley very fine in a food processor or by hand. Put the chopped vegetables and the parsley in a medium bowl and set aside.

---

* For garlic lovers only: use 4 large cloves garlic.

◆§ Using a paper towel, squeeze all the excess water from the tofu. Combine the tofu, garlic, yogurt, oil, mustard, and soy sauce in a food processor or blender. Purée until smooth and creamy.

◆§ Stir the tofu mixture into the finely chopped vegetables. Cover and store in the refrigerator until ready to serve. (Leftovers keep well.) Then assemble sandwiches, using the tofu spread, pita pockets, tomato slices, lettuce, and alfalfa sprouts. Serve each person 2 pockets.

Nutritional Analysis: 1 serving
cal 249; chol 0; fat-total 7.1 g; fat-mono 2.6 g+; fat-poly 0.9 g+; fat-sat 1.1 g+; protein 13.37 g; carbo 34.4 g; fiber 4.42 g+; calcium 120 mg; sodium 447 mg; fat 25%; protein 21%; carbo 54%

COOL MAGENTA BORSCHT

Borscht is an Eastern European soup made from beets. It is usually served cold but may also be heated. There are many versions of this simple soup. In this recipe the rich, ruby red color is transformed to a shocking pink, as yogurt is swirled through the icy cold soup.

4 large beets or 2 cups canned
   small whole beets, with liquid
1 teaspoon unsalted butter or
   margarine
1 small onion, chopped
½ – 1 cup vegetable broth
1 teaspoon honey
2 tablespoons lemon juice
Freshly ground black pepper to
   taste
Salt to taste (optional)
2 tablespoons chopped fresh
   chives or 1 tablespoon dried,
   plus extra for garnish

Serves 4
Prep: 10 – 45 minutes
Chill: 1 hour or more

½ teaspoon chopped fresh dill
   weed or ¼ teaspoon dried
1 cup nonfat plain yogurt

◆§ Wash the beets and steam or boil them until tender. Rinse the cooked beets under cool water and rub off the skins. (If you're using canned beets, save the liquid.)

◆§ Heat the butter in a small skillet and sauté the onion until soft.

◄§ Combine all the ingredients, except the yogurt, in a food processor or blender. (If you're using fresh, cooked beets, add ¾ to 1 cup vegetable broth. If you're using canned beets, add all the beet liquid and ½ cup vegetable broth.) Mix until the soup is very smooth.

◄§ Pour the soup into a bowl and refrigerate for 1 hour or until icy cold.

◄§ Serve the soup in individual bowls (the bright soup looks beautiful in white bowls) and spoon ¼ cup of the yogurt into the center of each. Top with a few extra chives.

Nutritional Analysis: 1 serving
cal 95; chol 4 mg; fat-total 1.2 g; fat-mono 0.3 g; fat-poly 0.1 g; fat-sat 0.7 g; protein 4.7 g; carbo 17.2 g; fiber 1.66 g+; calcium 142 mg; sodium 102 mg; fat 11%; protein 19%; carbo 70%

◆ With margarine instead of butter: chol 1 mg; fat-mono 0.5 g; fat-poly 0.4 g; fat-sat 0.3 g

BROWN RICE AND ARTICHOKE SALAD

This salad is a gentle blend of nutty brown rice and artichoke hearts. A highly aromatic rice, like basmati, creates an extra-special flavor.

2½ cups water or vegetable or
   chicken broth
1¼ cups long-grain brown rice
3 tablespoons olive oil
1 tablespoon white wine vinegar
2 cloves garlic, minced
3 shallots, chopped
1 can (14 ounces) artichoke
   hearts packed in water,
   drained, sliced
2 tablespoons chopped fresh
   parsley

Serves 6
Prep: 10 minutes
Cook: 35–45 minutes

4 tablespoons chopped pimientos
Lots of freshly ground black
   pepper
Salt to taste (optional)

◄§ Bring the water to a boil in a saucepan. Add the rice, bring to a boil again, and lower the heat to simmer. Cover and cook for 35 to 45 minutes or until the water has been absorbed.

⊷ While the rice is cooking, stir together the oil, vinegar, garlic, and shallots in a cup.

⊷ Toss the cooked rice in a bowl with the artichoke hearts, parsley, pimientos, pepper, and salt.

⊷ Add the oil and vinegar mixture to the rice and toss gently.

⊷ Cool to room temperature or chill. Adjust seasonings and serve.

Nutritional Analysis: 1 serving
cal 234; chol 0; fat-total 8 g; fat-mono 5.5 g+; fat-poly 0.8 g+; fat-sat 1.1 g+; protein 4.53 g; carbo 36.2 g; fiber 2.15 g+; calcium 29 mg; sodium 31 mg; fat 31%; protein 8%; carbo 61%

Nutritional Analysis for Lunch Meal: 1 serving
cal 578; chol 4 mg; fat-total 16.3 g; fat-mono 8.4 g+; fat-poly 1.8 g+; fat-sat 2.9 g+; protein 22.60 g; carbo 87.8 g; fiber 8.23 g; calcium 291 mg; sodium 580 mg; fat 25%; protein 15%; carbo 60%

◆ With margarine instead of butter: chol 1 mg; fat-mono 8.5 g+; fat-poly 2.1 g+; fat-sat 2.5 g+

⋐ Fruity Pasta Salad
Whole-Grain Bagels

Fruit, pasta, and yogurt are mixed into a bright, sweet-tasting salad. The colorful presentation is very appealing. Bagels make an excellent low-fat bread choice — store-bought or homemade. Try the Cinnamon Apple Bagels with this meal — a favorite in my house.

FRUITY PASTA SALAD

This is a refreshing summer salad that is at its best when a variety of fresh fruits is available. You may choose any combination of fruits, whatever is most ripe at the time. And many natural foods stores carry yogurt sweetened with fruit juice or honey instead of sugar. This salad is best served icy cold, so keep the fruit and yogurt refrigerated. This will help to decrease the time needed for chilling.

½ pound whole-grain vegetable
   rotini (spirals)
1½ cups nonfat vanilla yogurt
½ cup nonfat plain yogurt
Dash of cinnamon
Dash of nutmeg
4 cups mixed fruit, such as
   strawberries, blueberries,
   raspberries, melons, peaches or
   nectarines, bananas, apples,
   pears, and grapes, chopped if
   necessary

Serves 4
Prep: 15 minutes
Chill: ½ hour or more

8 leaves lettuce
Fresh mint or basil (optional)

- ⋐ Cook the pasta until al dente, about 8 to 10 minutes. Drain and rinse under cold water.
- ⋐ Mix the pasta with the yogurt and spices.
- ⋐ Gently toss in the fruit. Cover and refrigerate until icy cold.
- ⋐ Line 4 salad bowls with lettuce leaves and serve the pasta and fruit on top. Garnish each salad with a fresh mint or basil leaf.

Nutritional Analysis: 1 serving
cal 347; chol 4 mg; fat-total 2.2 g; fat-mono 0.5 g; fat-poly 0.3 g;

fat-sat 1 g; protein 13.76 g; carbo 67.6 g; fiber 2.63 g+; calcium 236 mg; sodium 60 mg; fat 6%; protein 16%; carbo 78%
◆ Analysis is based on 1 cup each of strawberries, blueberries, cantaloupe, and grapes.

WHOLE-GRAIN BAGELS

Bagels have become quite popular and are available in most grocery stores. If you're lucky enough to have a bagel shop in your area, look for bagels made with whole-wheat or rye flour. Here is my recipe for homemade Whole-Grain Bagels. They freeze well and taste great fresh or toasted.*

3 cups warm water (110–115°F)
3 tablespoons honey
2 tablespoons active dry yeast
1 teaspoon salt
8 cups whole-wheat flour
1 tablespoon cream of tartar
  (optional)
2 tablespoons baking soda
  (optional)

Makes 16 bagels
Bake: 15–20 minutes

⋯§ Pour the warm water and honey into a very large bowl. Sprinkle the yeast on top and let proof for 10 minutes.

⋯§ Add the salt and 3 cups of the flour. Beat with an electric mixer or vigorously by hand for 3 minutes.

⋯§ Slowly stir in enough of the remaining flour to form a stiff yet soft dough. Knead for 10 minutes.

⋯§ Place the dough in a large, lightly oiled bowl. Turn the dough to coat with oil. Cover and let rise in a warm place for about 1 hour or until doubled in size.

⋯§ Bring a very large pot of water to a boil. Add the cream of tartar and baking soda to the water. Very lightly oil a baking sheet and set aside. Preheat oven to 400°F.

⋯§ Punch down the dough and divide it into 16 pieces. Roll each piece into a strand seven to eight inches long. Put a drop of water

---

* See Chapter 7 for added tips and information on bread baking.

at each end and pinch gently to form a circle. Place the bagels on the baking sheet as you shape them.

◆§ Gently drop as many bagels into the boiling water as will fit (they expand, so don't crowd them). Boil for 2 minutes. Then, with a slotted spoon, turn each bagel over and boil for another 2 minutes. Remove the bagels from the water and place them on a wire rack to drain. Boil the remaining bagels in the same manner.

◆§ Place the bagels on the greased baking sheet and bake for 15 to 20 minutes.

Poppy Seed, Sesame Seed, Onion, or Garlic Bagels

◆§ Lightly beat 1 egg white and brush on top of each bagel before baking. Sprinkle with seeds, minced onion, or garlic.

Cinnamon Raisin Bagels

◆§ Add 1 tablespoon cinnamon, ¾ cup raisins, and a total of a ½ cup honey to the batter.

Cinnamon Apple Bagels

◆§ Follow directions for Cinnamon Raisin Bagels, substituting 2 cups peeled and chopped apples for the raisins.

Pumpernickel Bagels

◆§ Add 1 tablespoon molasses, 2 teaspoons caraway seeds, and 1 cup rye flour in the second step of the recipe.

Nutritional Analysis: 1 bagel, basic recipe
cal 215; chol 0; fat-total 1 g; fat-mono 0.2 g; fat-poly 0.6 g; fat-sat 0.2 g; protein 8.38 g; carbo 46.1 g; fiber 5.81 g; calcium 26 mg; sodium 136 mg; fat 4%; protein 15%; carbo 81%

Nutritional Analysis for Lunch Meal: 1 serving
cal 562; chol 4 mg; fat-total 3.3 g; fat-mono 0.6 g; fat-poly 0.8 g; fat-sat 1.1 g; protein 22.14 g; carbo 113.6 g; fiber 8.44 g+; calcium 262 mg; sodium 196 mg; fat 5%; protein 15%; carbo 80%

✺ Hummus-in-Pita Sandwiches
Israeli Salad

This sandwich-and-salad meal is easy to fix and keeps well in the refrigerator. Traditional hummus is made with quite a bit of oil and tahini and can be very high in fat. Here's a lower-fat variation.

HUMMUS-IN-PITA SANDWICHES

Hummus is a garbanzo bean and tahini (sesame seed paste) spread —the perfect filling for pita bread. This Middle Eastern sandwich is delicious any time of year. It's very easy to make, and a great fast meal with canned beans. Hummus is also good on crackers or whole-grain breads, or thinned with skim milk to make a dip for raw vegetables.

2 cups cooked garbanzo beans
  (⅞ cup raw)
¼ cup lemon juice
2 cloves garlic
2 tablespoons tahini
2 tablespoons fresh parsley
¼ teaspoon cumin
¼ teaspoon coriander
Freshly ground black pepper to
  taste
Cayenne pepper or Tabasco sauce
  to taste
Salt or soy sauce to taste
  (optional)
6 pieces whole-wheat pita bread

Serves 6
Prep: 15 minutes

Dijon-style mustard (optional)
Horseradish (optional)
3 tomatoes, sliced
½ onion, thinly sliced
12 leaves leaf lettuce
Alfalfa sprouts (optional)

✺ Combine the first 10 ingredients in a food processor or blender and purée until very smooth and creamy. If necessary add a little bean liquid or water to thin slightly.

✺ To make sandwiches, cut the pita bread in half to form 2 pockets. Spread hummus inside the pockets, along with some mustard and horseradish, if desired. Add tomato and onion slices, and fill with lettuce and sprouts.

Nutritional Analysis: 1 serving
cal 295; chol 0; fat-total 6.1 g; fat-mono 2.1 g+; fat-poly 2.5 g+; fat-sat 1.3 g+; protein 14 g; carbo 47.5 g; fiber 5.68 g+; calcium 61 mg; sodium 422 mg; fat 18%; protein 19%; carbo 63%

ISRAELI SALAD

When in season, the outdoor markets in Israel have an abundance of juicy, red tomatoes and crisp cucumbers. This salad is crisp, light, and refreshing — not oily.

2 large cucumbers, cubed
2 tomatoes, cubed
1 small onion, diced
1 green pepper, chopped
2 tablespoons olive oil
2 tablespoons lemon juice
1 large clove garlic, minced
1 teaspoon basil
½ teaspoon oregano
Salt to taste (optional)
Freshly ground black pepper to
    taste

Serves 6
Prep: 10 minutes
Chill: 1 hour or more

- ⊷ Combine all the vegetables in a large bowl.
- ⊷ Mix the remaining ingredients in a cup.
- ⊷ Pour the dressing over the vegetables and toss very gently.
- ⊷ Cover and let the salad marinate in the refrigerator for at least 1 hour. (The longer the salad marinates, the more flavor it will have.) Toss occasionally.
- ⊷ Taste to adjust seasonings before serving.

Nutritional Analysis: 1 serving
cal 212; chol 0; fat-total 6.9 g; fat-mono 3.9 g; fat-poly 1.5 g; fat-sat 0.9 g; protein 8.80 g; carbo 29.8 g; fiber 4.44 g+; calcium 71 mg; sodium 12 mg; fat 29%; protein 16%; carbo 55%

Nutritional Analysis for Lunch Meal: 1 serving
cal 508; chol 0; fat-total 13 g; fat-mono 6 g+; fat-poly 4 g+; fat-sat 2.2 g+; protein 22.79 g; carbo 77.2 g; fiber 10.12 g+; calcium 132 mg; sodium 433 mg; fat 23%; protein 18%; carbo 59%

৬৪ Greek Pasta Salad
Whole-Wheat French Bread

GREEK PASTA SALAD

This pasta dish is a meal in itself. Add a few slices of crusty whole-grain bread and you're set. (The recipe for Whole-Wheat French Bread is on page 181.) The salad actually improves in flavor over time, so it can be made in advance and kept refrigerated until you're ready to serve. A good-quality feta cheese packed in water is important for flavor in this recipe.

1 pound whole-grain spinach
  fettuccine
½ small red onion, very thinly
  sliced
3 tomatoes, chopped
½ pound spinach, chopped
18 black olives, sliced
4 ounces feta cheese, crumbled
2 tablespoons olive oil
2 tablespoons (or more to taste)
  balsamic vinegar
Several tablespoons feta cheese
  water, to taste

Serves 6
Prep: 15 minutes

Freshly ground black pepper to
  taste

ৡ৯ Cook the fettuccine until al dente, about 8 to 10 minutes.
ৡ৯ Meanwhile, toss the vegetables, olives, and feta in a large bowl.
ৡ৯ Drain the pasta and add it to the bowl. Sprinkle with the remaining ingredients and toss the whole salad very well.
ৡ৯ Taste to adjust seasoning.
ৡ৯ Cover and refrigerate until ready to serve. Flavor is best when well chilled.

Nutritional Analysis for Lunch Meal: 1 salad serving with 2 slices of Whole-Wheat French Bread
cal 637; chol 17 mg; fat-total 12.4 g; fat-mono 6.1 g; fat-poly 1.5 g; fat-sat 4 g; protein 23.75 g; carbo 109.1 g; fiber 8.94 g+; calcium 207 mg; sodium 849 mg; fat 17%; protein 15%; carbo 68%

✒ Chilled Fresh Peach Soup
Bibb Lettuce with Apricot Yogurt Dressing
Banana–Poppy Seed Muffins

This simple lunch with an elegant, fruity flair is the perfect meal to share with good friends on a hot summer day.

CHILLED FRESH PEACH SOUP

The sweet, juicy flavor of ripe summer peaches is combined with the low-fat creaminess of cottage cheese and yogurt. Lightly spiced with ginger, this soup is wonderful in a meal or as a simple dessert.

10 very ripe peaches, peeled,
   pitted, and sliced
2 cups tangerine or orange juice
¾ cup unsweetened pineapple
   chunks, drained, with ½ cup
   juice reserved
1 teaspoon ginger
½ cup nonfat plain yogurt
½ cup Cottage Cream (page 319)

Serves 4
Prep: 20 minutes
Chill until icy cold

- ✒ Set aside 8 thin peach slices and purée the rest with ½ cup of the tangerine juice in a blender or food processor. Pour this mixture into a bowl and stir in the remaining tangerine juice.
- ✒ Purée the pineapple chunks with ¼ cup of the pineapple juice. Stir this mixture into the peach purée.
- ✒ Whisk the ginger, yogurt, and cottage cheese into the purée. Slowly stir in enough of the remaining pineapple juice to get the consistency you want. Chill very well and serve with 2 sliced peaches floating in each bowl.

Nutritional Analysis: 1 serving
cal 223; chol 3 mg; fat-total 0.8 g; fat-mono 0.2 g+; fat-poly 0.1 g+; fat-sat 0.4 g+; protein 9.30 g; carbo 51.2 g; fiber 4.34 g+; calcium 109 mg; sodium 139 mg; fat 3%; protein 15%; carbo 82%

BIBB LETTUCE WITH APRICOT YOGURT DRESSING

Soft, buttery heads of Bibb lettuce are sliced in half and laced with a creamy dressing made from dried apricots.

¼ cup chopped dried apricots
¾ cup nonfat plain yogurt
1½ tablespoons walnut,
    hazelnut, almond, or extra-
    light olive oil
1 tablespoon apple cider vinegar
2 teaspoons honey
½ teaspoon celery seed
½ teaspoon minced onion
1/16 teaspoon dry mustard powder
3 heads Bibb, Boston, or
    buttercrunch lettuce
Nutmeg

Serves 6
Prep: 5 minutes

◄§ Purée the apricots and the yogurt in a food processor or blender until very smooth. Blend in the remaining ingredients, with the exception of the lettuce and nutmeg. Refrigerate until ready to serve.
◄§ Wash and dry whole lettuce heads. Cut each head in half and place in individual bowls.
◄§ Drizzle the chilled dressing over the lettuce. Sprinkle each serving with a little nutmeg.

Nutritional Analysis: 1 serving
cal 81; chol 1 mg; fat-total 3.9 g; fat-mono 2.6 g+; fat-poly 0.4 g+; fat-sat 0.6 g+; protein 2.85 g; carbo 10.2 g; fiber 1.88 g; calcium 89 mg; sodium 27 mg; fat 40%; protein 13%; carbo 47%

BANANA – POPPY SEED MUFFINS

These muffins are full of rich banana flavor and low-fat goodness. The poppy seeds add a special touch.

2 tablespoons unsalted butter or
margarine, softened
4 tablespoons honey or maple
syrup
2 teaspoons vanilla
1 egg or 2 egg whites or egg
replacer, beaten
4 very ripe bananas, mashed
¼ cup cultured nonfat buttermilk
1½ cups whole-grain flour
1 tablespoon poppy seeds
1 teaspoon baking powder

Makes 12 muffins
Prep: 15 minutes
Bake: 30–35 minutes

½ teaspoon baking soda
⅛ teaspoon nutmeg
⅛ teaspoon cinnamon

◆§ Preheat oven to 350°F. Line 12 muffin tins with paper cups.

◆§ Cream the butter in a large bowl. Beat in the sweetener, vanilla, egg, banana, and buttermilk.

◆§ Combine the remaining ingredients in a separate bowl.

◆§ Add the dry mixture to the wet and stir just well enough to incorporate all the ingredients.

◆§ Pour the batter into the muffin cups. Bake for 30 to 35 minutes, or until a toothpick inserted into the center of a muffin comes out almost dry (the muffins should be quite moist). Remove the muffins from the pan and cool on a rack.

Nutritional Analysis: 1 serving
cal 141; chol 28 mg; fat-total 3.3 g; fat-mono 0.8 g; fat-poly 0.5 g; fat-sat 1.5 g; protein 3.15 g; carbo 26.1 g; fiber 2.2 g; calcium 46 mg+; sodium 71 mg; fat 20%; protein 9%; carbo 71%
◆ With margarine and egg whites instead of butter and a whole egg: chol 0; fat-mono 0.9 g; fat-poly 1 g; fat-sat 0.5 g

Nutritional Analysis for Lunch Meal: 1 serving
cal 445; chol 31 mg; fat-total 7.9 g; fat-mono 3.7 g+; fat-poly 1 g+; fat-sat 2.5 g+; protein 15.30 g; carbo 87.5 g; fiber 8.42 g+; calcium 245 mg+; sodium 236 mg; fat 15%; protein 13%; carbo 72%
◆ With margarine and egg whites instead of butter and a whole egg: chol 3 mg; fat-mono 3.8 g+; fat-poly 1.5 g+; fat-sat 1.6 g+

Cool Weather Dinner
Menus and Recipes

◆◆

◆◆

✒ Saffron Bouillabaisse
Fresh Spinach and Garlic Sauté
Whole-Wheat French Bread

Enjoy this informal European meal with your family or transform it into an elegant menu for entertaining. The seafood you choose and the manner in which you set your table will create the ambiance you desire.

SAFFRON BOUILLABAISSE

Bouillabaisse (bool-ya-bays) is a light fish stew or chowder that originated in the Mediterranean coastal region of France. This dish is an experience — the ultimate in soup. And not only is it fast and easy to prepare, it's fun to eat as well. Cooks originally made bouillabaisse with the less desirable fish left in a fisherman's net after the better fish had been sold. Today it's made with whatever seafood is readily available. Choose your favorites. Be sure to serve bouillabaisse with enough bread to dip into and soak up the saffron-scented broth.

1 large leek, sliced
2 cloves garlic, sliced
1 – 2 tablespoons olive oil
1 can (28 ounces) Italian-style
   tomatoes, drained
3 cups fish stock, vegetable broth,
   or water
1 cup dry white wine

Serves 4
Prep and Cook: 30 –
40 minutes

(Ingredients continued on page 180)

1 teaspoon saffron threads
1 teaspoon thyme
Freshly ground black pepper to taste
2 tablespoons fresh minced parsley

2 slices whole-grain bread, crumbled (day-old is best if available)
1½ pounds mixed seafood,* cut into bite-size pieces
Salt to taste (optional)

◦§ Sauté the leek and garlic slices in oil in a large soup pot for 5 to 10 minutes. Add the tomatoes and crush them with a spoon. Cook for another 5 to 10 minutes.

◦§ Stir in all the remaining ingredients, except the seafood, and bring to a rapid boil.

◦§ Add the large pieces of seafood to the pot (those that are about 1 inch thick) and cook for 5 minutes. Now add the rest of the fish and continue cooking at a slower boil for another 5 minutes or until the fish is cooked through.

◦§ Remove the pot from the heat and divide the fish into 4 bowls. Top with broth and serve.

Nutritional Analysis: 1 serving
cal 354; chol 128 mg; fat-total 9.7 g; fat-mono 5.7 g+; fat-poly 1.6 g+; fat-sat 1.3 g+; protein 41.68 g; carbo 23.2 g; fiber 4.24 g+; calcium 150 mg; sodium 225 mg; fat 25%; protein 48%; carbo 27%
◆ Analysis is based on ½ pound each: halibut, shrimp, scallops and 2 tablespoons olive oil.

FRESH SPINACH AND GARLIC SAUTÉ

Two pounds of raw spinach may seem like a lot, but once cooked it shrinks to the perfect amount. The combination of olive oil, garlic, and spinach is perfection. This dish is a favorite in our home as well as in many restaurants. Try substituting other greens for the spinach, such as beet greens, kale, or escarole.

---

* *Seafood options:* Fresh or frozen tuna, sole, monkfish, sea bass, sea perch, lobster, shrimp, scallops, crab, crawfish, prawns, perch, mahimahi, swordfish, redfish, clams, mussels, oysters. Shellfish cooked with the shell should be soaked, scrubbed, and rinsed very well to remove all sand. Cook these 10 minutes.

Vegetarian alternative: Sautéed tempeh, tofu, and cooked beans in place of seafood

2 pounds spinach
2 tablespoons olive oil
4 large cloves garlic, thinly sliced
Freshly ground black pepper to
  taste
Salt to taste (optional)
Fructose or sugar (optional)

Serves 4
Prep: 10 minutes
Cook: 10 minutes

🍃 Wash and dry the spinach. Remove the stems and tear the leaves into big pieces.

🍃 Heat the oil in a very large skillet. Add the garlic and sauté until it's softened.

🍃 Stir in the spinach and toss over medium heat until the leaves shrink fully and are coated with garlic and oil.

🍃 Remove from heat and toss with black pepper and salt to taste. You may add a very light sprinkle of fructose to reduce any bitterness from the spinach.

Nutritional Analysis: 1 serving
cal 98; chol 0; fat-total 7.2 g; fat-mono 5.2 g; fat-poly 0.8 g; fat-sat 1 g; protein 3.95 g; carbo 6.5 g; fiber 3.05 g; calcium 191 mg; sodium 96 mg; fat 61%; protein 15%; carbo 24%

WHOLE-WHEAT FRENCH BREAD

Whole-wheat flour makes a heavier, denser bread than does white flour. It also has more flavor. Brick ovens are traditionally used to make French bread, giving it a tender inside and crispy crust. To create a crispy crust at home, I improvise by spraying the loaves with water while baking. If you can buy good French bread locally, that may be more convenient, although this recipe bakes 2 large loaves that freeze well. It's also easy to cut this recipe in half.*

2½ cups warm water (110–
  115°F)
2 tablespoons active dry yeast
6–8 cups whole-wheat flour
1 tablespoon salt

Serves 24
Bake: 25 minutes

---

* See Chapter 7 for added tips and information on baking bread.

◆ Pour water into a large bowl and sprinkle yeast on top. Let proof for 10 minutes.

◆ Slowly add 2 to 3 cups of flour and the salt to the yeast mixture and beat well for 3 minutes (I like to use an electric mixer). Slowly knead in enough of the remaining flour to form a soft, unsticky dough. Knead for 10 minutes.

◆ Place the dough in a very large bowl that you have rubbed with a little oil and turn the dough in the bowl to coat with the oil.

◆ Cover the bowl and set it aside in a warm place (80 to 85°F) to rise for 1 hour or until the dough is doubled in size.

◆ Punch down the dough, divide it into 2 pieces, and shape them into long, rounded loaves. Place the loaves in French bread pans if you have them, or sprinkle a baking sheet with corn meal and set the loaves on top. Cover the loaves lightly and let them rise in a warm place for 20 minutes or until doubled in size. Preheat oven to 450°F.

◆ Bake loaves for 25 minutes. Every 5 minutes during baking, open the oven door and spray the oven bottom, walls, and the bread lightly with water. A plant sprayer works best.

◆ Remove the bread from the oven and cool it on a rack.

Nutritional Analysis: 1 serving
cal 120; chol 0; fat-total 0.8 g; fat-mono 0.2 g; fat-poly 0.3 g; fat-sat 0.1 g; protein 4.92 g; carbo 25 g; fiber 3.4 g; calcium 16 mg; sodium 268 mg; fat 6%; protein 15%; carbo 79%

Nutritional Analysis for Dinner Meal: 1 serving (with 2 slices of bread)
cal 692; chol 128 mg; fat-total 18.5 g; fat-mono 11.3 g+; fat-poly 3 g+; fat-sat 2.6 g+; protein 55.47 g; carbo 79.8 g; fiber 14.07 g+; calcium 374 mg; sodium 857 mg; fat 24%; protein 31%; carbo 45%

◄§ Pasta Rustica
Red, White, and Green Salad with Creamy Garlic Dressing

This meal is fast and hearty with a European country flair. You can divide the recipes in half to make 3 servings instead of 6 — although you can reheat leftover pasta quickly for lunch.

PASTA RUSTICA

This chunky tomato-based sauce has the warmth and feeling of the country, yet it's anything but plain and simple. Try adding other vegetables, such as sun-dried tomatoes or *peperoncini*.

1 tablespoon olive oil
7 cloves garlic, sliced
1 onion, cut into strips
1 green pepper, sliced
1 can (28 ounces) tomato purée
1 can (6 ounces) tomato paste
½ cup dry red wine
1½ teaspoons basil
1½ teaspoons oregano
24 small black olives, pitted
16 small green olives, pitted
1 can (4 ounces) artichoke hearts
    packed in water, drained,
    sliced
¼ cup chopped fresh parsley

Serves 6
Prep: 15 minutes
Cook: 15 minutes

Freshly ground black pepper to
    taste
1 pound whole-grain pasta
    shells, gnocci, or other pasta
6 tablespoons grated Parmesan
    cheese

◄§ Heat the oil slightly in a medium saucepan. Sauté the garlic, onion, and green pepper for 5 to 10 minutes.

◄§ Stir in the remaining ingredients, except the pasta and cheese. Cover and simmer on medium-low heat for 15 minutes. Stir occasionally to prevent burning.

◄§ Cook the pasta until al dente, 8 to 10 minutes. Drain and toss the pasta with the sauce in a large bowl.

◄§ Serve the pasta in bowls, each topped with a tablespoon of Parmesan cheese.

Nutritional Analysis: 1 serving
cal 474; chol 4 mg; fat-total 9 g; fat-mono 4.7 g+; fat-poly 0.8 g+;
fat-sat 1.9 g+; protein 17.01 g; carbo 82.3 g; fiber 10.88 g+; calcium
188 mg; sodium 466 mg; fat 17%; protein 14%; carbo 69%

RED, WHITE, AND GREEN SALAD

3 small heads Bibb, Boston, or   *Serves 6*
  buttercrunch lettuce   *Prep: 10 minutes*
2 cups frozen peas, thawed
2 tomatoes, chopped
1 red pepper, sliced
6 radishes, sliced

∾§ Wash, dry, and cut the lettuce in half lengthwise. Spread the
lettuce leaves and place in 6 individual bowls.

∾§ Place the peas and tomatoes on top of each lettuce half. Decorate
the edges of the bowls with the pepper and radish slices.

Nutritional Analysis: 1 serving
cal 65; chol 0; fat-total 0.3 g; fat-mono 0; fat-poly 0.2 g; fat-sat 0 g;
protein 4.17 g; carbo 12.3 g; fiber 5.02 g; calcium 43 mg; sodium
55 mg; fat 4%; protein 24%; carbo 72%

CREAMY GARLIC DRESSING

Cottage cheese and yogurt form the base for this low-fat, low-calorie
dressing with a mild garlic flavor.

½ cup low-fat cottage cheese   *Serves 6*
½ cup nonfat plain yogurt   *Prep: 5 minutes*
1 clove garlic, minced
1 teaspoon parsley
1 teaspoon Dijon-style mustard
¼ teaspoon onion powder
¼ teaspoon freshly ground black
  pepper
Salt to taste (optional)

✺ Mix all the ingredients in a blender or food processor until smooth. If possible, refrigerate several hours before serving.

Nutritional Analysis: 1 serving
cal 29; chol 2 mg; fat-total 0.4 g; fat-mono 0.1 g; fat-poly 0; fat-sat 0.3 g; protein 3.70 g; carbo 2.4 g; fiber 0.01 g; calcium 53 mg; sodium 102 mg; fat 13%; protein 53%; carbo 34%

Nutritional Analysis for Dinner Meal: 1 serving
cal 568; chol 6 mg; fat-total 9.7 g; fat-mono 4.9 g+; fat-poly 1 g+; fat-sat 2.2 g+; protein 24.87 g; carbo 97 g; fiber 15.92 g+; calcium 284 mg; sodium 623 mg; fat 15%; protein 17%; carbo 68%

◆§ Risotto Vino Blanco
Warm Spinach Salad
Crostini

This Italian meal is quite hearty and rich-tasting. The entree and bread are low in fat, allowing for the special, higher-fat salad.

RISOTTO VINO BLANCO

Risotto is an Italian rice dish. Unlike the plain, dry rice that is popular in China, India, and America, the rice in *risotto* is tossed in oil and then cooked in a broth until it's chewy, al dente, as with pasta. *Risotto* is traditionally made with Arborio rice (an Italian round rice), but short-grain brown rice works very well. This recipe uses several readily available vegetables. Try adding any number of additional ingredients to create variety.* You can make *risotto* in a microwave oven or pressure cooker to quicken the cooking time.

1 tablespoon + 1 teaspoon olive oil	*Serves 6*
2 large onions, chopped	*Prep: 5 minutes*
4 large cloves garlic, minced	*Cook: 45 – 55 minutes*
2¼ cups short-grain brown rice	
5¾ cups vegetable or chicken broth	
¾ cup dry white wine	
1 teaspoon basil	½ pound mushrooms, sliced
½ teaspoon dry mustard powder	1½ cups frozen snow or green peas, thawed
Lots of freshly ground black pepper	4 ounces pimientos, chopped
Salt to taste (optional)	½ cup grated Parmesan cheese

◆§ Heat 1 tablespoon of the oil slightly in a large soup pot and sauté the onions and garlic for 5 minutes.

---

* You can precook and stir additional ingredients into the *risotto* just before serving or add them during the last few minutes of cooking: asparagus, broccoli, cauliflower, carrots, artichoke hearts, sun-dried tomatoes, wild mushrooms, pine nuts, fresh herbs, saffron, lemon juice, seafood or poultry, beans, tempeh, or tofu.

✧§ Stir in the rice and sauté for another 5 minutes or until the rice browns slightly. Pour in half of the broth, the wine, and seasonings.

✧§ Bring the mixture to a boil, stir, lower the heat to simmer, and cover. Cook the *risotto* for 30 to 45 minutes, stirring every 10 to 15 minutes.

✧§ Add the remaining broth when the risotto has cooked for 15 minutes. There should be a little liquid left.

✧§ Remove the pot from the heat and beat the rice with an electric mixer or a wooden spoon to create a creamy texture (about 3 minutes).

✧§ Lightly sauté the mushrooms in the remaining teaspoon of olive oil. Gently stir the mushrooms, peas, pimientos, and cheese into the *risotto.* Adjust seasonings to taste and serve steaming hot in bowls.

Nutritional Analysis: 1 serving
cal 390; chol 7 mg; fat-total 7.3 g; fat-mono 3.7 g+; fat-poly 0.9 g+; fat-sat 2.3 g; protein 12.38 g; carbo 68.4 g; fiber 8.36 g+; calcium 176 mg; sodium 204 mg; fat 17%; protein 13%; carbo 70%

WARM SPINACH SALAD

Raw spinach is topped with a warm red onion vinaigrette dressing and then tossed with a little feta cheese and some chickpeas. The combination of ingredients is unique and delicious.

1 pound spinach
2 ounces feta cheese
1½ cups cooked garbanzo beans
  (¾ cup raw)
2 tablespoons olive oil
2 tablespoons balsamic or red
  wine vinegar
1 red onion, thinly sliced
2 cloves garlic, minced
2 tablespoons grated Parmesan
  cheese

Serves 6
Prep: 15 minutes

Freshly ground black pepper to
  taste

◄§ Wash, dry, and remove stems from spinach, and place the leaves in a large salad bowl. Top with feta cheese and garbanzo beans.

◄§ Heat the oil and vinegar in a large skillet and sauté the onion and garlic for 3 to 5 minutes or until soft.

◄§ Add the onion-garlic sauté to the spinach and toss very well. Divide the salad among 6 plates and lightly sprinkle each serving with Parmesan cheese. Add pepper. Serve immediately.

Nutritional Analysis: 1 serving
cal 70; chol 10 mg; fat-total 8.4 g; fat-mono 4 g+; fat-poly 0.6 g+; fat-sat 2.4 g+; protein 9.05 g; carbo 17.5 g; fiber 5.54 g; calcium 180 mg; sodium 198 mg; fat 42%; protein 20%; carbo 38%

CROSTINI

Crostini are similar to American crackers or toast. In this recipe, whole-grain French or Italian bread is sliced and baked in the oven until crisp. This is a great way to use bread that is a few days old. Once the *crostini* cool, they keep well in a covered container. You can try other types of bread, too.

½-inch slices of Whole-Wheat   *Bake: 10 minutes*
   French Bread (page 181)

◄§ Preheat oven to 400°F. Place the slices of bread flat on a baking sheet. Bake 10 minutes or until lightly browned.

◄§ Cool before storing. Serve plain or with a variety of spreads.

Nutritional Analysis: 1 slice
cal 120; chol 0; fat-total 0.8 g; fat-mono 0.2 g; fat-poly 0.3 g; fat-sat 0.1 g; protein 4.92 g; carbo 25 g; fiber 3.4 g; calcium 16 mg; sodium 268 mg; fat 6%; protein 15%; carbo 79%

Nutritional Analysis for Dinner Meal: 1 serving
cal 680; chol 16 mg; fat-total 16.6 g; fat-mono 8 g+; fat-poly 1.9 g+; fat-sat 4.8 g+; protein 26.35; carbo 110.9 g; fiber 17.30 g+; calcium 372 mg; sodium 670 mg; fat 21%; protein 15%; carbo 64%

৵ Baked Potatoes with Tuna Tomato Sauce
Tossed Greens with Balsamic Splash
Country Farmhouse Bread

If you bake the potatoes in a microwave oven and buy bread (instead of using the recipe below), this family-style meal can be on the table in 30 minutes.

BAKED POTATOES WITH TUNA TOMATO SAUCE

These potatoes are overflowing with tuna fish cooked in tomato sauce. The sauce tastes great on pasta, too.

4 large potatoes	*Serves 4*
1 tablespoon olive oil	*Prep: 10 minutes*
3 large cloves garlic, minced	*Cook: 45 minutes – 1*
3 shallots or ½ small onion, chopped	*hour*
1 green pepper, chopped	
½ cup fresh parsley, chopped	
1 can (6½ ounces) tuna fish packed in water, drained, flaked	Freshly ground black pepper to taste
1 can (28 ounces) Italian-style tomatoes with liquid	Grated Parmesan cheese (optional)

৵ Preheat oven to 425°F. Wash the potatoes, poke several holes in each, and bake for 45 minutes to 1 hour or until tender.

৵ Heat the oil slightly in a medium saucepan and sauté the garlic, shallots, and green pepper for 5 minutes.

৵ Add the parsley and tuna. Cook for 2 minutes more. Chop the tomatoes and add to the saucepan along with the tomato liquid.

৵ Cook over medium heat for 20 minutes, stirring occasionally. Season to taste with pepper.

৵ Cut a large X into the top of each baked potato. Push into each potato, with both thumbs and forefingers on all sides of the X to squeeze the insides up and out of the opening. Serve the potatoes in bowls with sauce and a sprinkle of Parmesan cheese on top.

Nutritional Analysis: 1 serving
cal 384; chol 26 mg; fat-total 5.2 g; fat-mono 2.8 g+; fat-poly 0.8 g+; fat-sat 0.8 g+; protein 23.44 g; carbo 63.5 g; fiber 7.2 g; calcium 103 mg; sodium 297 mg; fat 12%; protein 24%; carbo 64%

TOSSED GREENS WITH BALSAMIC SPLASH

Balsamic vinegar is a dark, sweet, and syrupy vinegar made in Italy from special grapes that are cooked on a fire and aged in wooden casks. The unique flavor quickly becomes a favorite.

8 cups lettuce, such as Bibb, romaine, red leaf, and buttercrunch

Serves 4
Prep: 5 minutes

3 tablespoons balsamic vinegar
2 tablespoons olive oil
1 tablespoon dry white wine or water
1 clove garlic, minced
1 teaspoon mustard seeds
½ teaspoon mustard powder
¼ teaspoon honey
Freshly ground black pepper to taste

Grated Parmesan cheese (optional)

- ◄§ Wash, dry, and tear the lettuce into pieces. Place them in a salad bowl.
- ◄§ Combine the remaining ingredients in a separate bowl. Toss the dressing with the lettuce right before serving. If the vinegar flavor is a little too strong at first, add a bit more olive oil. Sprinkle with Parmesan cheese.

Nutritional Analysis: 1 serving
cal 91; chol 0; fat-total 7.5 g; fat-mono 5.3 g; fat-poly 0.8 g; fat-sat 1 g; protein 2.18 g; carbo 5.4 g; fiber 1.87 g; calcium 70 mg; sodium 10 mg; fat 68%; protein 9%; carbo 23%

COUNTRY FARMHOUSE BREAD

A true country bread with a crispy, floured crust and hearty whole-grain flavor.*

2 cups skim milk
½ cup water
2 tablespoons unsalted butter or
  margarine
1 tablespoon honey
1 tablespoon active dry yeast
5 – 6 cups whole-wheat flour
2 teaspoons salt

Serves 12
Bake: 40 minutes

◆§ Heat milk, water, butter, and honey to 110 to 115°F. Pour the liquid into a large bowl and sprinkle yeast on top. Let proof for 10 minutes.

◆§ Slowly add 2 to 3 cups of flour and the salt to the yeast mixture and beat well for 3 minutes (I like to use an electric mixer). Slowly knead in enough of the remaining flour to form a soft, unsticky dough. Knead for 10 minutes.

◆§ Place the dough in a very large bowl that has been rubbed with a little oil and turn the dough in the bowl to coat with the oil.

◆§ Cover the bowl and set it aside in a warm place (80 to 85°F) to rise for 1 hour or until doubled in size.

◆§ Punch down the dough and shape it into a round loaf. Place the loaf on a lightly oiled baking sheet sprinkled with flour. Brush the top of the loaf with water, dust with flour, and make a few ¼-inch-deep slashes from end to end. Cover the loaf lightly and let it rise in a warm place for 45 minutes or until about doubled in size.

◆§ Preheat oven to 375°F. Bake for 35 to 40 minutes or until the loaf is browned and sounds hollow when tapped on the bottom.

◆§ Remove the bread from the baking sheet and cool on a rack.

Nutritional Analysis: 1 serving
cal 238; chol 6 mg; fat-total 2.9 g; fat-mono 0.7 g; fat-poly 0.6 g; fat-sat 1.4 g; protein 9.58 g; carbo 46.2 g; fiber 5.81 g; calcium 78 mg; sodium 379 mg; fat 11%; protein 15%; carbo 74%

---

* See Chapter 7 for added tips and information on baking bread.

◆ With margarine instead of butter: chol 1 mg; fat-mono 1 g; fat-poly 1.1 g; fat-sat 0.6 g

Nutritional Analysis for Dinner Meal: 1 serving
cal 714; chol 31 mg; fat-total 15.6 g; fat-mono 8.8 g+; fat-poly 2.2 g+; fat-sat 3.2 g+; protein 35.20 g; carbo 115.1 g; fiber 14.88 g; calcium 251 mg; sodium 686 mg; fat 19%; protein 19%; carbo 62%
◆ With margarine instead of butter: chol 26 mg; fat-mono 9.1 g+; fat-poly 2.7 g+; fat-sat 2.4 g+

◀§ *Savory Soybeans au Gratin*
   Crunchy Tossed Salad with
      Blackberry-Pecan Vinaigrette
   Sprouted Wheat-Berry Bread

This is a wonderful meal for a cold winter's eve. The creamy soybean casserole is contrasted with the crunchy texture of the salad and the bright flavor of the blackberry-pecan dressing. The Sprouted Wheat-Berry Bread is especially delicious, but if time is a factor, you can substitute any whole-grain bread.

SAVORY SOYBEANS AU GRATIN

Cooked soybeans have a firm texture and rich flavor that are enhanced by the *au gratin* (breaded) crust. You need to do some advance planning for this meal since it's important that the beans soak overnight and cook fully. But when you taste this dish, I think you will agree that it's well worth planning ahead.

1½ cups soybeans
1 tablespoon olive oil
1 onion, chopped
4 cloves garlic, minced
1 green pepper, chopped
¼ pound mushrooms, sliced
⅓ cup whole-grain flour
1 tablespoon soy sauce
1 teaspoon basil
1 teaspoon parsley
½ teaspoon savory
¼ teaspoon sage
1½ cups evaporated skim milk

Serves 6
Soak: Overnight
Cook: 3 hours
Prep: 25 minutes
Bake: 15 minutes

½ cup grated part–skim milk
   Swiss or Cheddar cheese
¼ cup grated Parmesan cheese
½ cup whole-grain bread crumbs

◀§ Sort through the beans and remove any foreign material. Rinse and soak the beans in a large pot of water overnight.

◀§ Drain the beans and fill the cooking pot with fresh water. Bring to a boil, skim foam from the top of the pot, reduce the heat to medium-low, and cook, partially covered, for 3 hours or until the beans seem soft but not mushy. Taste one. It should be soft but still firm.

◆§ Heat the oil in a saucepan and sauté the onion, garlic, and pepper for 5 minutes. Add the mushrooms and cook for 5 minutes more. Stir in the flour, soy sauce, and herbs. Cook for 2 to 3 minutes. Slowly add the milk, stirring to avoid lumps in the sauce. Simmer the mixture for 10 minutes or until slightly thickened.

◆§ Mix the cheeses and bread crumbs in a separate bowl. Preheat oven to 350°F. Very lightly oil a 9 × 13-inch baking dish.

◆§ When the beans are cooked, drain them well and mix with the sauce. Pour into the baking dish and sprinkle the cheese mixture evenly on top of the casserole. Bake for 15 minutes or until lightly browned on top. Let cool slightly before serving.

Nutritional Analysis: 1 serving
cal 310; chol 9 mg; fat-total 12.4 g; fat-mono 3.8 g; fat-poly 3.8 g; fat-sat 3.1 g; protein 21.65 g; carbo 30.5 g; fiber 2.57 g+; calcium 302 mg; sodium 381 mg; fat 35%; protein 27%; carbo 38%

CRUNCHY TOSSED SALAD WITH BLACKBERRY-PECAN VINAIGRETTE

Fresh or frozen blackberries and pecans are blended into a sweet and tangy dressing. You can use any mild oil in this dressing, but the ones I've chosen create the nicest flavor.

6 cups romaine lettuce

1 cup red cabbage, thinly sliced

½ red onion, thinly sliced

1 carrot, grated

½ green pepper, sliced

6 radishes, sliced

3 scallions, sliced lengthwise

1½ cups frozen blackberries, thawed

3 tablespoons white wine vinegar

3 tablespoons water

1 tablespoon extra-light olive, canola, walnut, or hazelnut oil

½ tablespoon honey or fructose

¼ teaspoon thyme

¼ teaspoon freshly ground black pepper

5 pecan halves

Salt to taste (optional)

Serves 6
Prep: 20 minutes

◈§ Wash, dry, and tear the lettuce into pieces. Place them in a large salad bowl. Add the other vegetables in the order given.

◈§ Combine the remaining ingredients in a blender or food processor until very smooth. Chill the dressing thoroughly before serving with the salad.

Nutritional Analysis: 1 serving
cal 79; chol 0; fat-total 3.6 g; fat-mono 2.2 g; fat-poly 0.5 g; fat-sat 0.4 g; protein 1.82 g; carbo 11.4 g; fiber 4.06 g; calcium 48 mg; sodium 11 mg; fat 38%; protein 9%; carbo 53%

SPROUTED WHEAT-BERRY BREAD

This bread has a sweet, nutty flavor and a nice chewy texture. It's also a great sandwich bread. Several days' advance planning is needed to make this bread because the wheat berries need 2 to 3 days to sprout.*

⅓ cup wheat berries (whole-
  wheat kernels)
3 cups warm water (110 – 115°F)
2 tablespoons honey
1 tablespoon active dry yeast
6 – 7 cups whole-wheat flour
1 tablespoon salt

Serves 16
Bake: 45 – 50 minutes

◈§ Two or three days before making this bread, soak the wheat berries overnight in a sealed jar filled with water. In the morning, drain the water, rinse the berries, and place a screen, cheesecloth, or mesh over the top of the jar and secure it with a rubber band. Leave the jar on a counter and each morning and evening rinse the berries and drain well. In a few days you will see little white sprouts. The berries are now ready to be eaten.

◈§ Mix the warm water and honey in a large bowl. Sprinkle the yeast on top and let proof for 10 minutes.

◈§ Add 2 cups of the whole-wheat flour and beat for 3 minutes with an electric mixer or vigorously by hand.

---

* See Chapter 7 for added tips and information on bread baking.

◦ Stir in the sprouted wheat berries and salt. Slowly knead in enough of the remaining flour to form a smooth, elastic dough. Knead for 10 minutes.

◦ Very lightly oil a large bowl. Place the dough in the bowl and turn it to coat with oil. Cover and let rise in a warm place for 1 hour or until about doubled in size. Lightly oil 2 loaf (9 × 5 inches) pans.

◦ Punch down the dough and divide it in half. Shape 2 loaves and place them in the pans. Cover and let rise in a warm place for 30 minutes. Preheat oven to 500°F.

◦ Place the loaves in the oven and immediately turn the heat down to 375°F. Bake for 45 to 50 minutes or until the loaves sound hollow when tapped on the bottom. Remove the loaves from the pans and let them cool on a rack.

Nutritional Analysis:* 1 serving
cal 184; chol 0; fat-total 0.9 g; fat-mono 0.1 g; fat-poly 0.5 g; fat-sat 0.1 g; protein 7.19 g; carbo 39.5 g; fiber 5.08 g; calcium 24 mg; sodium 402 mg; fat 4%; protein 15%; carbo 81%

Nutritional Analysis for Dinner Meal:* 1 serving
cal 573; chol 9 mg; fat-total 16.9 g; fat-mono 6.2 g; fat-poly 4.7 g; fat-sat 3.6 g; protein 30.66 g; carbo 81.4 g; fiber 11.72 g+; calcium 375 mg; sodium 794 mg; fat 25%; protein 20%; carbo 55%

---

* Possible underestimate in nutrients due to a lack of available USDA data for sprouted wheat berries.

ເⴺ Squash and Cheese Casserole
Mixed Greens with Poppy Seed – Tahini Dressing
Honey – Cracked Wheat Bread

This smooth, creamy casserole is best served with mixed greens that are flavorful and crunchy. Some of my favorites are Belgian endive, romaine lettuce, radicchio, and arugula.

SQUASH AND CHEESE CASSEROLE

The rich creamy texture of cooked squash is enhanced by the addition of vegetables and cheeses, which are then baked into a casserole. The combination of acorn and butternut squash gives it a nice flavor. Try adding other vegetables as well.

6 pounds acorn or butternut
  squash
1 teaspoon olive oil
1 onion, chopped
4 cloves garlic, minced
1 green pepper, chopped
2 eggs or 4 egg whites or egg
  replacer, beaten
½ cup cultured nonfat buttermilk
½ cup nonfat plain yogurt
4 ounces feta cheese, crumbled
1 cup grated part–skim milk
  Cheddar cheese
¼ cup picante sauce or salsa
1 cup frozen corn, thawed

Serves 6
Prep: 45 minutes
Bake: 40 minutes

1 cup frozen peas, thawed
1 tablespoon cooking sherry
1 teaspoon basil
Lots of freshly ground pepper to
  taste
Salt to taste (optional)
1 teaspoon paprika

ເⴺ Preheat oven to 450°F. Lightly oil a 9 × 13-inch baking dish.

ເⴺ Cut the squash in half lengthwise. Scoop out seeds and fibers and place the cut side down on a jelly roll pan (or any baking pan that will catch the squash juice to prevent it from spilling). Bake for 45 minutes or until soft. Then lower the oven temperature to 375°F.

ເⴺ Meanwhile, heat the oil in a small saucepan and sauté the onion, garlic, and pepper for 5 minutes.

ເⴺ Mix the remaining ingredients, except paprika, in a large bowl.

◆§ Scoop the squash from its shell and mix into the large bowl of ingredients.

◆§ Pour the mixture into the prepared pan and sprinkle the top with paprika. Bake at 375°F for 40 minutes or until the top is slightly browned and the casserole seems set.

◆§ Let cool for several minutes before serving.

Nutritional Analysis: 1 serving
cal 393; chol 119 mg; fat-total 10.9 g; fat-mono 3.1 g; fat-poly 0.8 g; fat-sat 5.8 g; protein 19.09 g; carbo 61.7 g; fiber 8.92 g; calcium 458 mg; sodium 433 mg; fat 23%; protein 18%; carbo 59%
◆ With egg whites instead of whole eggs: chol 27 mg; fat-mono 2.4 g; fat-poly 0.5 g; fat-sat 5.2 g

MIXED GREENS WITH POPPY SEED – TAHINI DRESSING

Many varieties of delicious greens can be used in salads. Some are not yet very popular in America but are commonly eaten in Europe. The flavors and textures vary from sweet, juicy, and crunchy to pleasantly bitter and soft. Add small amounts of new varieties to your current favorites. Tahini (ground sesame seeds) is sold in natural foods stores and many progressive markets. It has a wonderfully nutty flavor. In this recipe tahini is mixed into a slightly sweet dressing studded with poppy seeds.

Quantity of greens: usually 1 – 2 heads of lettuce, or 9 – 12 cups, yields about 6 servings

Serves 6
Prep: 10 minutes

Greens

Romaine	Curly endive	Mustard greens
Leaf	(chicory)	Spinach
Boston	Escarole	Dandelion greens
Bibb	Radicchio	Beet greens
Buttercrunch	Arugula	Turnip greens
Belgian endive	Mâche	Kale

Dressing

2 tablespoons tahini	2 tablespoons plain nonfat yogurt
3 tablespoons lemon juice	1 tablespoon olive oil
½ cup water	1 tablespoon tomato juice

1 tablespoon honey
1 teaspoon soy sauce
1 tablespoon poppy seeds

◆§ Wash, dry, and tear the greens into pieces.
◆§ Combine all the dressing ingredients, except the poppy seeds, in a blender or food processor until smooth. Stir in the poppy seeds and refrigerate until ready to serve. Thin with a small amount of water before serving if necessary.
◆§ Place the greens on individual plates and serve the dressing on the side.

Nutritional Analysis: 1 serving
cal 95; chol 0; fat-total 6 g; fat-mono 2.8 g; fat-poly 1.9 g; fat-sat 0.8 g; protein 3.6 g; carbo 8.8 g; fiber 1.72 g+; calcium 97 mg; sodium 72 mg; fat 52%; protein 14%; carbo 34%
◆ Analysis is based on romaine and leaf lettuce.

HONEY-CRACKED WHEAT BREAD

The addition of cracked wheat gives this mildly sweet bread a crunchy texture. The hearty loaves make great sandwich bread as well as toast. By varying the ingredients you can create a number of different flavors and textures. Try rolled oats instead of oat bran or substitute sunflower seeds for sesame seeds.*

2 cups warm water (110–115°F)   *Serves 20*
2 tablespoons active dry yeast   *Bake: 30–45 minutes*
4½–5½ cups whole-wheat flour
1 cup cracked wheat
½ cup oat bran
⅓ cup sesame seeds
⅓ cup honey
2 tablespoons molasses
1 tablespoon corn oil (or other
   lightly flavored oil)
2 teaspoons salt

---

* See Chapter 7 for added tips and information on bread baking.

⁄ Pour warm water into a large bowl. Sprinkle yeast on top and let proof for 10 minutes.

⁄ Add 1½ cups of the whole-wheat flour and beat for 3 minutes with an electric mixer or vigorously by hand.

⁄ Stir in the remaining ingredients, except the flour. Then slowly knead in enough of the remaining flour to form a smooth, elastic dough. Knead for 10 minutes.

⁄ Very lightly oil a large bowl. Add the dough and turn it in the bowl to coat with oil. Cover the bowl and let the dough rise in a warm place for 1 hour or until about doubled in size. Lightly oil 2 loaf (9 × 5 inches) pans.

⁄ Punch down the dough and divide it in half. Shape into 2 loaves and place them in the prepared pans. Cover the pans and let the dough rise in a warm place for 30 to 45 minutes.

⁄ Preheat oven to 375°F. Bake for 30 to 45 minutes or until the loaves sound hollow when tapped on the bottom. Remove the bread from the pans and let cool on a rack.

Nutritional Analysis: 1 serving
cal 183; chol 0; fat-total 2.6 g; fat-mono 0.7 g+; fat-poly 1.3 g+; fat-sat 0.4 g+; protein 6.4 g; carbo 35.6 g; fiber 3.22 g; calcium 35 mg; sodium 219 mg; fat 12%; protein 13%; carbo 75%

Nutritional Analysis for Dinner Meal: 1 serving
cal 650; chol 119 mg; fat-total 19.4 g; fat-mono 6.7 g+; fat-poly 3.9 g+; fat-sat 6.9 g+; protein 27.76 g; carbo 102.3 g; fiber 12.33 g; calcium 583 mg; sodium 701 mg; fat 25%; protein 16%; carbo 59%
◆ With egg whites instead of whole eggs: chol 27 mg; fat-mono 5.9 g+; fat-poly 3.7 g+; fat-sat 6.3 g+

✒ Mexican Bean and Cheese Enchiladas Grated Mixed Vegetable Salad with Spicy Tomato Dressing

This meal looks most appealing if each serving — 2 enchiladas and salad — is placed on a large plate. For a little added crunch, Whole-Grain Pita Chips are excellent served on the side.

MEXICAN BEAN AND CHEESE ENCHILADAS

These enchiladas are soft and mild. They're made with refried beans and cheese rolled inside corn tortillas. The whole casserole is then smothered in a slightly spicy ranchero sauce. You can use homemade (page 96) or canned refried beans in this recipe. For hotter enchiladas, add chilis to the filling and a dash of extra chili powder or a touch of cayenne pepper to the sauce. You may also add cooked ground turkey breast, diced chicken, or rice to the filling for variety. Spoon a little Guacamole or Cottage Cream on top if desired.

Sauce
1 tablespoon olive oil
1 onion, finely chopped
2 cloves garlic, minced
2 cups tomato sauce
1 can (28 ounces) tomato purée
2 tablespoons chili powder

Serves 4
Prep: 30 minutes
Bake: 25 – 30 minutes

2 teaspoons oregano
2 teaspoons cumin
3 tablespoons cornmeal

Filling
3 cups Mexican Refried Beans
1 cup frozen corn, thawed
4 ounces part – skim milk
 Cheddar cheese, grated

¼ cup green chilis, diced
 (optional)
12 black olives, sliced (optional)

8 corn tortillas

✒ Heat the oil in a medium saucepan and sauté the onion and garlic for 3 minutes. Add the remaining sauce ingredients, except the cornmeal, and cook on medium-low heat for 15 minutes.

✒ Mix a small amount of the sauce into the cornmeal. Then slowly pour the cornmeal mixture into the remaining sauce while stirring. Cook for 5 to 10 minutes more.

ఆ§ Mix filling ingredients in a bowl.

ఆ§ Preheat oven to 350°F. Pour a small amount of sauce to cover the bottom of a 9 × 13-inch baking dish.

ఆ§ Divide the filling among the tortillas. Roll the tortillas and place them folded side down in the baking dish.

ఆ§ Spread the remaining sauce over the top of the enchiladas, covering each completely.

ఆ§ Bake for 25 to 30 minutes. Let cool slightly before serving each person 2 enchiladas.

Nutritional Analysis: 1 serving
cal 683; chol 15 mg; fat-total 14.3 g; fat-mono 5.3 g+; fat-poly 3.4 g+; fat-sat 4.3 g+; protein 33.07 g; carbo 114.8 g; fiber 16.36 g+; calcium 494 mg; sodium 1900 mg; fat 18%; protein 18%; carbo 64%

GRATED MIXED VEGETABLE SALAD

The combination of textures and colors in this recipe makes for a bright and crunchy salad.

1 large carrot, grated
1 zucchini, grated
1 small red pepper, finely
    chopped
1 stalk celery, finely chopped
½ cup frozen corn, thawed
½ cup frozen peas, thawed
½ cucumber, thinly sliced or
    chopped
¼ cup minced fresh parsley

Serves 4
Prep: 10 minutes

ఆ§ Toss all the ingredients in a salad bowl. Keep chilled until ready to serve.

Nutritional Analysis: 1 serving
cal 56; chol 0; fat-total 0.2 g; fat-mono 0; fat-poly 0.1 g; fat-sat 0; protein 2.6 g; carbo 12 g; fiber 3.61 g; calcium 27 mg; sodium 37 mg; fat 3%; protein 17%; carbo 80%

SPICY TOMATO DRESSING

1 small clove garlic
½ tomato
1½ tablespoons olive oil
2 teaspoons apple cider vinegar
1 teaspoon soy sauce
½ teaspoon honey
¼ teaspoon celery seed   ·
⅛ teaspoon thyme

Serves 4
Prep: 5 minutes

✒ Combine the garlic and tomato in a food processor or blender. Add the remaining ingredients and blend very well. Chill until ready to serve.

Nutritional Analysis: 1 serving
cal 55; chol 0; fat-total 5.3 g; fat-mono 3.9 g; fat-poly 0.5 g; fat-sat 0.7 g; protein 0.3 g; carbo 2 g; fiber 0.14 g; calcium 6 mg; sodium 88 mg; fat 84%; protein 2%; carbo 14%

Nutritional Analysis for Dinner Meal: 1 serving
cal 794; chol 15 mg; fat-total 19.8 g; fat-mono 9.2 g+; fat-poly 4 g+; fat-sat 5.1 g+; protein 35.97 g; carbo 128.7 g; fiber 20.11 g+; calcium 527 mg; sodium 2024 mg; fat 21%; protein 17%; carbo 62%

~§ Portuguese Potato and Artichoke Pie
Spanish Rice
Fresh Green Bean Salad

With both the pie and the rice, a microwave oven can shorten the cooking time. Leftover salad from this meal has an excellent flavor from marinating overnight, and the pie and rice reheat quickly and easily.

PORTUGUESE POTATO AND ARTICHOKE PIE

In Spain and Portugal, artichokes, potatoes, and olives are inexpensive and abundant. This recipe is a wonderful combination of these ingredients.

2 teaspoons garlic powder
1 tablespoon olive oil
1 red onion, thinly sliced
5 medium potatoes, thinly sliced
2 teaspoons basil
1 can (14 ounces) artichoke
 hearts packed in water,
 drained, sliced
18 black olives, thinly sliced
Freshly ground black pepper to
 taste

Serves 6
Prep: 10 minutes
Bake: 40 minutes

¼ cup grated Parmesan cheese
1 teaspoon paprika

- ~§ Preheat oven to 400°F. Oil the bottom and sides of an 8 X 12-inch baking dish and sprinkle with garlic powder.
- ~§ Heat the olive oil in a large skillet and sauté the onion over medium heat for 3 minutes.
- ~§ Add the potatoes and basil to the sauté. Toss well and remove from the heat. Gently stir in the artichoke hearts and olives.
- ~§ Spoon the mixture into the baking dish. Cover with aluminum foil and bake for 30 minutes.
- ~§ Remove the dish from the oven, uncover, and sprinkle with cheese and paprika.
- ~§ Return the pie to the oven and bake for another 10 minutes. Let cool slightly before cutting. (This pie freezes and reheats very well. Cover before reheating to prevent drying out.)

Nutritional Analysis: 1 serving
cal 280; chol 3 mg; fat-total 6.1 g; fat-mono 3.4 g+; fat-poly 0.6 g+;
fat-sat 1.5 g+; protein 7.73 g; carbo 50.6 g; fiber 6.12 g; calcium
115 mg; sodium 181 mg; fat 19%; protein 11%; carbo 70%

SPANISH RICE

This rice dish is lightly seasoned and cooked in a tomato-based
sauce. For a spicier flavor, add additional green chilis, pepper, and
chili powder.

1 tablespoon olive oil
1 onion, chopped
1 small green pepper, chopped
¼ cup mild green chilis, chopped
1 cup long-grain brown rice
1 can (28 ounces) Italian-style
    tomatoes, with liquid, chopped
¾ cup vegetable broth
1 tablespoon Worcestershire
    sauce or soy sauce
1 teaspoon chili powder
1 teaspoon honey or fructose

Serves 6
Prep: 10 minutes
Cook: 1 hour

½ teaspoon oregano
Freshly ground black pepper to
    taste

◄§ Heat the oil in a large skillet and sauté the onion and pepper for 3
minutes. Add the green chilis and the rice. Cook for 3 more
minutes, stirring often.

◄§ Add the remaining ingredients, stir once, and bring the mixture
to a boil. Lower the heat to simmer, cover, and cook for 1 hour, or
until all the liquid has been absorbed and the rice is soft.

◄§ Remove the skillet from the heat and let it sit, covered, until
you're ready to serve. Then toss the rice gently with a fork. (You
can easily reheat leftovers in a skillet, oven, or microwave.)

Nutritional Analysis: 1 serving
cal 187; chol 0; fat-total 3.7 g; fat-mono 2.1 g; fat-poly 0.6 g; fat-sat
0.5 g; protein 4.81 g; carbo 34.8 g; fiber 3.66 g+; calcium 60 mg;
sodium 751 mg+; fat 17%; protein 10%; carbo 73%

FRESH GREEN BEAN SALAD

This marinated salad tastes best with fresh green beans, although you may use frozen beans, too. The longer the salad marinates, the more flavor it will have.

4 cups fresh green beans
2 tablespoons olive oil
2 tablespoons red wine vinegar
2 tablespoons dry white wine or
  water
1 clove garlic, minced
1 tablespoon chives
½ teaspoon honey or fructose
½ teaspoon paprika
½ teaspoon soy sauce (optional)
¼ teaspoon Dijon-style mustard
Freshly ground black pepper to
  taste

1 large tomato, chopped
½ cup cooked garbanzo beans
  (¼ cup raw)

Serves 6
Prep: 20 – 25 minutes
Chill: 1 – 2 hours or
  more

◦§ Remove the ends of the green beans and cut or snap into bite-size pieces. Steam the beans until bright green and tender, 15 to 20 minutes.

◦§ Mix the remaining ingredients, except the tomato and garbanzo beans, very well.

◦§ Combine the warm green beans, tomato, garbanzo beans, and dressing in a medium bowl. Toss gently.

◦§ Cover the salad and refrigerate until well chilled, at least 1 to 2 hours. Stir several times while cooling.

Nutritional Analysis: 1 serving
cal 147; chol 0; fat-total 5.9 g; fat-mono 3.7 g; fat-poly 1 g; fat-sat 0.8 g; protein 5.29 g; carbo 20 g; fiber 4.38 g; calcium 64 mg; sodium 10 mg; fat 34%; protein 14%; carbo 52%

Nutritional Analysis for Dinner Meal: 1 serving
cal 614; chol 3 mg; fat-total 15.7 g; fat-mono 9.2 g+; fat-poly 2.2 g+; fat-sat 2.8 g+; protein 17.84 g; carbo 105.4 g; fiber 14.16 g+; calcium 239 mg; sodium 942 mg+; fat 22%; protein 11%; carbo 67%

◅ Simple Salmon Loaf with Lemon Mustard Sauce Brussels Sprouts in White Wine Honey Dinner Rolls

Canned salmon is the base of this moist loaf, which is topped with a cool, creamy sauce. For a different flavor, serve the salmon loaf with ketchup. And if Brussels sprouts aren't a family favorite, try serving this meal with Honey-Glazed Carrots.

SIMPLE SALMON LOAF

This basic salmon loaf with a rich flavor is both easy and fast to make. You can use either pink or red salmon. The nutritional analysis is calculated using pink salmon since it's lower in fat as well as price.

1 can (15½ ounces) salmon,
   bones, skin, and liquid
   discarded
1 onion, chopped
1 stalk celery, chopped
1 cup skim milk
1 cup bread crumbs
1 egg or 2 egg whites or egg
   replacer, beaten
1 tablespoon parsley
1 teaspoon garlic powder
½ teaspoon dill weed

Serves 6
Prep: 10 minutes
Bake: 45 minutes

½ teaspoon basil
½ teaspoon freshly ground black
   pepper

◅ Preheat oven to 350°F. Lightly oil a 9 × 5-inch loaf pan.

◅ Mix all the ingredients in a large bowl and pour the mixture into the pan.

◅ Smooth out the top and sides and bake for 45 minutes.

Nutritional Analysis: 1 serving
cal 205; chol 76 mg; fat-total 6.1 g; fat-mono 1.9 g; fat-poly 2.1 g; fat-sat 1.3 g; protein 19.03 g; carbo 17 g; fiber 1.73 g+; calcium 229 mg; sodium 531 mg; fat 28%; protein 38%; carbo 34%

◆ With egg whites instead of a whole egg: chol 30 mg; fat-sat 1.1 g; fat-mono 1.5 g; fat-poly 1.9 g

LEMON MUSTARD SAUCE

The creamy, tangy flavor of this sauce is a perfect complement to the Simple Salmon Loaf.

¼ cup low-fat cottage cheese
¼ cup skim milk
2 tablespoons lemon juice
2 teaspoons Dijon-style mustard
1 clove garlic, minced
1 teaspoon honey
½ teaspoon salt (optional)
½ teaspoon dill weed
Freshly ground black pepper to
   taste

Serves 6
Prep: 5 minutes

৵৪ Combine all the ingredients in a blender or food processor and mix until smooth.

Nutritional Analysis: 1 serving
cal 20; chol 1 mg; fat-total 0.3 g; fat-mono 0.1 g; fat-poly 0; fat-sat 0.1 g; protein 1.69 g; carbo 2.5 g; fiber 0.01 g+; calcium 24 mg; sodium 65 mg; fat 12%; protein 36%; carbo 52%

BRUSSELS SPROUTS IN WHITE WINE

Brussels sprouts are cooked in white wine to form a glazed coating that enhances the flavor of this little, cabbagelike vegetable. Make sure the Brussels sprouts cook long enough — this creates a milder flavor.

2 pounds Brussels sprouts
2 cups vegetable or chicken broth
1 cup dry white wine
2 tablespoons unsalted butter or
   margarine

Serves 6
Prep: 10 minutes
Cook: 25 minutes

¼ teaspoon freshly ground black
   pepper
Salt to taste (optional)

⋐ Wash, trim off outer leaves, and cut an X into the root side of
   each Brussels sprout.
⋐ Combine all the ingredients in a large pot. Most of the Brussels
   sprouts should be in a single layer on the bottom of the pot.
⋐ Bring the ingredients to a boil, reduce heat, then simmer on
   medium for about 20 minutes. Stir to coat the sprouts with glaze
   and cook until most of the liquid has evaporated. Serve immediately.

Nutritional Analysis: 1 serving
cal 94; chol 10 mg; fat-total 4.7 g; fat-mono 1.2 g; fat-poly 0.5 g;
fat-sat 2.6 g; protein 4 g; carbo 13 g; fiber 7.2 g; calcium 57 mg;
sodium 34 mg; fat 38%; protein 15%; carbo 47%
◆ With margarine instead of butter: chol 0; fat-mono 1.8 g; fat-poly
   1.6 g; fat-sat 0.9 g

HONEY DINNER ROLLS

These little rolls are very tasty and quite light for a whole-grain
bread.*

1 cup warm water (110–115°F)   *Serves 10*
1 tablespoon active dry yeast   *Bake: 20–30 minutes*
¼ cup honey
3 cups whole-wheat flour
¼ cup nonfat dry milk powder
1 egg or 2 egg whites or egg
   replacer, beaten
2 tablespoons unsalted butter or
   margarine, melted
1 teaspoon salt

⋐ Pour the water into a large bowl and sprinkle yeast on top. Let
   proof for 10 minutes.

---

* See Chapter 7 for added tips and information on baking bread.

ᴥᔆ Slowly add the honey and 1 cup of the flour to the yeast mixture and beat well for 3 minutes (I like to use an electric mixer).

ᴥᔆ Beat in the remaining ingredients, except the flour. Turn the dough out onto a floured surface and knead in enough of the remaining flour to form a soft, unsticky dough. Knead for 10 minutes.

ᴥᔆ Place the dough in a large, lightly oiled bowl. Turn the dough in the bowl to coat with oil.

ᴥᔆ Cover the bowl and set it aside in a warm place (80 to 85°F) to rise for 1 hour or until the dough is doubled in size.

ᴥᔆ Punch down the dough, divide it into 10 pieces, and shape each into a roll. Place on a lightly oiled baking sheet, cover gently, and let rise in a warm place for 45 minutes to 1 hour, or until the rolls are about doubled in size.

ᴥᔆ Preheat oven to 375°F. Bake the rolls for 20 to 30 minutes or until lightly browned.

ᴥᔆ Remove the rolls from the baking sheet and cool on a rack.

Nutritional Analysis: 1 roll
cal 182; chol 34 mg; fat-total 3.4 g; fat-mono 1 g; fat-poly 0.5 g; fat-sat 1.7 g; protein 6.33 g; carbo 33.8 g; fiber 3.49 g; calcium 41 mg; sodium 232 mg; fat 16%; protein 13%; carbo 71%
◆ With margarine and egg whites instead of butter and a whole egg: chol 0; fat-mono 1.1 g; fat-poly 1 g; fat-sat 0.5 g

Nutritional Analysis for Dinner Meal: 1 serving
cal 501; chol 121 mg; fat-total 14.5 g; fat-mono 4.2 g; fat-poly 3.1 g; fat-sat 5.7 g; protein 31.05 g; carbo 66.3 g; fiber 12.43 g+; calcium 351 mg; sodium 862 mg; fat 25%; protein 24%; carbo 51%
◆ With margarine and egg whites instead of butter and a whole egg: chol 31 mg; fat-mono 4.5 g; fat-poly 4.6 g; fat-sat 2.7 g

✍§ Lasagna Rolls with Two Sauces
Festive Italian Salad with Creamy Lemon Mustard Vinaigrette

This is a light yet filling meal with a beautiful presentation. The lasagna can be prepared in the traditional manner, layer upon layer, although the rolls and two sauces are unique. You can add a wide variety of additional filling ingredients to the lasagna, creating your own special dish. To complete the meal, add a few slices of whole-grain bread.

LASAGNA ROLLS WITH TWO SAUCES

This very special low-fat lasagna features filling that is rolled inside the noodles instead of layered in between. And look at all the filling choices! If you prefer, make these rolls with just the spinach-ricotta filling. Although the recipe has quite a few steps, it's really very simple.

12 whole-wheat lasagna noodles

Filling
10 ounces frozen chopped
    spinach, thawed
1¼ cups part–skim milk ricotta
    cheese
1 cup part–skim milk mozzarella
    cheese, grated
4 tablespoons bread crumbs
1 teaspoon garlic powder
1 teaspoon parsley
1 teaspoon oregano
Freshly ground black pepper to
    taste

Additional Fillings (optional)
Pesto Sauce (page 322), cooked
    ground turkey breast or
    seafood, sautéed vegetables,
    spinach, or other ingredients
    you like

Serves 6
Prep: 25–30 minutes
Bake: 30 minutes

Sauces
1 tablespoon unsalted butter or
    margarine
3 tablespoons whole-grain flour
1 teaspoon basil
½ teaspoon garlic powder
½ teaspoon freshly ground black
    pepper
1½ cups evaporated skim milk
4 cups tomato sauce
Dash of oregano

⋖ⴷ Bring a large pot of water to a boil. Cook the noodles until al dente, about 10 minutes. Pour off the hot water, add cold, and let the noodles sit until ready to use.

⋖ⴷ In the meantime, combine the filling ingredients and set aside.

⋖ⴷ Prepare an additional filling of your choice. Set aside.

⋖ⴷ Melt the butter in a double boiler and stir in the flour with a fork or whisk. Add basil, garlic powder, and pepper. Slowly stir in the milk and let the sauce cook on medium heat until it's slightly thickened and ready to use.

⋖ⴷ Preheat oven to 375°F.

⋖ⴷ To assemble: Spread ½ cup of the tomato sauce on the bottom of a 9 × 13-inch baking dish. Lay the noodles out on a counter. Divide the spinach-ricotta filling among the noodles, spreading a thin layer down the center of each. Add the additional filling on top of the spinach-ricotta filling. Roll the noodles up lengthwise.

⋖ⴷ Place each roll in the baking dish, seam side down. Pour the remaining tomato sauce over rolls and spoon the white sauce over the top of each. Sprinkle with a dash of oregano.

⋖ⴷ Bake for 30 minutes. Serve each person 2 rolls. (Leftovers freeze well and reheat easily. Cover before reheating to prevent drying out.)

Nutritional Analysis: 1 serving

cal 421; chol 33 mg; fat-total 10.1 g; fat-mono 2.9 g; fat-poly 0.5 g; fat-sat 6 g; protein 24.98 g; carbo 57.6 g; fiber 3.34 g+; calcium 568 mg; sodium 1292 mg; fat 22%; protein 24%; carbo 54%

◆ With margarine instead of butter: chol 28 mg; fat-mono 3.1 g; fat-poly 1.0 g; fat-sat 5.2 g

◆ Analysis does not include an additional filling.

FESTIVE ITALIAN SALAD

This colorful salad has a festive presentation, hence the name.

1 head leaf lettuce
1 small red onion, thinly sliced
2 tomatoes, chopped
1 green pepper, chopped
1 red pepper, chopped
6 artichoke hearts packed in
    water, drained, sliced

Serves 6
Prep: 10 minutes

◆§ Wash, dry, and tear the lettuce into pieces and place in a large bowl or 6 individual bowls.

◆§ Sprinkle the next 4 ingredients on top of the lettuce in the order given. Garnish with the artichoke hearts.

Nutritional Analysis: 1 serving
cal 66; chol 0; fat-total 0.6 g; fat-mono 0; fat-poly 0.2 g+; fat-sat 0; protein 3.88 g; carbo 12.5 g; fiber 3.4 g; calcium 62 mg; sodium 41 mg; fat 7%; protein 22%; carbo 71%

CREAMY LEMON MUSTARD VINAIGRETTE

Lemon and mustard are combined with yogurt to create this light and tangy low-fat dressing.

2 tablespoons olive oil   *Serves 6*
4 tablespoons lemon juice   *Prep: 5 minutes*
1 clove garlic, minced
1 tablespoon Dijon-style mustard
3 tablespoons nonfat plain yogurt

◆§ Combine the ingredients in a blender until very smooth. Store in the refrigerator until ready to serve.

Nutritional Analysis: 1 serving
cal 52; chol 0; fat-total 4.8 g; fat-mono 3.5 g; fat-poly 0.4 g; fat-sat 0.6 g; protein 0.48 g; carbo 1.6 g; fiber 0.01 g+; calcium 18 mg; sodium 37 mg; fat 84%; protein 4%; carbo 12%

Nutritional Analysis for Dinner Meal: 1 serving (with 1 slice Whole-Wheat French Bread)
cal 634; chol 34 mg; fat-total 16.1 g; fat-mono 6.6 g+; fat-poly 1.5 g+; fat-sat 6.7 g+; protein 33.26 g; carbo 90.7 g; fiber 8.94 g+; calcium 653 mg; sodium 1144 mg; fat 23%; protein 21%; carbo 56%
◆ With margarine instead of butter: chol 28 mg; fat-mono 6.9 g+; fat-poly 2 g+; fat-sat 5.9 g

◈ American Tuna Noodle Casserole
Crunchy Tossed Salad with Tangy
Tomato Dressing
Whole-Wheat Monkey Bread

This meal happens to be one of my husband's favorites. You can cook the casserole in a microwave and serve store-bought whole-grain bread to shorten your time in the kitchen. Leftover dressing keeps well and the casserole reheats easily.

AMERICAN TUNA NOODLE CASSEROLE

This casserole uses low-fat dairy products with whole-grain noodles to create a nutritious version of an American classic.

4 cups whole-grain spinach
   noodles
1 tablespoon olive oil
½ onion, chopped
2 stalks celery, chopped
4 tablespoons whole-grain flour
1½ cups evaporated skim milk
¾ cup skim milk
1 teaspoon oregano
1 teaspoon basil
½ teaspoon garlic powder
Worcestershire sauce or soy sauce
   to taste (optional)
Freshly ground black pepper to
   taste
6 ounces part–skim milk Swiss
   cheese, grated

Serves 6
Prep: 20 minutes
Bake: 25 minutes

2 cans (6½ ounces each) tuna fish
   packed in water, drained,
   flaked
1 cup frozen peas, thawed
4 ounces pimientos, chopped
¼ cup grated Parmesan cheese

◈ Bring a large pot of water to a boil and cook the noodles until al dente, 8 to 10 minutes. Drain.

◈ Preheat oven to 375°F. Lightly oil a 1½-quart baking dish.

◈ Heat the olive oil in a saucepan and sauté the onion and celery until softened. Stir in the flour and cook for 2 minutes.

✻ Slowly pour in all the milk, oregano, basil, garlic powder, Worcestershire sauce, and pepper. Continue cooking until the sauce thickens slightly.

✻ Stir in the Swiss cheese and cook until melted.

✻ Toss the noodles, tuna, peas, and pimientos in a bowl with the sauce. Pour this mixture into the baking dish and sprinkle with Parmesan.

✻ Bake for 25 minutes. Let cool slightly before serving.

Nutritional Analysis: 1 serving
cal 430; chol 56 mg; fat-total 9.9 g; fat-mono 3.7 g+; fat-poly 0.7 g+; fat-sat 4.6 g; protein 43.03 g; carbo 40.4 g; fiber 2.71 g+; calcium 537 mg; sodium 695 mg; fat 21%; protein 41%; carbo 38%

CRUNCHY TOSSED SALAD

8 cups romaine lettuce
1 cup thinly sliced red cabbage
1 red onion, thinly sliced
2 carrots, thinly sliced
1 green pepper, sliced
6 radishes, sliced
3 scallions, sliced lengthwise

Serves 6
Prep: 10 minutes

✻ Wash, dry, and tear the lettuce into pieces and place in a large salad bowl. Add the remaining ingredients on top of the lettuce in the order listed. Keep chilled until ready to serve.

Nutritional Analysis: 1 serving
cal 41; chol 0; fat-total 0.4 g; fat-mono 0; fat-poly 0.1 g+; fat-sat 0; protein 2.28 g; carbo 7.9 g; fiber 2.89 g; calcium 49 mg; sodium 17 mg; fat 8%; protein 20%; carbo 72%

TANGY TOMATO DRESSING

This salad dressing is an adaptation of one we've had at a tiny clam bar out on Long Island. Here's my own version of this low-fat, chunky, salsa-like salad dressing.

¼ cup coarsely chopped onion
¼ green pepper, coarsely chopped
1 clove garlic
¼ cup fresh parsley
1 tomato, chopped
½ cup chili sauce
3 tablespoons tomato paste
3 tablespoons red wine vinegar
1 tablespoon ketchup
½ teaspoon freshly ground black
  pepper
Tabasco sauce to taste

Serves 6
Prep: 10 minutes

🍃 Place the onion, green pepper, garlic, and parsley in a food processor and chop finely. Add the remaining ingredients and process for a few more seconds. Don't overchop. Pour into a serving bowl and chill.

Nutritional Analysis: 1 serving
cal 43; chol 0; fat-total 0.2 g; fat-mono 0+; fat-poly 0.1 g+; fat-sat 0+; protein 1.16 g; carbo 10.4 g; fiber 1.10 g; calcium 17 mg; sodium 275 mg; fat 4%; protein 10%; carbo 86%

WHOLE-WHEAT MONKEY BREAD

This bread is very special, not because of the ingredients but for the way in which the dough is shaped and eaten. It's torn into pieces, dipped in a small amount of butter or margarine, and piled into a pan. The baked bread is never cut but is torn from the bumpy loaf. You can use any bread recipe, although this one is my favorite. There are special pans made for baking monkey bread, but any small bundt or tube pan will do.*

¼ cup honey
1 cup warm skim milk (110–
  115°F)
1 tablespoon active dry yeast
½ teaspoon salt

Serves 6
Bake: 30–40 minutes

---

* See Chapter 7 for added tips and information on baking bread.

3 cups whole-wheat flour
1 tablespoon unsalted butter or
  margarine, melted

৺ Stir the honey into the milk and pour the mixture into a large
bowl. Sprinkle the yeast on top and let proof for 10 minutes.

৺ Slowly stir in the salt and 1½ cups of the flour. Beat for 3 minutes
(I like to use an electric mixer).

৺ Knead in enough of the remaining flour to form an unsticky and
light dough. Knead for 10 minutes.

৺ Very lightly oil a large bowl and turn the dough in the bowl to
coat with oil. Cover and let rise in a warm place for 1 hour or
until the dough is doubled in size.

৺ Punch down the dough and break it into 12 pieces. Dip one side
of each piece in the melted butter and toss (literally) into the pan.

৺ Cover and let rise for 30 minutes more or until dough is about
doubled in size.

৺ Preheat the oven to 375°F. Bake for 30 to 40 minutes or until the
bread is lightly browned and sounds hollow when tapped.

৺ Remove the bread from the pan and cool slightly on a rack. Serve
steaming hot. Have each person pull a piece off the loaf.

Nutritional Analysis: 1 serving
cal 278; chol 6 mg; fat-total 2.9 g; fat-mono 0.7 g; fat-poly 0.6 g;
fat-sat 1.4 g; protein 9.83 g; carbo 56.3 g; fiber 5.81 g; calcium
78 mg; sodium 202 mg; fat 9%; protein 14%; carbo 77%
◆ With margarine instead of butter: chol 1 mg; fat-mono 1 g;
fat-poly 1.1 g; fat-sat 0.6 g

Nutritional Analysis for Dinner Meal: 1 serving
cal 792; chol 62 mg; fat-total 13.4 g; fat-mono 4.5 g+; fat-poly
1.5 g+; fat-sat 6 g+; protein 56.31 g; carbo 115.1 g; fiber 12.51 g+;
calcium 681 mg; sodium 1189 mg; fat 15%; protein 28%; carbo 57%
◆ With margarine instead of butter: chol 56 mg; fat-mono 4.8 g+;
fat-poly 2 g+; fat-sat 5.2 g+

❧ Pasta with Marinara Sauce
Spinach and Mushroom Salad with
Pignoli Dressing

Marinara sauce is extremely versatile and can be a delicious substitute in a recipe calling for tomato sauce. Complete this meal with a few slices of crusty whole-wheat bread.

PASTA WITH MARINARA SAUCE

Marinara traditionally means a sauce made with seafood. But it's the lightly sweet tomato sauce itself, minus the seafood, that has recently become known as the "marinara sauce." Here's a recipe for that special tomato sauce. You may add cooked seafood, beans, tempeh, tofu, poultry, or vegetables. This sauce is also wonderful on ravioli or tortellini and even on pizza.

1 tablespoon olive oil	*Serves 4*
1 small onion, chopped	*Prep: 15 minutes*
1 carrot, finely chopped	*Cook: 25 minutes*
4 large cloves garlic, minced	
1 can (28 ounces) tomato purée	
1 tablespoon dry red wine	
1 bay leaf	
1 teaspoon basil	
1 teaspoon thyme	Crushed red pepper to taste
12 ounces whole-grain pasta	Freshly ground black pepper to
1 teaspoon grated lemon rind	taste
2 tablespoons minced fresh	4 tablespoons grated Parmesan
parsley	cheese

❧ Heat the oil in a large skillet and sauté the onion, carrot, and garlic for 5 to 10 minutes.

❧ Add the tomato purée, wine, bay leaf, basil, and thyme. Cook, covered, on medium-low heat for 20 minutes.

❧ Cook the pasta until al dente, 8 to 10 minutes.

❧ Remove the bay leaf and add the lemon rind. Purée the mixture in a blender or food processor until smooth.

◆§ Return the sauce to the skillet and add the parsley and red and black pepper to taste. Simmer until ready to serve.

◆§ Pour the sauce over the pasta and sprinkle with the Parmesan cheese.

Nutritional Analysis: 1 serving
cal 471; chol 4 mg; fat-total 5.7 g; fat-mono 3 g+; fat-poly 0.4 g+; fat-sat 1.5 g+; protein 16.84 g; carbo 87.2 g; fiber 10.02 g+; calcium 168 mg; sodium 146 mg; fat 11%; protein 14%; carbo 75%

SPINACH AND MUSHROOM SALAD WITH PIGNOLI DRESSING

Pignoli (Italian for pine nuts, it's *piñones* in Spanish) have a mild, pleasant flavor that is the base of this dressing. These nuts are actually pine cone kernels. There are many varieties, some from the Mediterranean and others from the Rocky Mountain region of the United States. If raw pine nuts have a "piney" taste, try roasting them in the oven at 350°F for 5 to 10 minutes. Be careful not to overcook, or they will taste sharp and rancid. Although this recipe is relatively high in fat, it combines well with the low-fat entree to create a well-balanced meal.

¼ cup pine nuts
2 tablespoons olive oil
2 tablespoons white wine vinegar
¼ teaspoon grated lemon rind
¼ teaspoon tarragon
Salt to taste (optional)
Dash of nutmeg
1 pound spinach
¼ pound mushrooms, sliced

Serves 4
Prep: 15 minutes
Chill: 1 hour –
*   overnight*

◆§ Combine all but the spinach and the mushrooms in a blender or food processor until smooth. Add a little water if necessary to thin to a dressing consistency.

◆§ Chill overnight if possible, or for at least an hour.

◆§ Wash, dry, remove the stems from the spinach and tear it into pieces.

❧ Toss the spinach, mushrooms, and dressing in a large salad bowl. Serve immediately.

Nutritional Analysis: 1 serving
cal 130; chol 0; fat-total 11.5 g; fat-mono 6.8 g+; fat-poly 2.7 g+; fat-sat 1.6 g+; protein 5.15 g; carbo 6.9 g; fiber 3.81 g; calcium 112 mg; sodium 92 mg; fat 68%; protein 14%; carbo 18%

Nutritional Analysis for Dinner Meal: 1 serving
cal 602; chol 4 mg; fat-total 17.2 g; fat-mono 9.8 g+; fat-poly 3.1 g+; fat-sat 3.1 g+; protein 21.99 g; carbo 94.1 g; fiber 13.83 g+; calcium 280 mg; sodium 238 mg; fat 25%; protein 14%; carbo 61%

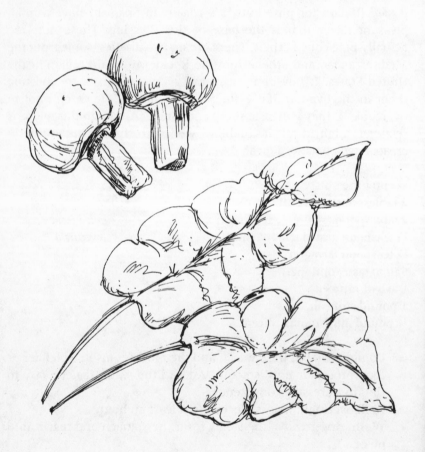

✌§ Picante Seafood Veracruz
Baked Sweet Potatoes with Nutmeg Cream
Seasonal Steamed Vegetables
Whole-Wheat and Honey Challah

You can make the Veracruz with tempeh or tofu rather than seafood for a vegetarian entree. Or replace the seafood with chicken cutlets. This menu combination is a festive arrangement of colors. Choose a bright and crisp green or other contrasting vegetable to complete the textural and visual appeal.

PICANTE SEAFOOD VERACRUZ

A mildly spicy tomato-based sauce cooks the seafood until tender. If you enjoy a more pronounced bite, add a little Tabasco to the sauce or use hot picante or salsa instead of mild. The seafood servings may seem small compared to restaurant portions, but the nutritional analysis shows that ¼ pound of seafood per person is a healthful amount.

1 tablespoon olive oil
1 small onion, chopped
½ green pepper, sliced
1 can (14 ounces) tomato purée or
  crushed tomatoes
3 tablespoons dry red wine
½ cup mild picante sauce or salsa
1 pound seafood, such as halibut,
  snapper, salmon, or swordfish
2 tablespoons minced fresh
  parsley

Serves 4
Prep: 15 minutes
Cook: 30 – 35 minutes

✌§ Heat the oil in a large skillet and sauté the onion and pepper for 5 minutes.

✌§ Stir in the tomato purée, wine, and picante sauce and simmer, covered, for 20 minutes.

✌§ Place the fish and parsley in the pan. Spoon some sauce over the fish, cover the pan, and cook for about 10 minutes per inch thickness of fish or until the fish flakes apart easily with a fork. Baste the fish several times during cooking.

◆§ Separate the fish into 4 portions and serve smothered in sauce.

Nutritional Analysis: 1 serving
cal 242; chol 47 mg; fat-total 6 g; fat-mono 3.3 g+; fat-poly 1.1 g+; fat-sat 0.7 g+; protein 31.73 g; carbo 15.3 g; fiber 5.66 g; calcium 92 mg; sodium 141 mg; fat 22%; protein 52%; carbo 26%
◆ Analysis is based on 1 pound of halibut.

BAKED SWEET POTATOES WITH NUTMEG CREAM

Sweet potatoes and yams are actually from different types of plants, although they are quite similar. True yams grow in Africa. There are two types of sweet potatoes grown in the United States. One has firm yellow flesh and is less sweet. The other has soft orange flesh and is quite sweet. We commonly refer to the second type as a yam, and I prefer it for this recipe.

4 sweet potatoes or yams	*Serves 4*
⅓ cup low-fat cottage cheese	*Prep: 5 minutes*
2 tablespoons nonfat plain yogurt	*Bake: 45 minutes – 1*
½ teaspoon nutmeg	*hour*

◆§ Preheat oven to 425°F. Wash the sweet potatoes and place them on a baking sheet. Bake for 45 minutes to 1 hour or until tender.

◆§ Combine the cottage cheese and yogurt in a blender or food processor until very creamy. Pour the mixture into a bowl and sprinkle with nutmeg. Keep chilled until ready to serve.

◆§ Cut a large X into each baked potato. Push into the potato with your thumbs and forefingers on all sides of the X to squeeze the insides up and out of the opening. Top each potato with an equal amount of Nutmeg Cream.

Nutritional Analysis: 1 serving
cal 137; chol 2 mg; fat-total 0.5 g; fat-mono 0.1 g; fat-poly 0.1 g; fat-sat 0.3 g; protein 5 g; carbo 29.3 g; fiber 2.65 g; calcium 60 mg; sodium 93 mg; fat 3%; protein 14%; carbo 83%

SEASONAL STEAMED VEGETABLES

By steaming instead of boiling, you can retain many vitamins and minerals, and much of the natural sweet flavor of fresh vegetables. All you need is a stainless steel steamer basket and a pot with a tight-fitting lid. There are many varieties of steamers available. Some large pots come with their own steamer basket inserts, a good investment. Microwave ovens offer another method of vegetable preparation.

A key to making steamed vegetables taste great is cooking them for just the right amount of time. You can serve any vegetable alone or with others for greater variety in taste and appearance. Always begin cooking the hardest vegetables first, adding each vegetable group according to length of cooking time needed. The thickness of the cut vegetable also determines the cooking time.

Always use a small amount of water on the bottom of the steamer pot, checking often to make sure the water doesn't evaporate and burn the bottom. Your basket should be raised above the water level so that you do steam, not boil, the vegetables. First bring the water to a full boil. Keep the vegetables in separate piles according to type and size. As you add the vegetables to the pot remember to time everything carefully — you don't want any of the vegetables overcooked — and be sure that the lid is on securely to hold in the steam.

Here are some general guidelines for several popular vegetables. Experiment. Because some people prefer certain vegetables cooked more or less than others, I've given no cooking times. Here is the order I suggest for putting the vegetables into the steamer. Remember that the order will vary depending on the size and shape of the cut vegetables. The fatter the cut, the longer the cooking time.

1. Root vegetables: potatoes, beets, carrots, parsnips, turnips, winter squash, yams, kohlrabi, Brussels sprouts
2. Cauliflower florets, broccoli stems, corn on the cob
3. Green beans, cabbage
4. Broccoli florets, zucchini
5. Spinach and other greens, fresh peas (You can also steam, rather than boil, frozen vegetables. Add them with this vegetable group.)

WHOLE-WHEAT AND HONEY CHALLAH

Challah is a traditional bread baked for the Jewish Sabbath meal. It is both incredibly delicious and one of the most beautiful of breads, shaped in a long braid, with a deep brown glaze, and usually sprinkled with poppy or sesame seeds. My recipe is made with whole-wheat flour and sweetened with honey. It makes a very large loaf, but you can cut the ingredients in half to make a small one. I do, however, suggest making the large loaf. Not only does my family eat this bread faster than any other I've ever baked, but leftovers are perfect for making Cinnamon Whole-Grain French Toast on the weekend.*

2 tablespoons honey
2 cups warm water (110–115°F)
2 tablespoons active dry yeast
½ teaspoon salt
7–9 cups whole-wheat flour
4 tablespoons unsalted butter or
    margarine, melted
3 eggs or 6 egg whites + 1 yolk
2 tablespoons poppy seeds or
    sesame seeds

Serves 24
Bake: 35–40 minutes

◦§ Stir the honey into the warm water and sprinkle the yeast on top. Let proof for 10 minutes.

◦§ Slowly stir in the salt and 2 to 3 cups of the flour. Beat with an electric mixer or vigorously by hand for 3 minutes. Add the butter and 2 eggs. Separate the third egg. Add the white to the batter and refrigerate the yolk for later. Beat the mixture for another 2 minutes. Stir in enough of the remaining flour to form a workable dough. Knead on a floured surface for 10 minutes, adding enough flour to form an unsticky and slightly firm dough.

◦§ Lightly oil a large bowl (this dough rises very high) and turn the dough in the bowl to coat with oil. Cover and let rise in a warm place for 1 hour or until the dough is about doubled in size. Lightly oil a baking sheet.

◦§ Punch down the dough and divide it into 4 equal pieces. Set 1 piece aside. Roll the other 3 pieces into long strands. Braid the

* See Chapter 7 for added tips and information on baking bread.

dough, pinch the ends of the strands together, and tuck them under the loaf. Place the braid on the baking sheet. Divide the remaining piece of dough into 3 more strands and braid to make a small loaf. Center this loaf on top of the large loaf. Cover and let rise in a warm spot for about 30 to 45 minutes. Preheat oven to 350°F.

৵§ Mix the remaining egg yolk with 2 tablespoons of water. Brush the raised loaf with egg wash and sprinkle with the seeds.

৵§ Bake for 40 to 45 minutes or until the crust is browned and the bread sounds hollow when tapped on the bottom.

৵§ Remove the bread from the baking sheet and cool slightly on a rack.

Nutritional Analysis: 1 serving
cal 179; chol 39 mg; fat-total 3.6 g; fat-mono 1 g; fat-poly 0.8 g; fat-sat 1.5 g; protein 6.8 g; carbo 32.1 g; fiber 4.16 g; calcium 33 mg; sodium 55 mg; fat 17%; protein 14%; carbo 69%
◆ With margarine, egg whites, and one egg yolk, instead of butter and whole eggs: chol 11 mg; fat-mono 1.1 g; fat-poly 1.2 g; fat-sat 0.6 g

Nutritional Analysis for Dinner Meal: 1 serving
cal 689; chol 88 mg; fat-total 12.2 g; fat-mono 4.4 g+; fat-poly 2.5 g+; fat-sat 2.7 g+; protein 55.53 g; carbo 102.7 g; fiber 24.88 g+; calcium 628 mg; sodium 337 mg; fat 15%; protein 30%; carbo 55%
◆ With margarine, egg whites, and one egg yolk, instead of butter and whole eggs: chol 60 mg; fat-mono 4.5 g+; fat-poly 3 g+; fat-sat 1.8 g+
◆ Analysis is based on 2 spears of broccoli and 1 cup cauliflower for Seasonal Steamed Vegetables.

৶ Pasta with Turkey Tomato Sauce
Vegetable Antipasto with Low-Fat
Blue Cheese Dressing

In this menu, I have transformed traditional recipes to fit today's nutritional recommendations — turkey replaces beef in the sauce, a variety of vegetables replace meat and cheeses in the antipasto, and the dressing is made with ingredients that retain all the flavor but not the fat.

PASTA WITH TURKEY TOMATO SAUCE

You can make this sauce with ground chicken breast, crabmeat, tempeh, tofu, or even beans in place of the turkey. The recipe makes enough for 12 servings of pasta and sauce. If you're not feeding a dozen people, make the full amount of sauce and refrigerate or freeze the leftovers. Adjust the amount of pasta to fit your needs; 1 pound feeds about 6 people.

2 tablespoons olive oil
4 cloves garlic, chopped
¼ cup chopped fresh parsley
1 pound ground turkey breast,
  skin and fat removed before
  grinding
2 cans (28 ounces each) crushed
  tomatoes or tomato purée
2 cups tomato sauce
¾ cup grated Parmesan cheese
3 tablespoons dry red wine
½ carrot
2 tablespoons basil
2 tablespoons Italian seasoning
  or oregano

Serves 12
Prep: 10 minutes
Cook: 2 hours

Lots of freshly ground black
  pepper to taste
2 pounds whole-grain pasta,
  such as shells, rotini, penne, or
  wagon wheels

৶ Heat the oil in a soup pot and sauté the garlic for 3 minutes. Stir in the parsley and ground turkey. Cook for 10 minutes or until the turkey is browned slightly.

~§ Mix in the remaining ingredients, except the pasta, cover, and simmer for 2 hours. Stir occasionally.

~§ Cook the pasta until al dente, 8 to 10 minutes. Toss with sauce and serve.

Nutritional Analysis: 1 serving
cal 408; chol 11 mg; fat-total 4.5 g; fat-mono 2.3 g; fat-poly 0.4 g; fat-sat 1.5 g; protein 17.27 g; carbo 72.9 g; fiber 6.54 g+; calcium 172 mg; sodium 952 mg; fat 10%; protein 17%; carbo 73%

VEGETABLE ANTIPASTO

Antipasto literally means "before the meal" and is served as an appetizer. It usually consists of salted fish, meats, cheeses, olives, and vegetables. My recipe naturally makes the most of the vegetables in the traditional version. Add or omit ingredients according to your tastes. Be creative.

6 small broccoli florets

3 cups cauliflower florets

2 carrots, cut into matchsticks

3 stalks celery, cut into 2-inch pieces

1 green pepper, cut into strips

1 red pepper, cut into strips

1½ cups artichoke hearts packed in water, drained, quartered

12 medium green olives

12 small black olives

6 radishes

Peperoncini (pickled Italian peppers, optional)

Sun-dried tomatoes (optional)

Dash of oregano

Serves 6
Prep: 15 minutes

~§ Arrange the vegetables decoratively on a large platter and sprinkle with the oregano.

~§ Serve with the Low-Fat Blue Cheese Dressing on the side.

Nutritional Analysis: 1 serving
cal 113: chol 0; fat-total 3.7 g; fat-mono 1.5 g+; fat-poly 0.6 g+; fat-sat 0.4 g+; protein 6.92 g; carbo 18.7 g; fiber 9.4 g; calcium 125 mg; sodium 298 mg; fat 25%; protein 20%; carbo 55%

LOW-FAT BLUE CHEESE DRESSING

Blue cheese and Roquefort are popular salad dressings that are usually made with lots of mayonnaise and sour cream, with a few little bits of cheese. I make my dressing with low-fat and nonfat dairy products as the base and lots of blue cheese to form a thick and rich lower-fat dressing. Ideal Cheese Shop in New York (see "Resources") sells an imported blue cheese that's especially tasty and has only 3 grams of fat and 8 milligrams of cholesterol per ounce, versus 12 grams of fat and 40 milligrams of cholesterol for common blue cheese. This recipe calls for regular blue cheese. If you do use the low-fat blue cheese, the fat total will decrease significantly. You may need to add a touch of sweetener and extra milk or yogurt.

⅓ cup low-fat cottage cheese
¼ cup nonfat plain yogurt
¼ cup skim milk
¼ teaspoon garlic powder
6 ounces blue cheese or
   Roquefort cheese

Serves 6
Prep: 5 – 10 minutes

◢§ Combine all ingredients, except blue cheese, in a blender or food processor until smooth.
◢§ Put 1½ ounces of the blue cheese into the blender and purée. Pour the dressing into a bowl and crumble in the remaining cheese. Stir with a fork to reach a desired consistency.
◢§ Taste to adjust flavor, adding more yogurt or milk to mellow the flavor or to thin. Chill until ready to serve.

Nutritional Analysis: 1 serving
cal 121; chol 22 mg; fat-total 8.3 g; fat-mono 2.3 g; fat-poly 0.2 g; fat-sat 5.5 g; protein 8.6 g; carbo 2.7 g; fiber 0; calcium 190 mg; sodium 460 mg; fat 62%; protein 29%; carbo 9%

Nutritional Analysis for Dinner Meal: 1 serving
cal 641; chol 33 mg; fat-total 16.5 g; fat-mono 6 g+; fat-poly 1.3 g+; fat-sat 7.4 g+; protein 32.79 g; carbo 94.3 g; fiber 15.94 g+; calcium 488 mg; sodium 1710 mg; fat 23%; protein 20%; carbo 57%

Warm Weather Dinner
Menus and Recipes

**◈ California Cutlets
Lemon Linguine Parmesan
Salad Nouveau with Creamy Watercress
Dressing**

This menu is appropriate for both fast family-style dining or elegant entertaining. Its origin is the light and flavorful California cuisine. The "Resources" section in the back of the cookbook can help if some of the ingredients are difficult to find. A loaf of crispy Whole-Wheat French Bread is always a nice addition to this meal.

CALIFORNIA CUTLETS

Raspberries, raspberry vinegar, and white wine are combined in an incredibly delicious sauce that is poured over lightly sautéed chicken breasts. For a vegetarian alternative, sauté ¼ pound tempeh or tofu per person and double the amount of sauce. This dish is fast, simple, and will please a variety of tastes.

1 tablespoon unsalted butter or
  margarine
4 chicken breast halves, skinned,
  boned, and slightly flattened
Freshly ground black pepper to
  taste
¼ cup dry white wine
2 tablespoons raspberry vinegar
1 cup fresh or frozen raspberries,
  thawed

Serves 4
Prep: 5 minutes
Cook: 25 minutes

231

◄§ Melt the butter in a large skillet and sauté the chicken until lightly browned on each side and cooked throughout.

◄§ Remove the chicken to a platter and keep warm.

◄§ Add the remaining ingredients to the skillet and cook on a high heat until the sauce thickens slightly.

◄§ Pour the sauce over warm chicken and serve immediately.

Nutritional Analysis: 1 serving

cal 170; chol 76 mg; fat-total 4.4 g; fat-mono 1 g; fat-poly 0.6 g; fat-sat 2.2 g; protein 27.50 g; carbo 4.3 g; fiber 2.27 g; calcium 23 mg; sodium 77 mg; fat 24%; protein 66%; carbo 10%

◆ With margarine instead of butter: chol 68 mg; fat-mono 1.6 g; fat-poly 1.3 g; fat-sat 1 g

LEMON LINGUINE PARMESAN

The flavor of this pasta dish is simple and delicate. Perfect served with California Cutlets.

1 tablespoon olive oil
2 cloves garlic, minced
½ cup skim milk or evaporated
  skim milk
¾ pound whole-grain linguine
½ cup lemon juice
⅓ cup grated Parmesan cheese
¼ cup minced fresh parsley
Lots of freshly ground black
  pepper

Serves 4
Prep: 5 minutes
Cook: 10 minutes

◄§ Heat the oil in a small skillet and sauté the garlic for a minute. Add the milk and heat gently.

◄§ Cook the pasta until al dente, 8 to 10 minutes. Drain and toss well with lemon juice.

◄§ Pour the garlic mixture over the pasta and toss. Add the Parmesan, parsley, and pepper and toss well again. Serve immediately.

Nutritional Analysis: 1 serving
cal 392; chol 7 mg; fat-total 6.1 g; fat-mono 3.3 g+; fat-poly 0.4 g+;
fat-sat 2.1 g+; protein 15.31 g+; carbo 65.5 g; fiber 0.15 g+;
calcium 194 mg; sodium 173 mg; fat 14%; protein 16%; carbo 70%

SALAD NOUVEAU

A true gourmet salad. Add whatever ingredients you like best.

4 cups mixed greens, such as	*Serves 4*
arugula, Belgian endive,	*Prep: 10 minutes*
leaf lettuce, and radicchio	
4 shallots, chopped	
12 spears asparagus, cooked	
4 tablespoons sliced pimientos	
Hearts of palm, sliced (optional)	
Sun-dried tomatoes, finely	
chopped (optional)	

❧ Wash and dry the greens. Divide among 4 bowls. Top with the
remaining ingredients in the order listed.

Nutritional Analysis: 1 serving
cal 36; chol 0; fat-total 0.4 g; fat-mono 0; fat-poly 0.2 g+; fat-sat 0;
protein 2.97 g; carbo 7.4 g; fiber 2.12 g+; calcium 44 mg; sodium
14 mg; fat 7%; protein 27%; carbo 66%
◆ Analysis is based on 1 cup leaf, 1 cup romaine, and 2 cups Bibb for
mixed greens.

CREAMY WATERCRESS DRESSING

¼ cup low-fat cottage cheese	*Serves 4*
¼ cup nonfat plain yogurt	*Prep: 5 minutes*
¼ cup watercress	*Chill: Several hours,*
2 teaspoons lemon juice	*if possible*
½ teaspoon parsley	
⅛ teaspoon onion powder	
Freshly ground black pepper to taste	
Salt to taste (optional)	

⋖§ Combine all the ingredients in a blender or food processor until smooth. If possible, refrigerate several hours to enhance the flavor.

Nutritional Analysis: 1 serving
cal 22; chol 1 mg; fat-total 0.3 g; fat-mono 0.1 g; fat-poly 0; fat-sat 0.2 g; protein 2.8 g; carbo 1.9 g; fiber 0.01 g+; calcium 41 mg; sodium 69 mg; fat 12%; protein 53%; carbo 35%

Nutritional Analysis for Dinner Meal: 1 serving
cal 620; chol 84 mg; fat-total 11.1 g; fat-mono 4.6 g+; fat-poly 1.1 g+; fat-sat 4.5 g+; protein 48.59 g; carbo 79 g; fiber 4.55 g+; calcium 302 mg; sodium 333 mg; fat 16%; protein 32%; carbo 52%
◆ With margarine instead of butter: chol 77 mg; fat-mono 5 g+; fat-poly 1.9 g+; fat-sat 3.2 g+

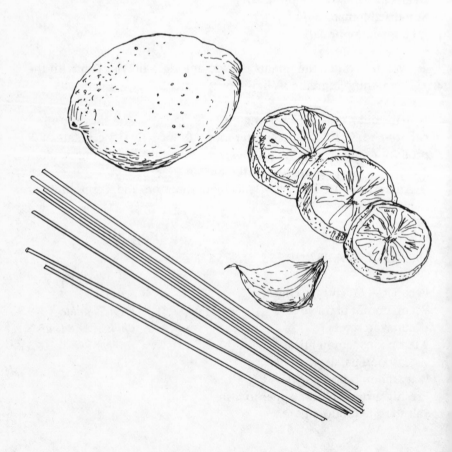

➳ Village Paella
Crisp Cos, Tomato, and Onion Salad
Spanish Country Bread

One of the key ingredients in *paella*, a Spanish rice dish, is saffron — the world's most expensive spice. It takes 75,000 crocus blossoms to make 1 pound of dried saffron. It's most often sold in small, 1-gram vials, plenty for this *paella* recipe. Be sure to buy true saffron threads — a much less costly saffron comes from Mexican saf-flowers, and it's similar but not quite so nice. Many grocery stores, gourmet shops, natural foods stores, as well as some of the compa-nies listed in the "Resources" section carry saffron.

VILLAGE PAELLA

Paella (pie-ay-a) is a combination of rice, seafood, poultry, and vegetables traditionally cooked in a special shallow iron pan with double handles. Indeed, the dish gets its name from the Latin *patella*, meaning "pan," but you can make a very successful *paella* in a large skillet. *Paella* is one of those dishes that have a few base ingredients, and the remaining additions are the chef's choice — hence, Village Paella. You may use any type of seafood or poultry. (Remember to soak shellfish, like clams or mussels, and rinse them very well to remove sand.) Create a vegetarian *paella* with tempeh, tofu, and vegetables such as asparagus and artichoke hearts. A few of the standard ingredients are short-grain rice, saffron, and green peas. In this recipe, I've used halibut, a chicken breast, shrimp, and scallops. Leftovers reheat very well.

2 tablespoons olive oil
1 onion, chopped
1 green pepper, thinly sliced
4 cloves garlic, thinly sliced
1 whole boneless chicken breast,
   skin discarded
1½ cups short-grain brown rice

Serves 6
Prep: 20 minutes
Cook: 45 minutes

(Ingredients continued on page 236)

1 cup canned Italian-style tomatoes, drained, quartered

1½ cups dry white wine

4 cups water or fish stock

1 teaspoon oregano

½ teaspoon saffron threads

½ pound halibut,* cut into bite-size pieces

½ pound scallops*

½ pound shrimp*

1 cup peas

Salt to taste (optional)

Freshly ground black pepper to taste

~§ Heat the oil in a *paella* pan or large skillet and sauté the onion, pepper, and garlic for 5 minutes. Cut the chicken into bite-size pieces, add to the skillet, and cook for 5 minutes more. Stir in the rice and cook for 3 minutes or until the rice browns slightly. Add the tomatoes, wine, water, and oregano. Bring to a boil, cover, reduce heat, and simmer for 45 minutes or until the rice is soft and all the water has been absorbed.

~§ Meanwhile soak the saffron in ¼ cup water and add to the skillet 15 minutes before the rice has finished cooking. Do not stir the rice until it's ready to be served.

~§ Add the raw seafood to the rice at least 10 minutes before the rice has finished cooking.

~§ Add the peas a few minutes before serving. Season with salt and pepper.

~§ Remove the *paella* from the heat and keep it covered until ready to serve. This dish looks beautiful when set in the center of the table and served right from the pan into individual bowls.

Nutritional Analysis: 1 serving
cal 422; chol 108 mg; fat-total 7.8 g; fat-mono 4.3 g; fat-poly 1.4 g; fat-sat 1.1 g; protein 40.06 g; carbo 46.2 g; fiber 5.02 g+; calcium 124 mg; sodium 172 mg; fat 17%; protein 39%; carbo 44%

CRISP COS, TOMATO, AND ONION SALAD

Cos, or romaine, lettuce has long, broad, upright leaves that are tender and green on the upper portions, and crisp, thick, and juicy near the base.

---

* If the fish is frozen, cook it in 4 cups of water until tender. Use this water as fish stock.

1 large head romaine lettuce
3 tomatoes, cut into small wedges
1 red onion, thinly sliced
3 tablespoons olive oil
2 tablespoons balsamic vinegar
3 tablespoons grated Parmesan
  cheese
Freshly ground black pepper to
  taste

Serves 6
Prep: 10 minutes

◆§ Wash, dry, and tear the lettuce into pieces. Place in a large salad bowl. Toss with tomatoes and onion.
◆§ Add oil and vinegar and toss the salad very well. Sprinkle on the Parmesan and pepper, toss, and serve.

Nutritional Analysis: 1 serving
cal 101; chol 2 mg; fat-total 8.1 g; fat-mono 5.3 g; fat-poly 0.7 g; fat-sat 1.5 g; protein 2.2 g; carbo 4.9 g; fiber 1.31 g; calcium 58 mg; sodium 55 mg; fat 72%; protein 9%; carbo 19%

SPANISH COUNTRY BREAD

This is a true European country bread — simple basic ingredients, crispy flour-dusted crust, and a wonderful, hearty, whole-grain flavor.*

1½ cups warm water (110 –
  115°F)
1 tablespoon warm skim milk
  (110 – 115°F)
1 tablespoon active dry yeast
3½ cups whole-wheat flour
1½ teaspoons salt

Serves 6
Bake: 30 – 40 minutes

◆§ Pour the warm water and milk into a large bowl and sprinkle the yeast on top. Let proof for 10 minutes.
◆§ Add 1½ cups of the flour and salt to the yeast mixture and beat well for 3 minutes (I like to use an electric mixer).

---

* See Chapter 7 for added tips and information on baking bread.

◆§ Slowly knead in enough of the remaining flour to form a soft, unsticky dough. Knead for 10 minutes.

◆§ Place the dough in a large, lightly oiled bowl and turn to coat with oil.

◆§ Cover the dough and set aside in a warm place to rise for 45 minutes or until the dough is doubled in size.

◆§ Punch down the dough, knead for a few minutes more, and shape into a round loaf. Very lightly oil a baking sheet and sprinkle it with flour. Set the loaf on the sheet, cover lightly, and let rise in a warm place for 15 to 30 minutes or until doubled in size.

◆§ Preheat oven to 450°F. Dust the top of the loaf with flour. Bake for 30 to 40 minutes. Remove the bread from the sheet and cool on a rack.

Nutritional Analysis: 1 serving
cal 238; chol 0; fat-total 1.2 g; fat-mono 0.2 g; fat-poly 0.6 g; fat-sat 0.2 g; protein 9.92 g; carbo 50.2 g; fiber 6.78 g; calcium 36 mg; sodium 537 mg; fat 4%; protein 16%; carbo 80%

Nutritional Analysis for Dinner Meal: 1 serving
cal 761; chol 110 mg; fat-total 17 g; fat-mono 9.9 g; fat-poly 2.7 g; fat-sat 2.8 g; protein 52.18 g; carbo 101.3 g; fiber 13.11 g+; calcium 218 mg; sodium 765 mg; fat 20%; protein 27%; carbo 53%

✑ Angel Hair Pasta with Fresh Tomato Sauce Mixed Greens Salad with Creamy Fresh Basil Dressing

ANGEL HAIR PASTA WITH FRESH TOMATO SAUCE

Angel hair pasta (also referred to as vermicelli or capellini) is a very thin spaghetti. It is a big favorite with my family. Angel hair cooks in about 3 minutes and comes in "nests" or long strands. Because the pasta's texture is so fine, it needs a light and fresh-tasting sauce like the one in this recipe, made from garden-fresh red tomatoes. You can serve this meal warm, immediately off the stove — or on a hot summer day, let the sauce come to room temperature and serve it over cooled pasta. Fresh herbs can enhance the flavor of the sauce.

2 tablespoons olive oil
6 cloves garlic, minced
8 large, ripe tomatoes, chopped
(about 7 cups)
½ cup dry white wine
1 teaspoon dried oregano or 1 tablespoon chopped fresh
1 teaspoon dried basil or 1 tablespoon chopped fresh
Lots of freshly ground black pepper to taste
Salt to taste (optional)

Serves 6
Prep: 10 minutes
Cook: 20 minutes

1 pound whole-grain angel hair pasta
¾ cup grated Parmesan cheese

✑ Heat the oil in a saucepan and sauté the garlic for 2 minutes. Add all but 1½ cups of the tomatoes to the saucepan, along with the wine and seasonings. Bring the sauce to a boil. Reduce the heat to medium and simmer for 20 minutes.

✑ Stir in the reserved tomatoes and remove from the heat. Cook the pasta until al dente, 2 to 3 minutes. Drain well and toss with half of the Parmesan cheese. Pour the sauce over the pasta and toss again.

✑ Serve pasta with the remaining Parmesan cheese sprinkled on top.

Nutritional Analysis: 1 serving
cal 399; chol 8 mg; fat-total 8.8 g; fat-mono 4.2 g; fat-poly 0.6 g; fat-sat 2.6 g; protein 14.9 g; carbo 61.6 g; fiber 1.36 g+; calcium 194 mg; sodium 201 mg; fat 21%; protein 15%; carbo 64%

MIXED GREENS SALAD

Many varieties of delicious salad greens are not yet very popular in America but are commonly eaten in Europe. The flavors and textures vary from sweet, juicy, and crunchy to pleasantly bitter and soft. Add small amounts of new varieties to your current favorites. A salad with a variety of greens not only tastes good but looks beautiful when served.

Usually 1 large head, 2 medium heads, or 9 to 12 cups yields about 6 servings.

Romaine
Leaf
Boston, Bibb, buttercrunch
Belgian endive
Curly endive (chicory)
Escarole
Radicchio
Arugula

Serves 6
Prep: 5 minutes

Nutritional Analysis: 1 serving
cal 20; chol 0; fat-total 0.2 g; fat-mono 0; fat-poly 0.1 g+; fat-sat 0; protein 2.30 g; carbo 3.8 g; fiber 2.19 g; calcium 71 mg; sodium 24 mg; fat 7%; protein 35%; carbo 58%
◆ Analysis is based on romaine and leaf lettuce.

CREAMY FRESH BASIL DRESSING

This low-fat cream dressing is deliciously scented and flavored with fresh basil. Don't try to use dried basil — the flavor is not nearly the same.

1 clove garlic, minced
½ cup nonfat plain yogurt
2–3 tablespoons chopped fresh
basil
2 tablespoons white wine
vinegar or champagne vinegar
1½ tablespoons olive oil
1½ teaspoons Dijon-style
mustard
½ teaspoon freshly ground black
pepper to taste
Salt to taste (optional)

Serves 6
Prep: 5 minutes
Chill: Several hours –
overnight

◦§ Combine all the ingredients in a blender or food processor until
very smooth and creamy.
◦§ Refrigerate in a covered jar or container for several hours, or for
the best flavor, overnight.

Nutritional Analysis: 1 serving
cal 46; chol 0; fat-total 3.6 g; fat-mono 2.6 g; fat-poly 0.3 g; fat-sat
0.5 g; protein 1.22 g; carbo 2.4 g; fiber 0.01 g; calcium 56 mg;
sodium 31 mg; fat 69%; protein 10%; carbo 21%

Nutritional Analysis for Dinner Meal: 1 serving
cal 465; chol 8; fat-total 12.7 g; fat-mono 6.9 g; fat-poly 1 g; fat-sat
3 g; protein 18.42 g; carbo 67.9 g; fiber 3.56 g+; calcium 321 mg;
sodium 256 mg; fat 25%; protein 16%; carbo 59%

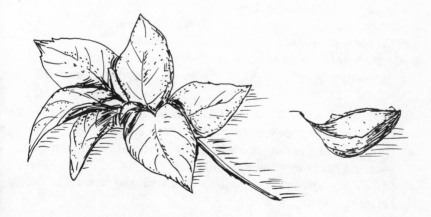

◦§ Turkey Burgers or Zucchini – Oat Bran Burgers
Spicy French Potatoes

Burgers and fries are an American favorite. Here is a low-fat, low-cholesterol version of this popular meal — turkey breast or vegetarian burgers replace beef, and oven-baked potatoes are substituted for traditional french fries.

TURKEY BURGERS

Unlike beef burgers, those made from ground turkey breast are low in fat and cholesterol. They have a mild flavor, so you can add a number of spices to create the burger that best suits your family's tastes. A food processor can chop the vegetables extra-fine in one quick step. For a great fast-meal option, make extra burgers, wrap them individually, and freeze. They thaw and cook quickly for a healthful meal in minutes.

1 pound ground turkey breast,
  skin and fat removed before
  grinding
½ onion, finely chopped
½ green pepper, finely chopped
2 cloves garlic, minced
¼ cup oat bran (optional)
Freshly ground black pepper to
  taste
Salt to taste (optional)
8 slices whole-wheat bread or 4
  whole-wheat buns

Serves 4
Prep: 10 minutes
Cook: 15 – 20 minutes

4 leaves leaf lettuce
4 slices tomato
4 tablespoons ketchup
4 teaspoons prepared mustard

◦§ Combine the first 7 ingredients in a bowl and mix very well. Form 4 patties. (For smaller burgers, form 6 patties.)

◦§ Grill or broil the patties until lightly browned, then turn them over and continue cooking until done.

◦§ Serve on whole-grain bread or a bun, with leaf lettuce, tomato, ketchup, and mustard.

Nutritional Analysis: 1 serving
cal 234; chol 17 mg; fat-total 2.5 g; fat-mono 1 g; fat-poly 0.7 g; fat-sat 0.9 g; protein 13.68 g; carbo 40.4 g; fiber 4.27 g; calcium 74 mg; sodium 832 mg; fat 9%; protein 23%; carbo 68%

ZUCCHINI–OAT BRAN BURGERS

These wonderful vegetarian burgers are so moist and flavorful that even my eleven-year-old son's friends enjoy them. You can freeze the burgers cooked or raw.

Serves 8
Prep: 15 minutes
Bake: 30 minutes

- 1 teaspoon olive oil
- ½ cup chopped onion
- 2 cups rolled oats
- 3 cups grated zucchini
- ½ cup grated part–skim milk mozzarella cheese
- ½ cup oat bran
- 1 egg or 2 egg whites
- 1½ tablespoons parsley
- ½ teaspoon garlic powder
- ⅛ teaspoon nutmeg
- Salt and pepper to taste (optional)
- 16 slices whole-wheat bread or 8 whole-wheat buns
- 8 leaves leaf lettuce
- 8 slices tomato
- 8 tablespoons ketchup
- 8 teaspoons prepared mustard

- Heat the oil in a small skillet and sauté the onion for 5 minutes. Preheat oven to 375°F. Very lightly oil a baking sheet.
- Combine all the ingredients in a bowl and mix well. Add a tiny bit of water to moisten the mixture if necessary.
- Form 8 burger patties and place them on the baking sheet. Bake 30 minutes.
- Serve on whole-grain bread or a bun with leaf lettuce, tomato, ketchup, and mustard.

Nutritional Analysis: 1 serving
cal 320; chol 38 mg; fat-total 6.7 g; fat-mono 2.1 g+; fat-poly 0.8 g+; fat-sat 1.9 g+; protein 14.57 g; carbo 51.9 g; fiber 5.13 g;

calcium 137 mg; sodium 634 mg; fat 18%; protein 18%; carbo 64%
◆ With egg whites instead of a whole egg: chol 4 mg; fat-mono
2.8 g+; fat-poly 0.7 g+; fat-sat 1.7 g+

SPICY FRENCH POTATOES

French fries were the inspiration for these potatoes. They are cut
thick, coated with olive oil and herbs, but baked — not fried.
Although they don't get very crispy, they are a real taste treat and go
well with burgers.

1 tablespoon olive oil

Serves 4

5 potatoes, cut lengthwise

Prep: 15 minutes

1 teaspoon garlic powder

Bake: 20 – 30 minutes

1 teaspoon paprika
1 teaspoon basil
Freshly ground black pepper to
taste
Salt to taste (optional)

✑ Preheat oven to 475°F.
✑ Heat the oil in a large skillet. Add the potatoes and sauté them
over medium heat, covered, for 5 to 10 minutes. Stir often with a
metal spatula, scraping the potatoes from the bottom of the pan.
(It helps to use a nonstick skillet or nonstick cooking spray.)
✑ Add the seasonings and cook for another 2 to 3 minutes, stirring
well.
✑ Spread the potatoes on a baking sheet in a single layer and bake
for 20 to 30 minutes.
✑ Line a large bowl with 3 layers of paper towels. Spoon the
potatoes into the bowl and serve warm.

Nutritional Analysis: 1 serving
cal 312; chol 0; fat-total 3.8 g; fat-mono 2.6 g; fat-poly 0.5 g; fat-sat
0.6 g; protein 6.3 g; carbo 65 g; fiber 6.15 g; calcium 36 mg; sodium
21 mg; fat 11%; protein 8%; carbo 81%

Nutritional Analysis for Dinner Meal with a Turkey Burger: 1 serving
cal 546; chol 7 mg; fat-total 6.3 g; fat-mono 3.6 g; fat-poly 1.2 g; fat-sat 1.5 g; protein 19.98 g; carbo 105.4 g; fiber 10.42 g; calcium 110 mg; sodium 852 mg; fat 10%; protein 14%; carbo 76%

Nutritional Analysis for Dinner Meal with a Zucchini–Oat Bran Burger: 1 serving
cal 632; chol 38 mg; fat-total 10.5 g; fat-mono 4.6 g+; fat-poly 1.3 g+; fat-sat 2.5 g+; protein 20.87 g; carbo 116.9 g; fiber 11.28 g; calcium 174 mg; sodium 655 mg; fat 15%; protein 13%; carbo 72%
◆ With egg whites instead of a whole egg: chol 4 mg; fat-mono 4.4 g+; fat-poly 1.2 g+; fat-sat 2.3 g+

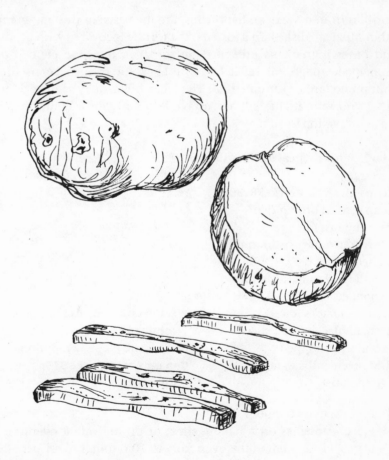

✑ *Garden Tostadas with Beans and Brown Rice*

This dish is a meal in itself. It's fresh and light but still filling. If you are unfamiliar with Mexican food, shop for a mild picante sauce or salsa. There are many varieties of picante and salsa on the market, each with its own flavor. Every member of my family has a different favorite, so I keep an assortment of salsas in the refrigerator. This is a wonderful low-fat, high-flavor addition to many recipes, and if you haven't tried it before it's worth purchasing, especially for this and other Mexican meals.

GARDEN TOSTADAS WITH BEANS AND BROWN RICE

Tortillas (round Mexican flat breads) are the basis for this and many other Mexican dishes. In a tostada, the tortilla is covered with beans, and other ingredients are piled on top. You may use canned or homemade (page 96) refried beans. Look for canned beans that contain no lard or saturated fat. The label will usually say "vegetarian," "no saturated fats," or "no cholesterol." For a lighter meal, leave off the top tortilla.

8 large whole-wheat tortillas or
  chapatis
4 cups Mexican Refried Beans
1 cup cooked brown rice
  (½ cup raw)
1 cup grated part–skim milk
  Cheddar cheese
1 small head romaine lettuce,
  chopped
2 large tomatoes, diced
12 small black olives, sliced
4 scallions, chopped
Mild green chilis to taste
  (optional)

Serves 4
Prep: 20 minutes

Picante sauce or salsa to taste
  (optional)
Guacamole (page 321, optional)
Cottage Cream (page 319,
  optional)

- ✑ Preheat oven to 400°F.
- ✑ Place 4 tortillas on a baking sheet or on individual ovenproof plates. Place them in the oven for 5 to 10 minutes to crispen. Be careful not to overcook.

◆§ Remove the tortillas from the oven and spread an equal amount of beans on each. Put the rice on top of the beans.

◆§ Press the remaining tortillas on top of the beans and rice. Sprinkle the cheese on the tortillas. Set the oven to broil.

◆§ Place the tostadas under the broiler for about a minute, or until the cheese is melted and the tortillas are crisp.

◆§ Top the tostadas with the remaining ingredients.

◆§ Serve at once with a knife and fork and pass the picante sauce or salsa.

Nutritional Analysis for Dinner Meal: 1 serving
cal 708; chol 15 mg; fat-total 16.4 g; fat-mono 3.4 g +; fat-poly 2 g +; fat-sat 3.9 g +; protein 34.74 g; carbo 113 g; fiber 5.18 g; calcium 458 mg; sodium 1758 mg; fat 20%; protein 19%; carbo 61%

∾§ *Linguine with Salmon Sauce*
Crudités with Dijon Dip
Bruschetta

The pasta dish in this meal is much less oily than the traditional version. The white wine helps to retain the moisture and flavor of the sauce. The crudités and *bruschetta* add crunch and color to the meal.

LINGUINE WITH SALMON SAUCE

This fast and simple pasta dish has a light sauce made from canned salmon and white wine. I use pink salmon because it's about half the price of red salmon and has a bit less fat. My husband really loves this meal, as does our cat (she gets the discarded salmon skin and bones).

1 can (15½ ounces) salmon with
   liquid, skin and bones removed
3 tablespoons olive oil
1 onion, chopped
7 large cloves garlic, minced
1½ cups dry white wine
2 teaspoons vegetable broth
   powder
1 teaspoon basil
1 teaspoon oregano
1 pound whole-grain linguine
½ cup chopped fresh parsley

Serves 6
Prep and Cook: 25
minutes

Lots of freshly ground black
   pepper to taste
6 tablespoons grated Parmesan
   cheese

∾§ Flake the salmon into a small bowl, saving the liquid and discarding the skin and bones. Set aside.

∾§ Heat the oil in a medium saucepan and sauté the onion and garlic for 5 minutes. Add the wine, broth powder, basil, and oregano. Bring the sauce to a boil, reduce the heat to simmer, and cook for 5 to 10 minutes.

∾§ Cook the pasta until al dente, about 8 to 10 minutes. Drain.

∾§ Add the parsley, pepper, and salmon with liquid to the sauce. Simmer for 5 minutes more.

∾§ Serve the pasta in bowls, topped with the sauce. Sprinkle each serving with a tablespoon of Parmesan cheese.

Nutritional Analysis: 1 serving
cal 472; chol 32 mg; fat-total 13.3 g; fat-mono 6.8 g+; fat-poly 2.4 g+; fat-sat 2.7 g+; protein 26.21 g; carbo 57.3 g; fiber 0.93 g+; calcium 264 mg; sodium 466 mg; fat 26%; protein 23%; carbo 51%

CRUDITÉS

Crudités is the French word for raw vegetables that are commonly served on a platter as an appetizer. Any assortment of vegetables will do. Add or subtract to the list below as you wish. You can serve any low-fat dip with the crudités. I've chosen a tangy mustard dip that complements the salmon in the pasta. You might also place a bowl of balsamic vinegar in the center of the table for dipping the vegetables.

3 broccoli florets   *Serves 6*
1½ cups cauliflower   *Prep: 15 minutes*
2 carrots, cut into sticks
1 red pepper, cut into strips
1 green pepper, cut into strips
2 stalks celery, cut into sticks

◦§ Decorate a large platter with assorted vegetables and serve in the center of the table.

Nutritional Analysis: 1 serving
cal 45; chol 0; fat-total 0.6 g; fat-mono 0; fat-poly 0.3 g; fat-sat 0.1 g; protein 3.17 g; carbo 9.3 g; fiber 4.88 g; calcium 56 mg; sodium 45 mg; fat 10%; protein 23%; carbo 67%

DIJON DIP

This quick and easy dip has a distinct mustard taste and a smooth creamy texture. Add extra yogurt if the mustard seems a bit strong, or try making one of the other dressings in this cookbook to use as a dip.

¼ cup nonfat plain yogurt   *Serves 6*
2 tablespoons Dijon-style   *Prep: 5 minutes*
   mustard
2 tablespoons chopped fresh
   chives or 1 tablespoon dried

◆§ Combine all the ingredients in a bowl and chill until ready to serve.

Nutritional Analysis: 1 serving
cal 11; chol 0; fat-total 0.2 g; fat-mono 0.2 g; fat-poly 0; fat-sat 0; protein 0.56 g; carbo 0.7 g; fiber 0.01 g; calcium 24 mg; sodium 70 mg; fat 27%; protein 31%; carbo 42%

BRUSCHETTA

This is a wonderful recipe that makes use of day-old (or several days old) bread, which is sliced and baked in the oven until crisp. The toasts are spread with a cooked garlic clove. Once the garlic is cooked, its bite mellows significantly and only the luscious flavor remains. Serve the crispy toasts in a basket with cooked garlic cloves beside it for each to spread individually. This recipe calls for a full loaf of bread, but you can cut as many slices as you like. Bake and serve 1 clove of garlic per slice of bread. (The toasts keep well in a covered container if they've been thoroughly dried in the oven.)

1 loaf whole-grain French or   *Serves 24*
   Italian bread   *Bake: 10 minutes*
24 small cloves garlic, unpeeled

◆§ Preheat oven to 400°F. Slice 1 to 2 pieces of bread per person.
◆§ Place the bread flat on a baking sheet, with the unpeeled cloves of garlic alongside them.
◆§ Bake for 10 minutes or until the bread is crisp and the garlic is soft.
◆§ Peel each garlic clove and rub on the toast or spread with a knife.

Nutritional Analysis: 1 serving
cal 106; chol 0; fat-total 0.5 g; fat-mono 0.1 g; fat-poly 0.3 g; fat-sat 0.1 g; protein 4.45 g; carbo 22.5 g; fiber 2.95 g; calcium 19 mg; sodium 269 mg; fat 4%; protein 16%; carbo 80%

Nutritional Analysis for Dinner Meal: 1 serving
cal 633; chol 33 mg; fat-total 14.6 g; fat-mono 7.1 g+; fat-poly 3 g+; fat-sat 2.9 g+; protein 34.38 g; carbo 89.8 g; fiber 8.77 g+; calcium 363 mg; sodium 850 mg; fat 21%; protein 22%; carbo 57%

⊷§ Cutlets or Filets with Fresh Tomato Relish
Fan Potatoes
Honey-Glazed Carrots
Whole-Grain Buttermilk Biscuits

This meal is elegant enough for entertaining yet basic and easy to prepare.

CUTLETS OR FILETS WITH FRESH TOMATO RELISH

Turkey breast, seafood steaks or filets, tempeh, and tofu all work as well as the chicken breasts with this fresh and bright-tasting salsa-like accompaniment. You can prepare the relish up to a day in advance and keep it refrigerated until you're ready to serve. Cold leftovers taste great with a salad.

2 tomatoes, chopped
4 scallions, diced
2 small cloves garlic, minced
2 teaspoons diced green chilis
1 tablespoon olive oil
1 tablespoon white wine vinegar
½ teaspoon lemon juice
Salt to taste (optional)
6 chicken breast halves, skinned
    and boned

Serves 6
Prep: 5 minutes

⊷§ Mix together all the ingredients, except the chicken, in a bowl. Set aside.

⊷§ Pound the chicken to flatten slightly and cook until tender. My favorite methods of preparation are grilling, broiling, and poaching.

⊷§ Spoon equal amounts of sauce over each chicken breast. Serve immediately.

Nutritional Analysis: 1 serving
cal 161; chol 68 mg; fat-total 3.8 g; fat-mono 2.1 g; fat-poly 0.6 g; fat-sat 0.7 g; protein 27.79 g; carbo 2.5 g; fiber 0.39 g; calcium 20 mg; sodium 80 mg; fat 22%; protein 71%; carbo 7%

FAN POTATOES

These potatoes are my son's favorite. I'm not sure if it's the flavor he prefers or their festive appearance.

6 baking potatoes
3 tablespoons water
2 tablespoons unsalted butter or
   margarine
1 tablespoon chives
1 teaspoon basil
¼ teaspoon tarragon
¼ teaspoon freshly ground black
   pepper or to taste
Salt to taste (optional)

Serves 6
Prep: 5–10 minutes
Bake: 1 hour

◦§ Preheat oven to 425°F. Lightly oil a baking dish big enough to hold the potatoes.

◦§ The unique quality of these potatoes is in the cut. Set a potato on a cutting board and slowly make several slices lengthwise along the top of the potato, about ¼ inch apart. Be careful to stop cutting ¼ inch from the potato bottom. As the potato cooks, the slices will spread apart and create a fan.

◦§ Heat the remaining ingredients in a small saucepan until the butter melts.

◦§ Brush the butter mixture over the potatoes and bake for 1 hour. Baste the potatoes every 15 minutes with the pan liquid.

Nutritional Analysis: 1 serving
cal 255; chol 10 mg; fat-total 3.9 g; fat-mono 1.1 g+; fat-poly 0.2 g+; fat-sat 2.5 g+; protein 5.06 g; carbo 51.2 g; fiber 4.92 g; calcium 27 mg; sodium 17 mg; fat 13%; protein 8%; carbo 79%
◆ With margarine instead of butter: chol 0; fat-mono 1.7 g+; fat-poly 1.3 g+; fat-sat 0.8 g+

HONEY-GLAZED CARROTS

Simple and slightly sweet, these carrots are sure to be loved by all.

3 tablespoons unsalted butter or
  margarine
2 tablespoons minced onion or
  shallot
6 large carrots, sliced
¾ cup vegetable or chicken broth
2 tablespoons honey
⅛ – ¼ teaspoon nutmeg
1 tablespoon chopped fresh
  parsley
Freshly ground black pepper to
  taste

Serves 6
Prep: 5 minutes
Cook: 15 minutes

⋖§ Melt the butter in a large saucepan and sauté the onion for 2 minutes.

⋖§ Stir in the carrots and broth. Bring to a boil, lower the heat to simmer, cover, and cook for 15 minutes or until just tender.

⋖§ Raise the heat to medium-high and add the remaining ingredients. Stir and cook, uncovered, until the sauce becomes syrupy.

Nutritional Analysis: 1 serving
cal 105; chol 16 mg; fat-total 5.6 g; fat-mono 1.7 g+; fat-poly 0.3 g+; fat-sat 3.6 g+; protein 1.1 g; carbo 13.4 g; fiber 2.37 g; calcium 24 mg; sodium 27 mg; fat 47%; protein 4%; carbo 49%
◆ With margarine instead of butter: chol 0; fat-mono 2.5 g+; fat-poly 1.9 g+; fat-sat 1.1 g+

WHOLE-GRAIN BUTTERMILK BISCUITS

Biscuits are usually made with white flour and lots of butter, creating a very tasty yet high-fat addition to a meal. I've worked years on developing a low-fat, whole-grain biscuit that has a light, airy texture and a traditional flavor. Here's the result, which has won rave reviews.

1¾ cups whole-wheat pastry flour	*Serves 12*
1 tablespoon baking powder	*Prep: 10 minutes*
1 teaspoon fructose or sugar	*Bake: 12–15 minutes*
¼ teaspoon baking soda	
¼ teaspoon salt	
2 tablespoons butter	
1 cup cultured nonfat buttermilk	

◆§ Sift the dry ingredients together in a large bowl.

◆§ Preheat oven to 450°F.

◆§ Cut the butter into the flour mixture to make a fine crumb. (A food processor works very well if you use a pulse — on-off, on-off — action several times.)

◆§ Very gently stir the buttermilk into the flour-butter mixture, using a fork. Stir only until mixed.

◆§ Drop 12 spoonfuls of batter onto an ungreased baking sheet and bake immediately for 12 to 15 minutes or until lightly browned on top.

◆§ Serve at once.

Nutritional Analysis: 1 serving
cal 88; chol 6 mg; fat-total 2.2 g; fat-mono 0.6 g; fat-poly 0.2 g; fat-sat 1.3 g; protein 3.42 g; carbo 14.4 g; fiber 1.69 g; calcium 105 mg; sodium 155 mg; fat 21%; protein 15%; carbo 64%
◆ With margarine instead of butter: chol 0; fat-mono 0.9 g; fat-poly 0.8 g; fat-sat 0.4 g

Nutritional Analysis for Dinner Meal: 1 serving
cal 609; chol 99 mg; fat-total 15.5 g; fat-mono 5.4 g+; fat-poly 1.3 g+; fat-sat 8 g+; protein 37.36 g; carbo 81.6 g; fiber 9.37 g+; calcium 177 mg; sodium 279 m+g; fat 23%; protein 24%; carbo 53%
◆ With margarine instead of butter: chol 68 mg; fat-mono 7.1 g; fat-poly 4.5 g; fat-sat 3.1 g

ᴥᔥ *Variety Kebabs*
Brown Rice and Barley Pilaf
European Mixed Vegetable Salad with Artichoke Vinaigrette

VARIETY KEBABS

This recipe is an adaptation of traditional shish kebab. It's called "variety" because of the options available. Instead of the typical beef, it can be made with vegetables, fish, tofu, tempeh, or chicken breasts. You'll need 6 metal skewers (wood will also work, but not as well). When choosing fish, pick one that has a firm flesh (halibut, tuna, monkfish, swordfish, shark, shrimp, scallops, cod, perch, or other fish) so that it won't flake and fall off the skewers. The kebabs are first marinated and then grilled. Try leftover kebabs in pita bread with lettuce for a great sandwich.

¼ cup olive oil
¼ cup red wine vinegar
¼ cup dry red wine
5 cloves garlic, minced
2 teaspoons basil
2 teaspoons oregano
2 teaspoons thyme
2 teaspoons savory
½ teaspoon dry mustard powder
24 ounces seafood, skinless and
   boneless chicken breast, tofu,
   or tempeh, cut into large cubes
1 red onion, cut into large chunks
1 large green pepper, cut into
   large chunks

3 tomatoes, quartered, or 12
   cherry tomatoes
18 mushrooms
3½ cups vegetable or chicken
   broth

Serves 6
Prep: 15 minutes
Marinate: 2–4 hours
Cook: 15–20 minutes

ᴥᔥ Mix the oil, vinegar, wine, and seasonings in a measuring cup. Set aside.

ᴥᔥ Combine the seafood, chicken, tofu, or tempeh in a very large, shallow bowl with the vegetables and mushrooms.

ᴥᔥ Pour the marinade over the kebab mixture, along with the broth. Toss gently. Cover and let marinate in the refrigerator for several hours. The longer the kebabs marinate, the more flavor they will have. Start a grill.

❧ Lace the kebabs tightly on 6 metal skewers, alternating colors and textures.

❧ Place the skewers on the grill (use metal holders to keep the kebabs raised above the grill and prevent sticking, if available). Brush some marinade over the kebabs and cook until the underside is lightly browned. Turn the skewers to cook the other side. Continue to brush the kebabs with marinade as you grill. If possible, cook with the grill covered.

❧ Serve on or off the skewers over a bed of Brown Rice and Barley Pilaf.

Nutritional Analysis: 1 serving
cal 180; chol 83 mg; fat-total 5.8 g; fat-mono 3.6 g; fat-poly 0.7 g; fat-sat 1 g; protein 22.56 g; carbo 8.5 g; fiber 2.28 g; calcium 47 mg+; sodium 107 mg; fat 30%; protein 51%; carbo 19%

◆ Analysis is based on only the amount of marinade absorbed by the food. The seafood used was mahimahi.

BROWN RICE AND BARLEY PILAF

Brown rice and barley are paired up in this flavorful grain dish. For a fluffy pilaf, be sure *not* to stir while cooking. Use pearl barley if hulled is unavailable.

1 tablespoon olive oil
1 small onion, chopped
3 large cloves garlic, minced
½ green pepper, chopped
½ red pepper, chopped
¼ pound mushrooms, sliced
½ cup long-grain brown rice
½ cup hulled barley
1 teaspoon thyme
1 teaspoon basil
1½ cups vegetable or chicken broth
½ cup dry white wine
¼ cup minced fresh parsley

Serves 6
Prep: 15 minutes
Cook: 45 minutes

Freshly ground black pepper to taste
Salt to taste (optional)

◆§ Heat the oil in a large skillet and sauté the onion, garlic, and green and red peppers for 5 minutes.

◆§ Add the mushrooms and cook for 3 minutes more. Stir in the brown rice, barley, thyme, and basil. Cook until the grains brown slightly.

◆§ Pour the broth and wine into the skillet. Bring to a boil, reduce the heat to simmer, and cover. Cook for 45 minutes or until the rice and barley have absorbed all the water. Gently toss in the parsley, black pepper, and salt with a fork. Cover and let sit off the heat until ready to serve.

Nutritional Analysis: 1 serving
cal 156; chol 0; fat-total 2.9 g+; fat-mono 1.9 g+; fat-poly 0.4 g+; fat-sat 0.4 g+; protein 3 g; carbo 29.3 g; fiber 3.94 g; calcium 32 mg; sodium 5 mg; fat 17%; protein 9%; carbo 74%
◆ Analysis is based on pearl barley.

EUROPEAN MIXED VEGETABLE SALAD

This decorative salad is made in individual bowls. Choose the vegetable combination that best suits your meal plan and tastes.

Lettuce	*Serves 6*
Corn, fresh or frozen	*Prep: 10–15 minutes*
Carrot, grated	
Beets, grated, or unsalted, unsweetened canned	
Zucchini, grated	
Green or red pepper, chopped	
Cherry tomatoes	
Cucumber, sliced	
Green beans, fresh or frozen	
Peas, fresh or frozen	Marinated salads (see index)
Artichoke hearts packed in water, drained, sliced	Olives
	Pimientos

◆§ Thaw any frozen vegetables.

◆§ Wash, dry, and tear lettuce into pieces. Place on the bottom of each bowl.

🍃 Add 3 or 4 vegetables of your choice, each in its own pile on top
of the lettuce. Garnish with a few olives, pimientos, or other
vegetable in the center.

Nutritional Analysis: 1 serving
cal 93; chol 0; fat-total 0.4 g; fat-mono 0; fat-poly 0.3 g+; fat-sat 0;
protein 5.58 g; carbo 20.1 g; fiber 7.13 g; calcium 90 mg; sodium
51 mg; fat 3%; protein 21%; carbo 76%
◆ Analysis is based on 12 cups leaf lettuce, 1½ cups corn, 1 carrot, 1
red pepper, and 1½ cups peas.

ARTICHOKE VINAIGRETTE

A unique, fresh-flavored dressing that uses white wine, artichoke
hearts, and olive oil as a base.

5 artichoke hearts packed in   *Serves 6*
  water, drained   *Prep: 5 minutes*
½ cup dry white wine, water, or
  vegetable broth
2 tablespoons olive oil
1 tablespoon white wine or
  champagne vinegar
1 clove garlic, minced
1 teaspoon oregano
¼ teaspoon coriander
Freshly ground black pepper to
  taste
Salt to taste (optional)

🍃 Combine all the ingredients in a blender until smooth. Taste to
adjust seasoning. Keep chilled until you're ready to serve.

Nutritional Analysis: 1 serving
cal 68; chol 0; fat-total 4.8 g; fat-mono 3.4 g+; fat-poly 0.4 g+;
fat-sat 0.6 g+; protein 0.66 g; carbo 3 g; fiber 0.18 g; calcium 12 mg;
sodium 12 mg; fat 62%; protein 4%; carbo 34%

Nutritional Analysis for Dinner Meal: 1 serving
cal 497; chol 83 mg; fat-total 13.9 g; fat-mono 9 g+; fat-poly 1.9 g+;
fat-sat 2.1 g+; protein 32.16 g; carbo 60.9 g; fiber 13.52 g; calcium
181 mg+; sodium 175 mg; fat 25%; protein 25%; carbo 50%

✍ Pasta with Sweet Pea and Pimiento Sauce
Saladier with Vinaigrette Fines Herbes

PASTA WITH SWEET PEA AND PIMIENTO SAUCE

Green peas create a light yet lively low-fat sauce for ziti or penne (tubular pasta). This uncooked sauce is fast and easy to make.

3 tablespoons unsalted butter or margarine
4 shallots or ¼ onion, chopped
6 cloves garlic, minced
3 cups fresh or frozen peas, cooked
¼ cup fresh parsley, lightly packed
1 teaspoon dried basil or 1 tablespoon fresh
1 teaspoon tarragon
1 teaspoon chives
¾ cup low-fat cottage cheese
Lots of freshly ground black pepper to taste

Serves 6
Prep: 15 minutes
Cook: 10 minutes

Tabasco sauce to taste
Salt to taste (optional)
1 pound whole-grain ziti or penne
4 tablespoons diced pimientos

✍ Heat the butter in a small skillet and sauté the shallots and garlic until soft but not browned.

✍ Combine the sauté and all the ingredients, except 1 cup of the peas, the pasta, and the pimientos, in a food processor or blender. Purée until very smooth and creamy.

✍ Cook the pasta until al dente, 8 to 10 minutes. Drain the pasta and put it in a large serving bowl. Add the remaining peas and toss the pasta with the sauce. Gently fold in the pimientos.

✍ Serve immediately.

Nutritional Analysis: 1 serving
cal 423; chol 18 mg; fat-total 6.3 g; fat-mono 1.8 g+; fat-poly 0.3 g+; fat-sat 4 g+; protein 17.9 g; carbo 69.9 g; fiber 4.73 g+; calcium 90 mg; sodium 193 mg; fat 14%; protein 18%; carbo 68%

◆ With margarine instead of butter: chol 2 mg; fat-mono 2.7 g+;
fat-poly 1.9 g+; fat-sat 1.5 g+

SALADIER WITH VINAIGRETTE FINES HERBES

Fines herbes — a combination of tarragon, chives, parsley, and
chervil — are mixed into a creamy vinaigrette that's tossed with the
salad before serving.

2 tablespoons olive oil

1–2 tablespoons white wine
vinegar

1 shallot, minced

1 clove garlic, minced

1 teaspoon Dijon-style mustard

2 teaspoons fines herbes (½
teaspoon each dried tarragon,
chives, parsley, and chervil) or
4 teaspoons fines herbes (1
teaspoon each fresh)

Freshly ground black pepper to
taste

Salt to taste (optional)

4 tablespoons nonfat plain yogurt

1 head romaine lettuce

1 small red onion, thinly sliced

1 red pepper, sliced

6 artichoke hearts packed in
water, drained, quartered

18 small black olives

2 tablespoons pine nuts

Serves 6

Prep: 15 minutes

◆§ Combine the first 8 ingredients in a large salad bowl. Stir in the
yogurt until blended well.

◆§ Wash, dry, and tear the lettuce into pieces. Toss the lettuce in the
dressing until well coated.

◆§ Add the remaining ingredients in the order listed, tossing with
each addition.

◆§ Serve immediately.

Nutritional Analysis: 1 serving
cal 110; chol 0; fat-total 8.3 g; fat-mono 5.3 g+; fat-poly 1.3 g+;
fat-sat 1.2 g+; protein 2.6 g; carbo 7.2 g; fiber 1.96 g; calcium 58 mg;
sodium 106 mg; fat 66%; protein 9%; carbo 25%

Nutritional Analysis for Dinner Meal: 1 serving
cal 532; chol 18 mg; fat-total 14.6 g; fat-mono 7.1 g+; fat-poly
1.6 g+; fat-sat 5.1 g+; protein 20.50 g; carbo 77 g; fiber 6.68 g+;
calcium 148 mg; sodium 299 mg; fat 25%; protein 16%; carbo 59%
◆ With margarine instead of butter: chol 3 mg; fat-mono 8 g+;
  fat-poly 3.2 g+; fat-sat 2.7 g+

ᴇᔓ Grilled Cutlets with Country
Mustard Marinade
Grilled Vegetables
Baked Potatoes with Cucumber Dill
Sauce

For many of us, grilling conjures up wonderful images of summer, including outdoor eating on warm evenings. But summertime and cooking outdoors are not absolutely necessary for this meal with some of the new kitchen tools for grilling indoors.

GRILLED CUTLETS WITH
COUNTRY MUSTARD MARINADE

Coarsely ground mustard creates a thick coating on the cutlets which grills beautifully. This recipe uses chicken — although you can substitute tempeh and tofu, which are also well suited for this marinade, as vegetarian alternatives.

¼ cup coarsely ground mustard
½ cup white wine or champagne
   vinegar
2 tablespoons finely chopped
   onion
2 cloves garlic, minced
¼ teaspoon crushed rosemary
4 chicken breast halves, skinned
   and boned

Serves 4
Prep: 5 minutes
Marinate: 1 hour or
   more
Cook: 10 – 20 minutes

ᴇᔓ Mix together all the ingredients, except the chicken, in a shallow bowl.

ᴇᔓ Add the chicken and coat it with the marinade. Refrigerate for at least 1 hour.

ᴇᔓ Grill chicken until tender, basting with marinade as it cooks.

Nutritional Analysis: 1 serving
cal 148; chol 68; fat-total 2.4 g; fat-mono 0.4 g+; fat-poly 0.4 g+; fat-sat 0.4 g+; protein 28.31 g; carbo 3.8 g; fiber 0.18 g+; calcium 37 mg; sodium 272 mg; fat 14%; protein 76%; carbo 10%

GRILLED VEGETABLES

You can grill just about any vegetable. For a delightfully different flavor, add wood chips to the coals. If your grill has a cover, use it. Here is a recipe for some of my favorite grilled vegetables. Cooking time varies according to the size, type, and cut of the vegetable. Adjust the times below if necessary.

4 thin carrots
4 broccoli florets
4 ears corn, in the husk, soaked
   in water for 15 minutes
2 tablespoons olive oil
2 onions, cut in half, tip to root
2 green or red peppers, cut in
   half, seeds removed

Serves 4
Prep: 10 minutes
Grill: 20 minutes

- Some vegetables need to be precooked a bit before grilling. Steam carrots for 10 minutes and broccoli for 5.
- Carefully peel back the corn husks and remove the silk. Lightly brush the corn with oil, replace the husks, and tie them closed at the tip. Then brush all the other vegetables with oil.
- Place the onion, cut side down, on the grill and cook for 20 minutes.
- Place the corn and partially cooked carrots on a hot part of the grill and cook for 12 minutes on each side.
- Add the broccoli and cook for 5 minutes on each side. Four minutes before other vegetables are cooked, add the pepper halves, flesh side down, and cook for 3 minutes. Turn the peppers onto the skin side and cook for 1 minute more.
- Time the vegetables so they are finished cooking at the same time and place them on a large serving platter.

Nutritional Analysis: 1 serving
cal 258; chol 0; fat-total 9.3 g; fat-mono 5.5 g; fat-poly 1.7 g; fat-sat 1.3 g; protein 9.5 g; carbo 42.5 g; fiber 13.74 g; calcium 124 mg; sodium 89 mg; fat 29%; protein 13%; carbo 58%

BAKED POTATOES WITH CUCUMBER DILL SAUCE

There are many methods for preparing baked potatoes. Here's my favorite, topped with a creamy low-fat sauce flavored with dill.

4 large baking potatoes
½ small onion
2 large cucumbers, peeled
1 cup nonfat plain yogurt
½ cup part–skim milk ricotta
  cheese
2 teaspoons dill weed

Serves 4
Prep: 10 minutes
Cook: 45 minutes – 1
hour

- ⌁ Preheat oven to 450°F. Wash the potatoes and poke several holes in them with a fork. Place the potatoes directly on the oven rack and bake for 45 minutes or until tender. Or place them on a grill and bake for at least an hour or until tender, turning often.
- ⌁ Chop the onion very fine in a food processor or blender. Add 1 cucumber, yogurt, ricotta, and dill. Blend until smooth.
- ⌁ Finely chop the remaining cucumber. Stir it into the sauce. Cover and refrigerate until chilled and ready to serve.
- ⌁ Cut a large X into each potato. With both thumbs and forefingers, push up on all 4 sides to squeeze the pulp out the opening, making it ready for the topping.

Nutritional Analysis: 1 serving
cal 321; chol 11 mg; fat-total 2.9 g; fat-mono 0.7 g; fat-poly 0.3 g; fat-sat 1.7 g; protein 12.79 g; carbo 62.3 g; fiber 6.13 g+; calcium 250 mg; sodium 102 mg; fat 8%; protein 16%; carbo 76%

Nutritional Analysis for Dinner Meal: 1 serving
cal 726; chol 79 mg; fat-total 14.6 g; fat-mono 6.5 g+; fat-poly 2.3 g+; fat-sat 3.4 g+; protein 50.6 g; carbo 108.6 g; fiber 20.04 g+; calcium 410 mg; sodium 462 mg; fat 17%; protein 26%; carbo 57%

✑ Chilled Tomato Cucumber Soup
White Bean and Red Onion Salad
Oatmeal Soda Bread

This meal is perfect for a hot summer's eve. Only the bread — which is quick to prepare — requires any baking. You can make the soup and salad ahead of time and chill them until you're ready to serve.

CHILLED TOMATO CUCUMBER SOUP

This creamy tomato soup is filled with chunks of vegetables and served chilled.

½ cup low-fat cottage cheese
4 cups unsalted tomato juice
½ cup nonfat plain yogurt
2 cucumbers, chopped
1 green pepper, finely chopped
1 red pepper, finely chopped
3 scallions, chopped
1 large clove garlic, minced
2 tomatoes, chopped
¼ cup minced fresh parsley
1 teaspoon honey
½ teaspoon dill weed
½ teaspoon basil
Freshly ground black pepper to taste

Serves 4
Prep: 15 minutes
Chill: 1 hour or more

Cayenne pepper or Tabasco sauce to taste
Homemade Croutons (page 326)
4 slices lemon (optional)

✑ Cream the cottage cheese until smooth in a blender or food processor.

✑ Combine all the ingredients, except the croutons and lemon slices, in a large bowl and mix very well. Refrigerate for 1 hour or more until well chilled.

✑ Serve in bowls and garnish with Homemade Croutons and a thin slice of lemon.

Nutritional Analysis: 1 serving
cal 138; chol 3 mg; fat-total 1 g; fat-mono 0.2 g+; fat-poly 0.4 g+; fat-sat 0.4 g+; protein 9.62 g; carbo 24.6 g; fiber 3.29 g+; calcium 148 mg; sodium 172 mg; fat 6%; protein 26%; carbo 68%

WHITE BEAN AND RED ONION SALAD

This popular combination of beans and onion is truly enhanced by the addition of fresh herbs — although dried may be substituted if necessary. As with most marinated dishes, the longer the salad marinates the more enhanced the flavor.

1 red onion, thinly sliced or
  finely chopped
3 tablespoons olive oil
1½ tablespoons lemon juice or
  white wine vinegar
1 tablespoon minced fresh
  parsley or 1 teaspoon dried
1 tablespoon minced fresh chives
  or 1 teaspoon dried
1 tablespoon minced fresh
  tarragon or 1 teaspoon dried
1 tablespoon minced fresh basil
  or 1 teaspoon dried
1 teaspoon dry mustard powder
1 teaspoon fructose or honey

Serves 4
Prep: 10 minutes
Chill: 2 hours or more

Lots of freshly ground black
  pepper to taste
Salt to taste (optional)
3 cups cooked navy, pea, or great
  northern beans (1¼ cups raw)
Pimientos for garnish (optional)

◆§ Combine all the ingredients, except the beans and pimientos in a medium bowl and mix well.
◆§ Add the beans to the bowl and toss very gently to coat well.
◆§ Cover the salad and refrigerate several hours or until well chilled. Garnish with pimientos.

Nutritional Analysis: 1 serving
cal 272; chol 0; fat-total 11.3 g; fat-mono 7.8 g+; fat-poly 1.4 g+; fat-sat 1.5 g+; protein 10.93 g; carbo 33.1 g; fiber 5.46 g+; calcium 90 mg; sodium 11 mg; fat 37%; protein 16%; carbo 47%

OATMEAL SODA BREAD

This is a quick and easy bread to make. As the name suggests, it's made with baking soda as a leavening agent. This recipe calls for whole-wheat pastry flour, but you can use any whole-grain flour. It has a very decorative crust, covered with rolled oats.

3 cups whole-wheat pastry flour

1 teaspoon baking soda

1 teaspoon baking powder

½ teaspoon salt

½ cup rolled oats

1½ cups cultured nonfat
   buttermilk

1 tablespoon unsalted butter or
   margarine, melted

Serves 6

Prep: 15 minutes

Bake: 30–40 minutes

◆§ Preheat oven to 375°F. Very lightly oil a baking sheet.

◆§ Combine the flour, baking soda, baking powder, salt, and ¼ cup
   of the oats in a large bowl. Mix well.

◆§ Make a well in the center of the flour mixture, pour in the
   buttermilk, and stir to combine.

◆§ Spread the remaining oats onto a counter. Turn the dough out
   onto the oats and knead a few times to create a smooth, round
   dough that's covered with a thick layer of oats.

◆§ Place the dough on the baking sheet and cut a big X, about
   ½-inch deep, across the top.

◆§ Bake for 30 to 40 minutes or until the bread sounds hollow when
   tapped on the bottom.

◆§ Remove the loaf from the baking sheet and place it on a cooling
   rack. Brush the top of the loaf with the melted butter and let cool
   slightly before slicing.

Nutritional Analysis: 1 serving

cal 265; chol 6 mg; fat-total 3.4 g; fat-mono 0.7 g+; fat-poly 0.6 g+;
fat-sat 1.4 g+; protein 11.08 g; carbo 50.2 g; fiber 6.19 g; calcium
145 mg; sodium 403 mg; fat 11%; protein 16%; carbo 73%

◆ With margarine instead of butter: chol 1 mg; fat-mono 1 g+;
   fat-poly 1.1 g+; fat-sat 0.6 g+

Nutritional Analysis for Dinner Meal: 1 serving

cal 674; chol 9 mg; fat-total 15.7 g; fat-mono 8.7 g+; fat-poly
2.4 g+; fat-sat 3.4 g+; protein 31.63 g; carbo 107.9 g; fiber
14.94 g+; calcium 377 mg; sodium 586 mg; fat 20%; protein 18%;
carbo 62%

◆ With margarine instead of butter: chol 4 mg; fat-mono 9 g+;
   fat-poly 2.9 g+; fat-sat 2.6 g+

⌖ Pasta Pizza
Stuffed Artichokes

This pizza recipe is really a pasta dish baked in a casserole with pizza toppings. It's a quick and easy recipe. The Stuffed Artichokes require a bit of time to prepare and cook. For a faster meal, try making Pasta Pizza with one of the salads in this cookbook.

PASTA PIZZA

You may vary the topping ingredients to create many different types of Pasta Pizza. In this recipe, I've included traditional pizza vegetables, although the addition of cooked poultry, seafood, and unique vegetables can create the gourmet pizza of your choice.

1 pound whole-grain spinach
  fettuccine
4 cups tomato sauce
2 cups grated part–skim milk
  mozzarella cheese
1 small onion, chopped
1 green pepper, chopped
½ pound mushrooms, thinly
  sliced
18 black or green olives, sliced
6 tablespoons grated Parmesan
  cheese
1 teaspoon oregano

Serves 8
Prep: 15 minutes
Bake: 20 minutes

⌖ Cook the pasta until al dente, 8 to 10 minutes, and drain. Preheat oven to 400°F.

⌖ Pour 1 cup of the tomato sauce onto the bottom of a 9 × 13-inch baking dish.

⌖ Spread the pasta in the baking dish over the tomato sauce. Pour the remaining sauce over the pasta, sprinkle with mozzarella cheese and then the onion, pepper, mushrooms, and olives. Top the pizza with the Parmesan cheese and oregano.

⌖ Bake for 20 minutes or until the cheese is melted and the sauce is bubbling.

⌖ Cut the pizza into squares and serve hot.

Nutritional Analysis: 1 serving

cal 365; chol 18 mg; fat-total 8.3 g; fat-mono 2.7 g; fat-poly 0.4 g; fat-sat 4.1 g; protein 18.75 g; carbo 53.3 g; fiber 3.6 g+; calcium 313 mg; sodium 1014 mg; fat 21%; protein 21%; carbo 58%

STUFFED ARTICHOKES

Stuffed vegetables look so beautiful when served. This recipe is no exception. The artichoke is first cooked and then stuffed and baked. Not only is the flowery appearance of the artichoke appealing, but eating it is fun. It's the ultimate in finger foods. The trick to eating the artichoke leaves is in using your teeth to scrape the tender edible portion and then discarding the remainder. Take each leaf and hold the outer tip in your fingers. The slight curl in the leaf should face down. Place the inner part (which was attached to the heart) of the leaf between your top and bottom teeth. Bite down gently and scrape the tender portion from the soft end of the leaf with your teeth. Continue munching the outer leaves and the stuffing until you reach the light-colored young leaves in the center. Pull out these leaves in one movement, scrape the remaining fuzzy center, and discard it. Use a fork and knife to cut and eat the final treasure — the heart and bottom. You can easily cut this recipe in half or a third.

6 globe artichokes
3 cloves garlic, cut in half
9 cups vegetable or chicken broth
2–3 cups dry white wine
4 cups whole-grain bread crumbs
1 cup grated Parmesan cheese
½ cup minced fresh parsley
1½ tablespoons oregano
1½ tablespoons basil
1 teaspoon garlic powder
1 teaspoon freshly ground black
  pepper
2 tablespoons paprika

Serves 6
Prep: 20 minutes
Cook: 20–25 minutes
Bake: 20–30 minutes

◦§ Cut the bottom stem off the artichokes. Use a kitchen scissors or a sharp knife to trim about ¼ to ½ inch off the top. Then trim the spiked tip off each leaf.

↩ Bring the garlic, broth, and wine to a boil in a pot large enough to fit all the artichokes. Place the artichokes in the pot and cook in the boiling liquid for 20 to 25 minutes.

↩ Mix together the remaining ingredients, except the paprika. Preheat oven to 425°F.

↩ Remove the cooked artichokes from the broth. Pour the broth into a deep baking pan large enough to hold all the artichokes. Stuff each with an equal amount of filling, spreading out the leaves to do so. Place the artichokes upright in the baking pan. Pour some of the cooking liquid over each artichoke and sprinkle the tops with paprika. Bake for 20 to 30 minutes. Serve the artichokes with a small amount of broth in individual bowls.

Nutritional Analysis: 1 serving
cal 409; chol 17 mg; fat-total 8.8 g; fat-mono 2.5 g+; fat-poly 1.2 g+; fat-sat 4.2 g+; protein 19.03 g; carbo 65.1 g; fiber 8.02 g; calcium 413 mg; sodium 884 mg; fat 19%; protein 18%; carbo 63%

Nutritional Analysis for Dinner Meal: 1 serving
cal 774; chol 35 mg; fat-total 17.1 g; fat-mono 5.3 g+; fat-poly 1.6 g+; fat-sat 8.3 g+; protein 37.78 g; carbo 118.4 g; fiber 11.62 g+; calcium 726 mg; sodium 1897 mg; fat 20%; protein 19%; carbo 61%

✌§ Seafood Filets or Steaks with Red Pepper Coulis
Specialty Green Beans
Mashed Potatoes with a Difference

This meal can be made with any type of seafood. And tempeh and tofu are good vegetarian substitutes. Chicken breasts also taste great with the purée of sweet red peppers. This is an excellent meal for company or family dining, and I've found it to be especially pleasing to children.

SEAFOOD FILETS OR STEAKS

There are many ways to cook seafood. The following methods don't require any added fat or seasoning. Lemon juice, dry white wine, and herbs enhance flavor without raising the fat content of the dish. Seafood can also be marinated (see specific salad and dressing recipes for ideas) before cooking. Depending on the size of the cut and the type of fish, cooking times for seafood vary greatly. A general rule for estimating time is 10 minutes per 1-inch thickness. When done, the fish should flake apart easily at the thickest point when split with a fork. Estimate ¼ pound of seafood per person. This amount is less than typical restaurant portions, but any more than 4 ounces of seafood per meal is quite a lot of protein. Make the appropriate adjustments to meet your own personal and family preferences.

Broil
✌§ Place the fish on a very lightly oiled broiler pan. Broil 4 to 6 inches from the heat.

Bake
✌§ Baked fish is usually made in a baking dish with some type of sauce. Bake at 350°F until the fish flakes easily when pierced with a fork. Wine- and broth-based sauces are best.

Poach
✌§ With this method, seafood is cooked in a pan on top of the range. Water, dry white wine, and tomato or other sauces may be used as the poaching liquid.

Steam
✌§ Many oriental dishes are made with steamed fish. Just place the

fish in a steamer basket and cook, covered, until the fish flakes easily when pierced with a fork.

Grill

⋙ Place the fish directly on a lightly oiled grill (skin side down if there is one). Cook, covered if possible, until the fish flakes easily when pierced with a fork. Grilled fish tastes best when wood chips are used in addition to the coals.

RED PEPPER COULIS

Sweet red bell peppers have such a nice flavor — one of my favorites. Here they are cooked and puréed into a smooth, mildly sweet sauce. It's delicious with thick pieces of fish, such as tuna, halibut, mahimahi, and swordfish, as well as chicken breasts, tempeh, or grilled tofu.

2 tablespoons olive oil
3 red peppers, chopped
6 cloves garlic, chopped
1 tablespoon balsamic vinegar
1 teaspoon fructose or sugar
Freshly ground black pepper to
    taste
Red pepper flakes to taste
8 leaves fresh basil
2 teaspoons chopped sun-dried
    tomatoes (optional)

Serves 6
Prep: 5 minutes
Cook: 40 minutes

Salt to taste (optional)
4 tablespoons nonfat plain yogurt

⋙ Heat the oil in a saucepan and sauté the red peppers and garlic for 15 minutes.

⋙ Stir in the vinegar and fructose and season with black pepper and red pepper flakes. Cook for 15 minutes more.

⋙ Add the basil, tomatoes, and salt. Cook for another 10 minutes.

⋙ Pour the entire sauce into a food processor or blender and purée until smooth.

⋙ Return the purée to the saucepan and whisk or stir in yogurt. Keep warm on the lowest heat possible until ready to serve.

⋙ Pour equal amounts of the sauce on each plate and serve the fish on top.

Nutritional Analysis: 1 serving
cal 208; chol 47 mg; fat-total 7 g; fat-mono 4.1 g; fat-poly 1.2 g; fat-sat 0.8 g; protein 30.53 g; carbo 5 g; fiber 0.94 g+; calcium 96 mg; sodium 87 mg; fat 31%; protein 59%; carbo 10%
◆ Analysis is based on 4 ounces of halibut per person.

SPECIALTY GREEN BEANS

The inspiration for this recipe is a dish served at one of my favorite restaurants specializing in grilled foods.

1½ pounds green beans
1 tablespoon olive oil
6 cloves garlic, thinly sliced
2 tablespoons soy sauce
Freshly ground black pepper to
    taste
Red pepper flakes to taste
1 teaspoon fructose

Serves 6
Prep: 10 minutes
Cook: 20 minutes

☙ Steam the beans until bright green and partially cooked, about 5 to 10 minutes. Drain well.
☙ Heat the oil in a skillet and sauté the garlic for 3 minutes.
☙ Stir in the beans and the remaining ingredients and toss until the beans are well coated. Cook, covered, for about 10 minutes or until the beans are tender. Stir often.

Nutritional Analysis: 1 serving
cal 77; chol 0; fat-total 2.6 g; fat-mono 1.7 g; fat-poly 0.4 g; fat-sat 0.4 g; protein 2.87 g; carbo 12.5 g; fiber 4.22 g; calcium 66 mg; sodium 348 mg; fat 28%; protein 13%; carbo 59%

MASHED POTATOES WITH A DIFFERENCE

My husband has fond childhood memories of mashed potatoes and finds the simplicity in itself flavorful. There are so many varieties, and each family has its favorite. Some are made with egg yolks, some with sour cream, mayonnaise, or just lots of butter. Potatoes can be beaten until smooth or left chunky, with or without the skins removed. Here's our family favorite, which is light in texture and much lower in fat than most recipes. Whether to serve them with or without the skins, mashed until smooth or chunky, I leave to your discretion. For a mild flavor twist, use half sweet potatoes and half regular potatoes or peel, cook, and mash a clove of garlic with the potatoes.

8 large baking potatoes
2 tablespoons unsalted butter or
   margarine
¼ cup nonfat plain yogurt
¼ cup evaporated skim milk
Lots of freshly ground black
   pepper to taste
Salt to taste (optional)

Serves 6
Prep: 5 minutes
Cook: 15 minutes

◆§ Wash the potatoes and cut them into cubes.
◆§ Boil or steam the potatoes for 15 minutes or until tender. Drain well.
◆§ Add the remaining ingredients in the order given. Beat or mash to a desired texture, adding more milk if necessary.
◆§ Taste to adjust seasoning and serve immediately.

Nutritional Analysis: 1 serving
cal 341; chol 11 mg; fat-total 4 g; fat-mono 1.1 g; fat-poly 0.3 g; fat-sat 2.5 g; protein 8 g; carbo 70.1 g; fiber 6.56 g; calcium 79 mg; sodium 42 mg; fat 10%; protein 9%; carbo 81%
◆ With margarine instead of butter: chol 1 mg; fat-mono 1.7 g; fat-poly 1.3 g; fat-sat 0.9 g

Nutritional Analysis for Dinner Meal: 1 serving
cal 626; chol 58 mg; fat-total 13.6 g; fat-mono 7 g; fat-poly 1.9 g; fat-sat 3.8 g; protein 41.39 g; carbo 87.6 g; fiber 11.72 g+; calcium 241 mg; sodium 477 mg; fat 19%; protein 26%; carbo 55%
◆ With margarine instead of butter: chol 48 mg; fat-mono 7.5 g; fat-poly 2.9 g; fat-sat 2.2 g

❧ Low-Fat Deep-Dish Pizza or Veggie-Rich Pita Pizza
Tossed Greens Salad

Pizza is a favorite food in America. It can be made in dozens of ways, with any number and combination of ingredients, to please just about everyone.

LOW-FAT DEEP-DISH PIZZA

This is one of my favorite meals. I love pizza! At first glance, the recipe may seem involved, but it's actually quite easy. And with all the topping possibilities, it's a meal in itself. The next time you make Marinara Sauce, Pesto, or other sauces, save some and try it on the pizza instead of tomato sauce. The seafood and poultry options will add some extra flavor along with protein and just a small amount of cholesterol. Vegetables and beans make each slice heartier and boost carbohydrate and fiber levels. Olives, on the other hand, will add extra fat. Try adding a little semolina flour for a crisper crust.*

Crust

2 cups warm water (110–115°F)
1 tablespoon honey
2 tablespoons active dry yeast
5 cups whole-wheat flour
1 tablespoon olive oil
1 teaspoon salt

Serves 8
Prep: 20 minutes
Crust: 1 hour
Bake: 20 minutes

Toppings

1 cup tomato sauce
2 cups grated part–skim milk
   mozzarella cheese
1 green pepper, chopped
1 onion, chopped
½ pound mushrooms, sliced
2 cups broccoli florets, sliced,
   blanched if desired

1 can (28 ounces) Italian-style
   tomatoes, drained, chopped
4 tablespoons grated Parmesan
   cheese
1 tablespoon oregano

*(Additional topping options on page
   276)*

* See Chapter 7 for added tips and information on baking bread.

Additional Topping Options

Artichoke hearts

Olives

Pimientos

Garlic, fresh or roasted

Cooked beans

Green chilis

Zucchini

Spinach

Peperoncini (pickled Italian
   peppers)

Fresh basil

Pineapple

Cooked ground turkey breast

Cooked chicken breast

Tofu

Cooked seafood

◆§ Mix the water and honey in a large bowl and sprinkle the yeast on top. Let proof for 10 minutes. Beat in 2 cups of the flour with an electric mixer or vigorously by hand for 3 minutes. Stir in the other crust ingredients, slowly working in enough of the remaining flour to form a firm dough. Knead on a floured surface for 5 to 10 minutes, adding more flour if necessary. You can also prepare this dough in a food processor with the kneading attachment.

◆§ Place the dough in a very lightly oiled bowl and turn it to coat with oil. Cover and let rise in a warm place for 45 minutes or until about doubled in size.

◆§ Very lightly oil a large deep-dish pizza pan or baking sheet and sprinkle it with cornmeal. Punch down the dough and roll it into a circle, using a rolling pin. Place the dough in the pan and crimp the edges slightly.

◆§ Preheat oven to 425°F. Spread an even layer of tomato sauce over the dough. Add half the mozzarella cheese, then the other toppings (except the Parmesan and oregano) and remaining mozzarella. (Drain vegetables well to prevent a soggy crust.) Sprinkle with Parmesan cheese and oregano. Bake for 20 minutes or until lightly browned. Cool the pizza slightly before slicing.

Nutritional Analysis: 1 large slice
cal 415; chol 17 mg; fat-total 9.4 g; fat-mono 3.1 g; fat-poly 1.1 g; fat-sat 4.1 g; protein 22.25 g; carbo 65.8 g; fiber 10.29 g; calcium 346 mg; sodium 662 mg; fat 19%; protein 20%; carbo 61%

VEGGIE-RICH PITA PIZZA

When you need a meal in minutes, this one is a great choice. It's similar to the previous recipe, but this crust requires no preparation time — it's made with whole-wheat pita bread.

1 piece whole-wheat pita bread	*Serves 1*
3 tablespoons tomato sauce	*Prep: 10 minutes*
Toppings as suggested for Low- Fat Deep-Dish Pizza	

◄§ Preheat oven to 350°F. Place pita bread on a baking sheet and bake for 5 to 10 minutes or until slightly crisp. Remove the pita from the oven and raise the temperature to 425°F.

◄§ Spread the tomato sauce on top of the pita bread. Add toppings, including cheeses and oregano. Bake for 15 minutes or until the cheese is melted and lightly golden.

TOSSED GREENS SALAD

We sometimes call this a Pseudo Caesar Salad. That's because the flavor is similar — although the fat content is much lower — and the lettuce is tossed with the dressing before serving. This salad is fast and easy. Try different types of vinegars for variety. If the flavor is a little sharp at first, add more oil — but then slowly decrease the oil each time you make the salad.

1 large head romaine lettuce	*Serves 4*
1 tablespoon olive oil	*Prep: 10 minutes*
2 tablespoons lemon juice or white wine vinegar	
1 clove garlic, minced	

1 tablespoon Worcestershire
  sauce or reduced-sodium soy
  sauce	

4 tablespoons nonfat plain yogurt	
Lots of freshly ground black pepper	

2 tablespoons grated Parmesan
  cheese
	1 cup Homemade Croutons (page
	  326)

◄§ Wash, dry, and tear the lettuce into pieces. Mix the oil, lemon juice, and garlic in a large salad bowl. Stir in the Worcestershire, yogurt, and pepper. Mix with a fork until smooth.

◄§ Toss in the lettuce until well coated. Add Parmesan and additional pepper to taste. Mix again, toss in the croutons, and serve.

Nutritional Analysis: 1 serving
cal 104; chol 2 mg; fat-total 5 g; fat-mono 3 g; fat-poly 0.5 g; fat-sat 1.2 g; protein 4.69 g; carbo 10.2 g; fiber 1.15 g+; calcium 98 mg; sodium 410 mg; fat 43%; protein 18%; carbo 39%

Nutritional Analysis for Dinner Meal: 1 serving
cal 519; chol 19 mg; fat-total 14.4 g; fat-mono 6.1 g; fat-poly 1.6 g; fat-sat 0.3 g; protein 26.94 g; carbo 76 g; fiber 11.44 g+; calcium 443 mg; sodium 1072 mg; fat 24%; protein 20%; carbo 56%

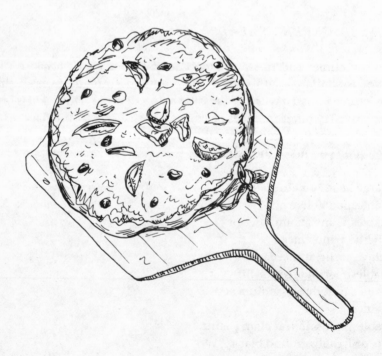

Snack and
Dessert Recipes

CHEWY OATMEAL RAISIN COOKIES

These cookies are low in fat, yet moist and chewy. A real favorite with all who have tried them.

4 tablespoons unsalted butter or margarine, melted

4 tablespoons maple syrup or honey

3 – 4 tablespoons skim milk

1 egg or 2 egg whites or egg replacer, beaten

2 tablespoons vanilla

1¼ cups rolled oats

1¼ cups whole-grain flour

¾ cup raisins

½ cup fructose or sugar

1 teaspoon baking powder

½ teaspoon baking soda

½ teaspoon cinnamon

½ teaspoon nutmeg

Makes 36 cookies
Prep: 10 minutes
Bake: 15 minutes

◦§ Preheat oven to 375°F. Lightly oil 2 baking sheets.

◦§ Mix the wet ingredients in a small bowl.

◦§ Mix the dry ingredients in a large bowl.

◦§ Stir the wet ingredients into the dry and mix just well enough to incorporate.

◦§ Drop the batter by rounded teaspoonfuls onto the prepared sheets, leaving an inch or so between the cookies to allow the dough to spread.

◦§ Bake for 15 minutes or until lightly browned. Remove the cookies from the sheets and cool on a rack.

Nutritional Analysis: 1 cookie
cal 64; chol 11 mg; fat-total 1.7 g; fat-mono 0.4 g+; fat-poly 0.1 g+; fat-sat 0.9 g+; protein 1.33 g; carbo 11.6 g; fiber 0.78 g; calcium 17 mg; sodium 24 mg; fat 23%; protein 8%; carbo 69%

◆ With margarine and egg whites instead of butter and a whole egg: chol 0; fat-mono 0.6 g; fat-poly 0.4 g; fat-sat 0.3 g

OLD-FASHIONED MOLASSES COOKIES

These cookies are light and flavorful. Traditionally, molasses cookies are drizzled with sugar syrup, which you may add if you like. Stir a small amount of warm skim milk into about a cup of powdered sugar (a fork works best) until it's a very thick consistency. Once the cookies have cooled, use a fork to drizzle a small amount of the syrup onto each cookie. The sugar will harden as it dries. These cookies stay quite moist and are best stored on a plate covered with plastic wrap.

¼ cup unsalted butter or
    margarine, softened
¾ cup honey
½ cup molasses
1 egg or 2 egg whites or egg
    replacer
3 cups whole-wheat pastry
    flour
1 teaspoon cinnamon
1 teaspoon baking soda
1 teaspoon ginger

¼ teaspoon cloves
½ cup currants (optional)
½ cup cultured nonfat buttermilk

Makes 50 cookies
Prep: 15–20 minutes
Bake: 12–15 minutes

◆§ Cream the butter in a large bowl until smooth. Beat in the honey, molasses, and egg.

◆§ Sift together the dry ingredients into a separate bowl.

◆§ Preheat oven to 350°F. Lightly oil 2 baking sheets.

◆§ Beat the buttermilk and flour mixture into the wet ingredients until well combined.

◆§ Drop the batter by teaspoonfuls onto the prepared sheets and bake for 12 to 15 minutes.

◆§ Remove the cookies from the baking sheets and cool on a rack.

Nutritional Analysis: 1 serving
cal 57; chol 8 mg; fat-total 1.1 g; fat-mono 0.3 g+; fat-poly 0.1 g+; fat-sat 0.6 g+; protein 1.18 g; carbo 11.3 g; fiber 0.7 g+; calcium 30 mg; sodium 23 mg; fat 17%; protein 8%; carbo 75%
◆ With margarine and egg whites instead of butter and a whole egg: chol 0; fat-mono 0.4 g+; fat-poly 0.4 g+; fat-sat 0.2 g+

OAT BRAN, DATE, AND CURRANT BITES

What a great way to eat oat bran and other high-fiber foods! These bite-size treats are loaded with chopped dates and currants, giving them a nice, sweet flavor and homespun texture.

1 cup oat bran
½ cup whole-grain flour
½ cup rolled oats
1½ teaspoons baking powder
1 teaspoon cinnamon
½ teaspoon nutmeg
¾ cup currants
¾ cup chopped dates
3 tablespoons unsalted butter or margarine, melted
4 tablespoons honey or maple syrup
1 egg or 2 egg whites or egg replacer, beaten

1 tablespoon vanilla
½ teaspoon grated lemon rind
½ cup skim milk

Makes 36 cookies
Prep: 10 minutes
Bake: 15 – 20 minutes

◄§ Preheat oven to 375°F. Lightly oil 2 baking sheets.
◄§ Mix the dry ingredients, including the currants and dates, in a large bowl.
◄§ Combine the remaining ingredients in a separate bowl. Stir the wet ingredients into the dry and mix well.
◄§ Drop the batter by teaspoonfuls onto the baking sheets. Flatten the cookies slightly with the back of the spoon.
◄§ Bake for 15 to 20 minutes. Remove the cookies from the baking sheets and cool on a rack.

Nutritional Analysis: 1 cookie
cal 59; chol 10 mg; fat-total 1.4 g; fat-mono 0.3 g+; fat-poly 0.1 g+; fat-sat 0.7 g+; protein 1.54 g; carbo 10.5 g; fiber 0.55 g+; calcium 23 mg; sodium 18 mg; fat 21%; protein 10%; carbo 69%
◆ With margarine and egg whites instead of butter and a whole egg: chol 0; fat-mono 0.4 g+; fat-poly 0.3 g+; fat-sat 0.2 g+

ALMOND AND HAZELNUT BISCOTTI

The mildly nutty flavor and crunchy texture of these Italian cookies make for a perfect after-dinner treat or midday snack.

2 ounces almonds (about ¼ cup)
1 ounce hazelnuts (about 26 nuts)
3½ cups whole-wheat pastry
  flour
½ teaspoon baking powder
½ teaspoon baking soda
½ teaspoon cinnamon
⅛ teaspoon allspice
2 tablespoons unsalted butter or
  margarine, softened
1½ cups fructose or sugar
3 egg whites
1 egg or 2 egg whites or egg
  replacer

Makes 40 cookies
Prep: 20 minutes
Bake: 25–30 minutes
Rebake: 15 minutes

1 teaspoon vanilla
1 teaspoon grated orange or
  lemon rind

- ⋅§ Chop the nuts in a food processor or by hand.
- ⋅§ Mix the ground nuts, flour, baking powder, baking soda, and spices.
- ⋅§ Beat the butter in a large bowl until smooth. Beat in the remaining ingredients in the order given.
- ⋅§ Preheat oven to 375°F. Lightly oil a baking sheet.
- ⋅§ Stir the dry mixture into the wet ingredients. Knead the dough in the bowl until the mixture is well combined.
- ⋅§ Divide the dough in half. With floured hands, form each half into a rough 5 × 12-inch rectangle on the baking sheet.
- ⋅§ Bake in the top third of the oven for 25 to 30 minutes or until a toothpick inserted into the center comes out dry.
- ⋅§ Remove the *biscotti* from the oven and lower the temperature to 325°F. Slice each rectangle crosswise into 20 pieces. Arrange the *biscotti* on the baking sheet, cut side up, and bake again in the upper third of the oven for 15 minutes.
- ⋅§ Transfer the *biscotti* to a rack and cool completely. They will harden as they cool. Store in an airtight container.

Nutritional Analysis: 1 cookie
cal 85; chol 8 mg; fat-total 2.1 g; fat-mono 1.1 g; fat-poly 0.3 g; fat-sat

0.5 g; protein 2.18 g; carbo 15.4 g; fiber 1.27 g; calcium 14 mg; sodium 26 mg; fat 21%; protein 10%; carbo 69%
◆ With margarine and egg whites instead of butter and a whole egg: chol 0; fat-mono 1.1 g; fat-poly 0.5 g; fat-sat 0.2 g

WHOLE-GRAIN MANDELBROT

Mandelbrot is a slightly sweet, crisp cookie. A perfect snack with a warm cup of tea or cold glass of skim milk for dunking. Traditionally, *mandelbrot* is made with additional butter, eggs, and sometimes candied fruit and nuts. My version is much lower in fat and calories but not flavor. Before baking, sprinkle the *mandelbrot* with some cinnamon and fructose if you like.

3 cups whole-grain flour
¾ cup fructose or sugar
1 tablespoon baking powder
1 teaspoon cinnamon
½ cup raisins
½ cup currants
½ cup chopped dates
4 tablespoons unsalted butter or margarine, melted
2 teaspoons vanilla
½ teaspoon almond extract
⅓ cup skim milk
2 eggs or 4 egg whites or egg replacer, beaten

Makes 24 cookies
Prep: 10 minutes
Bake: 30 minutes
Rebake: 5 minutes

᠊ᔥ Preheat oven to 350°F. Lightly oil a baking sheet.
᠊ᔥ Mix the dry ingredients, including the dried fruits, in a large bowl.
᠊ᔥ Mix the butter, vanilla, almond extract, and milk in a small bowl.
᠊ᔥ Add the eggs and butter mixture to the flour mixture. Stir just well enough to incorporate all the ingredients.
᠊ᔥ Turn the dough out onto a counter and knead a few times.
᠊ᔥ Separate the dough into 3 pieces. Shape the pieces into flat, oblong loaves and place them on the baking sheet with several inches between them.
᠊ᔥ Bake for 30 minutes or until lightly browned.
᠊ᔥ Remove the loaves from the oven and slice each one horizontally into 8 pieces while still hot.

⋖§ Separate the pieces and turn each onto its side. Return the *mandelbrot* to the oven for another 5 minutes. Remove and let cool on the cookie sheet. When fully cooled, store in a covered container.

Nutritional Analysis: 1 cookie
cal 127; chol 28 mg; fat-total 2.6 g; fat-mono 0.8 g+; fat-poly 0.3 g+; fat-sat 1.4 g+; protein 2.92 g; carbo 24.7 g; fiber 2 g+; calcium 50 mg; sodium 48 mg; fat 18%; protein 9%; carbo 73%
◆ With margarine and egg whites instead of butter and whole eggs: chol 0; fat-mono 0.9 g; fat-poly 0.7 g; fat-sat 0.4 g

GINGERSNAPS

Molasses and ginger are combined to make a light and low-fat cookie. Use several different cookie cutters. Kids love to pick their favorite shapes.

4 tablespoons unsalted butter or
   margarine, softened
6 tablespoons molasses
6 tablespoons maple syrup or
   honey
1 egg or 2 egg whites or egg
   replacer, beaten
2 tablespoons skim milk

Makes 24 cookies
Prep: 15–20 minutes
Bake: 5–10 minutes

1¼ cups brown rice flour
1 cup oat, barley, or whole-wheat pastry flour
2½ teaspoons cinnamon

2 teaspoons ginger
1 teaspoon baking soda
½ teaspoon cloves
½ teaspoon nutmeg

⋖§ Preheat oven to 375°F.
⋖§ Cream the butter and beat in the molasses, maple syrup, egg, and milk.
⋖§ Combine all the dry ingredients in a medium bowl.
⋖§ Add the wet ingredients to the dry and mix well.
⋖§ Knead the dough a few times and roll it out on a lightly floured surface to ⅛-inch thickness. Cut into shapes with a cookie cutter or knife.

◄§ Place the cookies on an ungreased baking sheet. Bake for 5 to 10 minutes or until lightly browned.

◄§ Remove the cookies from the baking sheet and cool on a rack.

Nutritional Analysis: 1 cookie
cal 82; chol 17 mg; fat-total 2.3 g; fat-mono 0.7 g+; fat-poly 0.2 g+; fat-sat 1.3 g+; protein 1.81 g; carbo 14.3 g; fiber 1.09 g+; calcium 50 mg; sodium 45 mg; fat 24%; protein 8%; carbo 68%

◆ With margarine and egg whites instead of butter and a whole egg: chol 0; fat-mono 0.9 g+; fat-poly 0.7 g+; fat-sat 0.4 g+

FENNEL, ANISE, AND ALMOND COOKIES

These cookies have a lightly sweet licorice taste and are perfect for dunking into a warm cup of tea.

3 cups whole-grain flour
2 teaspoons baking powder
1½ teaspoons fennel seeds,
  slightly crushed
5 tablespoons unsalted butter or
  margarine, melted
½ cup skim milk
½ cup maple syrup or honey
1 tablespoon vanilla
¼ teaspoon almond extract
¼ teaspoon anise extract
Slivered almonds (optional)

Makes 30 cookies
Prep: 15 minutes
Bake: 20 minutes

◄§ Preheat oven to 375°F. Lightly oil 2 baking sheets.

◄§ Mix the dry ingredients in a large bowl. Mix the wet ingredients in a small bowl.

◄§ Pour the wet ingredients into the dry and mix well. Knead the dough a few times and roll it out on a floured surface to ¼-inch thickness. Cut the dough into shapes or form the dough into round balls and flatten them with your palm.

◄§ Place the cookies on the baking sheets and press an almond sliver into the center of each one. Bake for 15 to 20 minutes or until lightly browned. Remove them from the baking sheets and cool on a rack.

Nutritional Analysis: 1 cookie
cal 71; chol 5 mg; fat-total 2 g; fat-mono 0.6 g; fat-poly 0.2 g; fat-sat
1.2 g; protein 1.73 g; carbo 12.1 g; fiber 1.16 g; calcium 32 mg;
sodium 24 mg; fat 25%; protein 9%; carbo 66%
◆ With margarine instead of butter: chol 0; fat-mono 0.9 g; fat-poly
0.7 g; fat-sat 0.4 g

RASPBERRY CURRANT SCONES

Scones are originally from Britain and are commonly eaten at
teatime. These scones have a cookie crust surrounding a spoonful of
raspberry jam. Experiment with other filling flavors.

3 cups whole-grain flour
5 teaspoons baking powder
½ teaspoon nutmeg
5 tablespoons unsalted butter or
   margarine
¼ cup fructose, honey, or maple
   syrup
⅓ cup currants
½ cup skim milk
16 teaspoons unsweetened
   raspberry jam, fruit spread,
   conserve, or jelly

Makes 16 scones
Prep: 15 minutes
Bake: 20 minutes

◦§ Preheat oven to 350°F. Lightly oil a baking sheet.
◦§ Mix the flour, baking powder, and nutmeg in a medium bowl.
Cut in the butter with a knife or a food processor to form a fine
crumb. Stir in the currants and the fructose (if this is your
sweetener).
◦§ Mix the maple syrup or honey (if you haven't used fructose) into
the dry ingredients with enough of the milk to form a stiff dough.
◦§ Roll the dough into 16 balls. Place the balls on the baking sheet.
Use your thumb to make a well in the center of each ball, being
careful not to touch bottom. Smooth out the edges and fill each
hole with a teaspoon of raspberry jam.
◦§ Bake for 20 minutes or until golden brown.

Nutritional Analysis: 1 scone
cal 155; chol 10 mg; fat-total 3.9 g; fat-mono 1.1 g+; fat-poly 0.3 g+;
fat-sat 2.3 g+; protein 3.44 g; carbo 28.2 g; fiber 2.18 g+; calcium
99 mg; sodium 104 mg; fat 22%; protein 9%; carbo 69%
◆ With margarine instead of butter: chol 0; fat-mono 1.6 g; fat-poly
  1.3 g; fat-sat 0.8 g

VERY BERRY MUFFINS

A versatile muffin chock-full of juicy berries. Use any type of berry,
fresh or frozen. You can keep most berries whole, but cut strawberries, for instance, into pieces.

1½ cups whole-grain flour
4 tablespoons honey, fructose, or
  maple syrup
2 teaspoons baking powder
1 teaspoon baking soda
Dash of nutmeg
¾ cup skim milk
2 tablespoons unsalted butter or
  margarine, melted
2 tablespoons lemon juice
2 teaspoons vanilla
½ teaspoon grated lemon rind or
  ¼ teaspoon lemon extract

1 egg or 2 egg whites or egg
  replacer, beaten
1¼ cups blueberries, raspberries,
  blackberries, strawberries, or
  other berries

Makes 12 muffins
Prep: 10 minutes
Bake: 20–25 minutes

◦§ Preheat oven to 350°F. Line 12 muffin tins with paper cups.
◦§ Mix all the dry ingredients in a large bowl.
◦§ Mix all the wet ingredients, except the berries, in another bowl.
◦§ Combine the wet mixture with the dry ingredients and mix the
   batter just well enough to incorporate.
◦§ Gently fold in the berries. Spoon the batter into the muffin tins.
◦§ Bake for 20 to 25 minutes or until a toothpick inserted into the
   center of a muffin comes out dry. Remove the muffins from the
   tins and cool on a rack.

Nutritional Analysis: 1 muffin
cal 110; chol 28 mg; fat-total 2.7 g; fat-mono 0.8 g; fat-poly 0.3 g;
fat-sat 1.4 g; protein 3.12 g; carbo 19.6 g; fiber 1.97 g+; calcium
69 mg; sodium 137 mg; fat 21%; protein 11%; carbo 68%

◆ With margarine and egg whites instead of butter and a whole egg: chol 0; fat-mono 0.9 g; fat-poly 0.8 g; sat-fat 0.4 g
◆ Analysis is based on fresh blueberries.

MULTIGRAIN CURRANT MUFFINS

These muffins are filled with whole-grain goodness. The variety of flours gives them a wonderful flavor and texture.

1 cup oat flour   *Makes 18 muffins*
1 cup barley flour   *Prep: 10 minutes*
1 cup brown rice flour   *Bake: 25 minutes*
¼ cup oat bran
¼ cup millet flour
½ cup currants
2 tablespoons baking powder
½ teaspoon nutmeg
¼ teaspoon cinnamon
2 cups skim milk
6 tablespoons maple syrup or
  honey   2 eggs or 4 egg whites or egg
5 tablespoons unsalted butter or   replacer, beaten
  margarine, melted   1 tablespoon vanilla

◆§ Preheat oven to 350°F. Line 18 muffin tins with paper cups.
◆§ Mix the dry ingredients in a large bowl.
◆§ Mix the wet ingredients in a small bowl.
◆§ Add the wet ingredients to the dry. Mix just well enough to incorporate. Spoon the batter into the muffin tins.
◆§ Bake for 25 minutes or until a toothpick inserted into the center of a muffin comes out dry. Remove the muffins from the tins and cool on a rack.

Nutritional Analysis: 1 muffin
cal 154; chol 40 mg; fat-total 4.3 g; fat-mono 1.2 g+; fat-poly 0.4 g+; fat-sat 2.3 g+; protein 4.95 g; carbo 25.3 g; fiber 2.1 g+; calcium 138 mg; sodium 129 mg; fat 24%; protein 12%; carbo 64%
◆ With margarine and egg whites instead of butter and whole eggs: chol 0; fat-mono 1.5 g+; fat-poly 1.2 g+; fat-sat 0.7 g+

CRANBERRY CURRANT MUFFINS

These muffins are a seasonal treat unless you remember to freeze a few packages of cranberries during the holidays. Tart cranberries and tiny currants are a perfect contrast to the sweet, whole-grain batter.

6 ounces cranberries
2 cups whole-grain flour
½ cup currants
1½ teaspoons baking powder
1 teaspoon baking soda
½ teaspoon nutmeg
¾ cup maple syrup or honey
½ cup orange juice
3 tablespoons unsalted butter or margarine, melted
1 tablespoon grated orange rind
1 egg or 2 egg whites or egg replacer, beaten
1 teaspoon vanilla

Makes 12 muffins
Prep: 15 minutes
Bake: 15 – 20 minutes

◆§ Wash the cranberries. Bring several cups of water to a boil, add the cranberries, and cook for 5 minutes. Drain well. Preheat the oven to 350°F. Line 12 muffin tins with paper cups.
◆§ Mix the dry ingredients in a large bowl.
◆§ Mix the remaining ingredients, except the cranberries, in another bowl.
◆§ Add the wet ingredients to the dry. Mix batter just well enough to incorporate all the ingredients.
◆§ Gently fold in the cranberries. Spoon the batter into the muffin tins.
◆§ Bake for 15 to 20 minutes or until a toothpick inserted into the center of a muffin comes out dry. Remove the muffins from the tins and cool on a rack.

Nutritional Analysis: 1 muffin
cal 176; chol 31 mg; fat-total 3.7 g; fat-mono 1.1 g+; fat-poly 0.3 g+; fat-sat 2 g+; protein 3.56 g; carbo 34.2 g; fiber 2.11 g+; calcium 70 mg; sodium 118 mg; fat 18%; protein 8%; carbo 74%
◆ With margarine and egg whites instead of butter and a whole egg: chol 0; fat-mono 1.3 g+; fat-poly 1.1 g+; fat-sat 0.6 g+

BLUEBERRY CORN MUFFINS

The unusual combination of blueberries and cornmeal is very special. Try using blue cornmeal for a beautiful, light purple muffin studded with dark purple berries.

1 cup cornmeal
1 cup whole-grain flour
⅓ cup fructose or sugar
2½ teaspoons baking powder
Dash of nutmeg
1 cup skim milk
3 tablespoons unsalted butter or
   margarine, melted
1 egg or 2 egg whites or egg
   replacer, beaten
1½ cups blueberries

Makes 12 muffins
Prep: 10 minutes
Bake: 25 – 30 minutes

- Preheat oven to 375°F. Line 12 muffin tins with paper cups.
- Mix the dry ingredients in a large bowl. Mix the wet ingredients, except the blueberries, in a separate bowl.
- Add the wet ingredients to the dry. Stir just well enough to incorporate all the ingredients. Gently fold in the blueberries.
- Spoon the batter into the muffin tins. Bake for 25 to 30 minutes or until a toothpick inserted into the center of a muffin comes out dry. Remove the muffins from the tins and cool on a rack.

Nutritional Analysis: 1 muffin
cal 141; chol 31 mg; fat-total 4 g; fat-mono 1.1 g; fat-poly 0.5 g; fat-sat 2 g; protein 3.54 g; carbo 23.9 g; fiber 3.15 g; calcium 85 mg; sodium 83 mg; fat 25%; protein 10%; carbo 65%
◆ With margarine and egg whites instead of butter and a whole egg: chol 0; fat-mono 1.4 g; fat-poly 1.2 g; fat-sat 0.6 g

CINNAMON RAISIN QUICK BREAD

This slightly sweet, brown quick bread has a cakey texture and is studded with raisins. Use this recipe to make 2 loaves or cinnamon raisin muffins.

1½ cups skim milk
¾ cup maple syrup or honey
6 tablespoons unsalted butter or
  margarine, melted
1 egg or 2 egg whites or egg
  replacer, beaten
1 tablespoon vanilla
3 cups whole-grain flour
2 teaspoons baking powder
1½ teaspoons baking soda
1½ teaspoons cinnamon
¼ teaspoon nutmeg
1½ cups raisins

Serves 20
Prep: 10 minutes
Bake: 40–45 minutes

᪣ Preheat oven to 350°F. Lightly oil 2 loaf (9 × 5 inches) pans.
᪣ Combine the wet ingredients in a small bowl.
᪣ Mix the dry ingredients in a large bowl. Stir in the raisins.
᪣ Add the wet mixture to the dry. Mix just well enough to incorporate all the ingredients.
᪣ Pour equal amounts of batter into both loaf pans. Bake for 40 to 45 minutes or until a toothpick inserted into the center comes out dry. Remove the loaves from the pans and cool on a rack.

Nutritional Analysis: 1 serving
cal 163; chol 23 mg; fat-total 4 g; fat-mono 1.2 g; fat-poly 0.3 g; fat-sat 2.3 g; protein 3.68 g; carbo 30.2 g; fiber 2.52 g; calcium 76 mg; sodium 111 mg; fat 21%; protein 9%; carbo 70%
◆ With margarine and egg whites instead of butter and a whole egg: chol 0; fat-mono 1.6 g; fat-poly 1.3 g; fat-sat 0.8 g

OATMEAL DATE BREAD

Chewy dates and oatmeal make this sweet, high-fiber bread rich and moist. To save time, buy chopped dates.

1⅔ cups chopped pitted dates
1½ cups rolled oats
6 tablespoons unsalted butter or margarine
2 cups boiling water
2 cups whole-grain flour
1½ teaspoons baking soda
1½ teaspoons baking powder
1½ teaspoons cinnamon

Serves 20
Prep: 15 minutes
Bake: 50 minutes – 1 hour

2 eggs or 4 egg whites or egg replacer, beaten
1 cup honey or maple syrup
1 tablespoon vanilla

◦§ Preheat oven to 350°F. Lightly oil 2 loaf (9 × 5 inches) pans.
◦§ Mix the dates, oats, and butter in a large bowl. Stir in the boiling water and set aside.
◦§ Stir together the flour, baking soda, baking powder, and cinnamon in a small bowl.
◦§ Mix the eggs, honey, and vanilla into the oat mixture.
◦§ Add the flour mixture to the wet ingredients and stir just well enough to incorporate.
◦§ Pour the batter into the pans and bake for 50 minutes to 1 hour. Remove the loaves from the pans and cool on a rack.

Nutritional Analysis: 1 serving
cal 194; chol 37 mg; fat-total 4.6 g; fat-mono 1.3 g+; fat-poly 0.3 g+; fat-sat 2.4 g+; protein 3.56 g; carbo 37.8 g; fiber 2.83 g; calcium 37 mg; sodium 96 mg; fat 20%; protein 7%; carbo 73%
◆ With margarine and egg whites instead of butter and whole eggs: chol 0; fat-mono 1.5 g+; fat-poly 1.2 g+; fat-sat 0.7 g+

SWEET SODA BREAD

This slightly sweet soda bread is made with currants, caraway or poppy seeds, and any variety of whole-grain flours. It's a delicious snack served steaming hot from the oven, plain or spread with a bit of honey. To make muffins, cut this recipe in half, add a little extra milk, and pour the batter into a muffin pan lined with paper cups.

7 cups whole-grain flour
1¾ cups currants
1 tablespoon caraway or poppy
  seeds
1½ teaspoons baking soda
1⅓ cups cultured nonfat
  buttermilk
1¼ cups skim milk
½ cup unsalted butter or
  margarine, melted

Serves 24
Prep: 15 minutes
Bake: 45 minutes

4 tablespoons maple syrup or
  honey
1 tablespoon grated lemon rind

- Preheat oven to 375°F. Lightly oil a baking sheet and sprinkle it with flour.
- Mix the flour, currants, caraway seeds, and baking soda in a large bowl.
- Combine the remaining ingredients in a small bowl.
- Add the wet ingredients to the dry and mix just well enough to incorporate.
- Divide the dough in half. Gently knead each piece a few times and shape into 2 round loaves.
- Place the loaves on the prepared baking sheet several inches apart. Using a sharp knife, slash an X across the top of each loaf.
- Bake immediately for about 45 minutes or until the crust is hard and lightly browned.
- Remove the bread from the baking sheet and cool on a rack.

Nutritional Analysis: 1 serving
cal 196; chol 11 mg; fat-total 4.4 g; fat-mono 1.2 g+; fat-poly 0.5 g+; fat-sat 2.5 g+; protein 6.02 g; carbo 35.6 g; fiber 3.39 g+; calcium 63 mg; sodium 69 mg; fat 19%; protein 12%; carbo 69%
◆ With margarine instead of butter: chol 0; fat-mono 1.8 g+; fat-poly 1.5 g; fat-sat 0.9 g+

ZUCCHINI SPICE BREAD

The zucchini creates a nice texture. This bread is moist and has a fabulous aroma.

3 cups whole-wheat pastry flour
1 tablespoon cinnamon
1½ teaspoons baking powder
1½ teaspoons baking soda
1 teaspoon nutmeg
2 eggs or 4 egg whites or egg
   replacer
2 cups unpeeled, grated zucchini
1 cup honey or maple syrup
6 tablespoons unsalted butter or
   margarine, melted
1 tablespoon vanilla

Serves 20
Prep: 15 minutes
Bake: 35–45 minutes

◦§ Preheat oven to 350°F. Lightly oil 2 loaf (9 × 5 inches) pans.
◦§ Mix the dry ingredients together in a large bowl.
◦§ Beat the eggs in a small bowl and stir in the remaining ingredients.
◦§ Stir the wet ingredients into the dry and mix just well enough to incorporate.
◦§ Pour the batter into the prepared pans. Bake for 35 to 45 minutes or until a toothpick inserted into the center comes out dry.
◦§ Cool slightly in pans. Remove the bread from the pans and continue cooling on a rack.

Nutritional Analysis: 1 serving
cal 155; chol 37 mg; fat-total 4.3 g; fat-mono 1.3 g; fat-poly 0.4 g; fat-sat 2.4 g; protein 3.36 g; carbo 28 g; fiber 1.86 g; calcium 38 mg; sodium 96 mg; fat 23%; protein 8%; carbo 69%
◆ With margarine and egg whites instead of butter and whole eggs: chol 0; fat-mono 1.5 g; fat-poly 1.2 g; fat-sat 0.7 g

PUMPKIN BREAD

Enjoy this autumn treat year-round by using canned pumpkin.
Double the recipe to make full use of a 16-ounce can.

1½ cups whole-wheat pastry
  flour
1 teaspoon cinnamon
1 teaspoon baking soda
½ teaspoon baking powder
½ teaspoon cloves
½ teaspoon nutmeg
½ cup raisins
1 cup unsweetened canned
  pumpkin
¾ cup honey
1 egg or 2 egg whites or egg
  replacer

Serves 10
Prep: 15 minutes
Bake: 1 hour

3 tablespoons unsalted butter or
  margarine, melted
1 tablespoon vanilla

⋅§ Preheat oven to 350°F. Lightly oil a 9 X 5-inch loaf pan.
⋅§ Mix all the dry ingredients and sift them into a large bowl. Gently
  toss in the raisins.
⋅§ Combine the wet ingredients in a separate bowl.
⋅§ Stir the wet ingredients into the dry and mix just well enough to
  incorporate.
⋅§ Pour the batter into the prepared pan and bake for 1 hour or until
  a toothpick inserted into the center comes out dry.
⋅§ Cool the bread in the pan slightly, then remove and cool on a
  rack.

Nutritional Analysis: 1 serving
cal 207; chol 37 mg; fat-total 4.4 g; fat-mono 1.3 g; fat-poly 0.4 g;
fat-sat 2.4 g; protein 3.63 g; carbo 41.8 g; fiber 2.7 g; calcium 37 mg;
sodium 111 mg; fat 18%; protein 7%; carbo 75%
◆ With margarine and egg whites instead of butter and a whole egg:
  chol 0; fat-mono 1.6 g; fat-poly 1.3 g; fat-sat 0.8 g

APPLE SPICE CAKE

A light cake filled with bits of fresh apple and a very special topping.
This recipe also makes great muffins.

3 tablespoons unsalted butter or
margarine, softened
1 cup + 1 tablespoon fructose or
sugar
1 egg or 2 egg whites or egg
replacer
¾ cup skim milk
1½ tablespoons vanilla
2 cups whole-grain flour
1 teaspoon baking powder
1 teaspoon baking soda
2½ teaspoons cinnamon
½ teaspoon nutmeg

¼ teaspoon cloves
¼ teaspoon allspice
2 cups diced apples
2 tablespoons finely ground
pecans

Serves 12
Prep: 10 minutes
Bake: 30–45 minutes

- ◆§ Preheat oven to 350°F. Lightly oil a 9 × 5-inch loaf pan or line 12 muffin tins with paper cups.
- ◆§ Cream the butter in a medium bowl. Beat in 1 cup of the fructose, the egg, milk, and vanilla.
- ◆§ Combine the flour, baking powder, baking soda, 2 teaspoons of the cinnamon, the nutmeg, cloves, allspice, and apples. Stir the flour mixture into the liquid mixture, stirring just well enough to incorporate all the ingredients. Pour the batter into the prepared pan.
- ◆§ Mix the pecans, the remaining 1 tablespoon fructose, and the remaining ½ teaspoon cinnamon. Sprinkle the nut mixture on top of the batter.
- ◆§ Bake the loaf cake for about 45 minutes, or muffins for about 30, or until a toothpick inserted into the center comes out dry. Remove the cake or muffins from the pan and cool on a rack.

Nutritional Analysis: 1 serving
cal 194; chol 31 mg; fat-total 4.4 g; fat-mono 1.5 g; fat-poly 0.5 g; fat-sat 2.1 g; protein 3.76 g; carbo 36.9 g; fiber 2.48 g; calcium 59 mg; sodium 111 mg; fat 20%; protein 7%; carbo 73%
- ◆ With margarine and egg whites instead of butter and a whole egg: chol 0; fat-mono 1.8 g; fat-poly 1.3 g; fat-sat 0.7 g

CARROT PINEAPPLE CAKE

Little chunks of pineapple make this carrot cake unique. This recipe makes great muffins too. Try topping them with Lemon Ricotta Icing (page 313) for delicious cupcakes.

3 cups whole-grain flour
¼ cup nonfat dry milk powder
2 teaspoons baking powder
1 teaspoon cinnamon
1 teaspoon nutmeg
1 teaspoon baking soda
¼ teaspoon cloves
¼ teaspoon allspice
½ cup currants
6 tablespoons unsalted butter or margarine, melted
2 eggs or 4 egg whites or egg replacer, beaten
1 cup skim milk
2 cups loosely packed, grated carrots

Serves 20
Prep: 15 minutes
Bake: 40 – 45 minutes

1 cup honey or maple syrup
1 tablespoon vanilla
8½ ounces unsweetened crushed pineapple, with juice

- ◄§ Preheat oven to 350°F. Lightly oil 2 loaf (9 X 5 inches) pans, one bundt pan, or line muffin tins with paper cups.
- ◄§ Mix all the dry ingredients in a large bowl. Stir in the currants.
- ◄§ Mix the butter, honey, vanilla, eggs, and milk in a small bowl.
- ◄§ Add the wet ingredients, carrots, and pineapple to the dry. Mix just well enough to incorporate all the ingredients.
- ◄§ Pour the batter into the prepared pans.
- ◄§ Bake 40 to 45 minutes for loaves (less time for muffins or slightly more time for one large cake), or until a toothpick inserted into the center comes out dry.

Nutritional Analysis: 1 serving
cal 180; chol 37 mg; fat-total 4.3 g; fat-mono 1.3 g+; fat-poly 0.4 g+; fat-sat 2.4 g+; protein 4.06 g; carbo 33.8 g; fiber 2.2 g+; calcium 71 mg; sodium 97 mg; fat 20%; protein 9%; carbo 71%
- ◆ With margarine and egg whites instead of butter and whole eggs: chol 0; fat-mono 1.6 g+; fat-poly 1.3 g+; fat-sat 0.8 g+

CAROB COCOA CAKE

This quick and easy cake is very versatile. Make it into cupcakes, squares, or double the recipe for a 9-inch layer cake or 10-inch tube cake. The flavor is rich and chocolaty, without a lot of fat. Use carob powder, cocoa powder, or a combination of both.

1¼ cups whole-wheat pastry
  flour
¼ cup carob powder, cocoa
  powder, or a combination of
  both
1 cup fructose or sugar
1 teaspoon baking soda
1 teaspoon baking powder
1 cup skim milk
4 tablespoons unsalted butter or
  margarine, melted
1 tablespoon vanilla
1 tablespoon white wine vinegar

Serves 9
Prep: 15 minutes
Bake: 35 – 40 minutes

◆§ Mix the dry ingredients and sift into a large bowl.

◆§ Combine the wet ingredients in a small bowl.

◆§ Preheat oven to 350°F. Lightly oil an 8 X 8-inch baking dish or other pan.

◆§ Stir the wet ingredients into the dry and mix until the batter is smooth.

◆§ Pour the batter into the prepared pan. Bake for 35 to 45 minutes, depending on your pan size, or until a toothpick inserted into the center comes out almost dry. Be careful not to overbake, or the cake will be dry.

◆§ Cool on a rack until ready to serve. (Cover the cake tightly to prevent it from drying out.)

Nutritional Analysis: 1 serving
cal 203; chol 14 mg; fat-total 5.2 g; fat-mono 1.5 g; fat-poly 0.3 g; fat-sat 3.2 g; protein 3.28 g; carbo 39 g; fiber 1.61 g+; calcium 80 mg; sodium 144 mg; fat 22%; protein 6%; carbo 72%
 ◆ With margarine instead of butter: chol 0; fat-mono 2.3 g; fat-poly 1.8 g; fat-sat 1.1 g

CAROB ANGEL FOOD CAKE

Angel food cake is special because it's made without added fat. Egg whites create the airy, delicate texture. In this recipe, whole-grain flour makes for a slightly heartier cake than does the traditional white flour, and fructose replaces sugar (although sugar may be used if necessary). You may substitute cocoa powder for the carob, or combine the two. Although the ingredients are basic, there are quite a few steps to follow because of the cake's delicate nature. For a fancy nonfat treat, serve a slice with fresh berries and a little Creamy Low-Fat Dessert Topping (page 314).

¾ cup whole-wheat pastry flour
1¼ cups fructose or sugar
¼ cup carob powder
10 egg whites
1 teaspoon cream of tartar
1 teaspoon vanilla
½ teaspoon lemon extract

Serves 12
Prep: 20 minutes
Bake: 45 minutes

- Sift the flour, ¼ cup of the fructose, and the carob powder together 6 times.
- Sift the remaining 1 cup of fructose into a separate bowl.
- Beat the egg whites until foamy and add the cream of tartar. Whip until the egg whites are stiff but not dry.
- Fold in the 1 cup of fructose, 1 tablespoon at a time. Add the vanilla and lemon extract.
- Preheat the oven to 350°F.
- Slowly sift small amounts of the flour mixture over the batter and fold it in, until all the flour has been incorporated.
- Pour the batter into an ungreased 10-inch tube pan and bake for 45 minutes.
- Remove the pan from the oven and turn it upside down to cool for 1½ hours. I like to invert the pan and place the tube over a bottle neck to prevent the cake from shrinking as it cools.
- When the cake is fully cooled, use a knife to cut around the edges to remove it from the pan.

Nutritional Analysis: 1 serving
cal 123; chol 0; fat-total 0.1 g; fat-mono 0; fat-poly 0.1 g; fat-sat 0; protein 3.63 g; carbo 28.7 g; fiber 0.73 g+; calcium 15 mg; sodium 43 mg; fat 1%; protein 11%; carbo 88%

APPLE CRUMB PIE

This apple pie has a special crumb crust and topping that combine wonderfully with the spicy filling. We can hardly wait for apple season each year — we never tire of this pie. It's delicious warm or cold. Try it à la mode with frozen yogurt.

Crust
2½ cups whole-grain flour
½ cup fructose or sugar
1 teaspoon cinnamon
4 tablespoons unsalted butter or
   margarine
2 tablespoons honey

Serves 10
Prep: 15 minutes
Bake: 45 minutes
Cool: 1 hour

Filling
8–9 tart apples, thinly sliced,
   peeled or with the skin left on
½ cup fructose or sugar
4 tablespoons whole-grain flour

2 tablespoons vanilla
3 teaspoons cinnamon
1 teaspoon nutmeg

- For the crust, mix the flour, ½ cup fructose, and cinnamon. Using a food processor or 2 knives, cut in the butter and honey to form a fine crumb. Pat two-thirds of the crust on the bottom and sides of an oiled 9- or 10-inch springform pan.
- Preheat oven to 425°F.
- Toss together all the filling ingredients and spoon into the crust. Bake for 25 minutes.
- Remove the pie from the oven and top with the remaining crust. Pat down gently. Sprinkle the top with a small amount of cinnamon. Return the pie to the oven and bake for another 20 minutes or until golden. Let cool for at least 15 minutes before removing the sides of the pan. Let the pie cool for another hour before slicing.

Nutritional Analysis: 1 serving
cal 356; chol 12 mg; fat-total 5.9 g; fat-mono 1.4 g; fat-poly 0.6 g; fat-sat 3.1 g; protein 4.41 g; carbo 76.4 g; fiber 7.07 g; calcium 40 mg; sodium 3 mg; fat 14%; protein 5%; carbo 81%
- With margarine instead of butter: chol 0; fat-mono 2.1 g; fat-poly 1.9 g; fat-sat 1.1 g

LOW-FAT LEMON MERINGUE PIE

Not only is this pie lower in fat than the traditional version, but it has been very popular with people who haven't liked lemon meringue pie in the past. This recipe does need the whole egg to achieve the custard filling. You may substitute margarine for butter. To lower the fat content even more, make the filling in individual baking cups without the crust. Or eliminate the butter or margarine from the filling. But as the nutritional analysis shows, the total fat and cholesterol in each serving are low enough for most people to enjoy an occasional slice. For variety, try lime filling rather than lemon.

Crust
1 cup bread crumbs
¼ cup fructose or sugar
2 tablespoons unsalted butter or
 margarine
1 teaspoon cinnamon

Serves 8
Prep: 30 minutes
Chill: 2 hours or more

Filling
1 cup fructose or sugar
6 tablespoons arrowroot or
 cornstarch
2 cups evaporated skim milk
2 yolks
2 tablespoons unsalted butter or
 margarine
⅓ cup lemon juice
2 tablespoons grated lemon rind

Meringue
2 egg whites
¼ teaspoon cream of tartar
½ teaspoon vanilla
3 tablespoons fructose

◆§ Preheat oven to 350°F. Lightly oil a 9-inch pie plate.

◆§ Combine the crust ingredients in a food processor and incorporate thoroughly. Press the dough evenly on the bottom and sides of the pie plate.

◆§ Bake the crust for 10 minutes, remove from oven, and let cool.

◆§ For the filling, mix the fructose and the arrowroot in a double boiler over high heat. Slowly pour in the milk and cook for 15 minutes. Stir often as the mixture thickens.

◆§ Once the milk mixture is very thick, beat a small amount of it into the egg yolks. Then stir the egg yolks into the thickened milk. Cook for 6 minutes more.

◆§ Remove the mixture from the heat and stir in the butter, lemon juice, and lemon rind. Let cool slightly.

◆§ In a separate bowl, beat the egg whites until foaming. Beat in the cream of tartar and vanilla until stiff, while slowly adding 3 tablespoons of fructose. Don't overbeat.

◆§ Pour the lemon filling into the baked crust and top with the meringue. Make meringue peaks by touching the top of the pie with a spatula and lifting up.

◆§ Bake for 15 minutes or until the peaks are lightly browned. Let cool and refrigerate until well chilled.

Nutritional Analysis: 1 serving
cal 330; chol 87 mg; fat-total 7.9 g; fat-mono 2.5 g; fat-poly 0.5 g; fat-sat 4.2 g; protein 7.94 g; carbo 58.6 g; fiber 0.61 g+; calcium 215 mg; sodium 184 mg; fat 21%; protein 9%; carbo 70%
◆ With margarine instead of butter: chol 71 mg; fat-mono 3.3 g; fat-poly 2.1 g; fat-sat 1.8 g

CHERRY PIE

This recipe for cherry pie is made with fructose and arrowroot instead of sugar and cornstarch. Rolled pie crusts are generally difficult to make with whole-grain flour, especially if they are to be low in fat. This recipe achieves excellent results with both less fat and whole grains. For a nonfat variation, try baking the cherry filling in ovenproof cups and serve the "Baked Cherries" like pudding — without the crust.

Filling
2 cans (1 pound each)
   unsweetened red tart pitted
   cherries
⅔ cup fructose or sugar
½ cup arrowroot
3 – 4 drops almond extract

Serves 8
Prep: 20 minutes
Bake: 50 minutes
Chill: 3 hours or more

Crust

4 tablespoons unsalted butter or margarine	2 tablespoons fructose or sugar
1 cup whole-wheat pastry flour	4–8 tablespoons ice water
	Salt to taste (optional)

◞§ For the filling, drain the cherries and reserve the liquid.

◞§ Combine ⅓ cup of fructose and the arrowroot in a small saucepan. Pour in the reserved cherry juice. Cook on a medium heat, stirring often, until the mixture is thick and bubbly. Preheat oven to 375°F.

◞§ Stir in the remaining ⅓ cup fructose, cherries, and almond extract. Cook and stir for another 3 minutes, remove from the heat, and set aside.

◞§ For the crust, use a food processor or 2 knives to cut the butter into the flour and fructose. When the butter is cut into small bits, slowly stir in a tablespoon of water at a time. Stir in only enough water to form a stiff dough.

◞§ Roll out dough to fit a lightly oiled 9-inch pie plate. Press the dough into the plate and flute the edges.

◞§ Pour the filling into the pie crust, place a cookie sheet under the pie to catch any filling that may overflow, and bake for 50 minutes. Remove the pie from oven and cool on a rack. Chill before serving.

Nutritional Analysis: 1 serving
cal 249; chol 16 mg; fat-total 5.9 g; fat-mono 1.7 g; fat-poly 0.4 g; fat-sat 3.6 g; protein 3 g; carbo 48.2 g; fiber 2.71 g+; calcium 21 mg; sodium 10 mg; fat 21%; protein 5%; carbo 74%
◆ With margarine instead of butter: chol 0; fat-mono 2.6 g; fat-poly 2 g; fat-sat 1.2 g

RHUBARB CRUMB PIE

This pie makes use of springtime's abundance of rhubarb. But you can make it a year-round treat because most markets now sell frozen rhubarb. Try strawberries in place of half the rhubarb for a straw-berry rhubarb crumb pie. And to lower the fat, bake the filling in individual cups; make half the crust for a crumb topping.

Filling
2½ pounds rhubarb
  (approximately 7 cups
  chopped)
1¼ cups fructose or sugar
5 tablespoons arrowroot
1 tablespoon vanilla
1 teaspoon cinnamon
½ teaspoon nutmeg

Serves 8
Prep: 20 minutes
Bake: 45 minutes

Crust
1¾ cups whole-grain flour
¾ cup fructose or sugar
4 tablespoons unsalted butter or
  margarine
2 tablespoons honey

◦§ Wash, dry, and chop the rhubarb into 1-inch pieces. Preheat the oven to 425°F. Lightly oil a 10-inch deep-dish pie pan.

◦§ Combine the filling ingredients in a large bowl. Toss the mixture well.

◦§ For the crust, mix the flour and fructose. Cut in the butter and honey, using a food processor or 2 knives, to form a fine crumb. Press two-thirds of the crumb crust in the bottom and sides of the baking dish.

◦§ Pour the filling into the pie pan and smooth out the top. Place the pie on top of a baking sheet to catch any filling that may overflow. Bake for 25 minutes.

◦§ Remove the pie from oven and crumble on the remaining crust. Pat down gently and return the pie to the oven.

◦§ Bake for another 20 minutes. Remove the pie from the oven and let cool for at least 1 hour before slicing.

◦§ Serve warm or chilled.

Nutritional Analysis: 1 serving
cal 389; chol 16 mg; fat-total 6.2 g; fat-mono 1.7 g+; fat-poly 0.4 g+; fat-sat 3.7 g+; protein 4.46 g; carbo 82.1 g; fiber 3.29 g+; calcium 109 mg; sodium 8 mg; fat 14%; protein 4%; carbo 82%

◆ With margarine instead of butter: chol 0; fat-mono 2.6 g+; fat-poly 2 g+; fat-sat 1.2 g+

FRESH BERRY COBBLER

This is a real treat during berry season, but you can also use frozen berries. Blueberries are especially good in this recipe. Our favorite combination is blueberries and raspberries. Try topping a warm piece of cobbler with nonfat or low-fat frozen yogurt for Fresh Berry Cobbler à la mode.

Cake Layer
2 tablespoons unsalted butter or margarine, softened
¼ cup honey or maple syrup
1 egg or 2 egg whites or egg replacer
½ cup nonfat plain yogurt
2 tablespoons skim milk

2 teaspoons vanilla
1¼ cups whole-grain flour
1 teaspoon baking powder

Serves 9
Prep: 20 minutes
Bake: 35 minutes

Filling
4 cups berries

Crumb Topping
½ cup whole-grain flour
3 tablespoons fructose or sugar
2 tablespoons unsalted butter or margarine

1 tablespoon honey
½ teaspoon cinnamon
½ teaspoon nutmeg

- Lightly oil an 8 × 8-inch baking dish.
- For the cake, cream the butter. Beat in the honey, egg, yogurt, milk, and vanilla.
- Mix the flour with the baking powder and stir into the liquid ingredients.
- Spread the mixture into the baking dish. Preheat oven to 350°F.
- Top the batter with the berries.
- Combine the topping ingredients and cut into a fine crumb, using a food processor or 2 knives.
- Pat the crumbs on top of the berries. Bake the cobbler for about 35 to 40 minutes. Serve warm or cold.

Nutritional Analysis: 1 serving
cal 223; chol 45 mg; fat-total 6.5 g; fat-mono 1.8 g; fat-poly 0.6 g;

fat-sat 3.5 g; protein 5.09 g; carbo 39.2 g; fiber 5.39 g; calcium 80 mg; sodium 58 mg; fat 25%; protein 9%; carbo 66%
◆ With margarine and egg whites instead of butter and a whole egg: chol 0; fat-mono 2.3 g; fat-poly 2 g; fat-sat 1.1 g

BLUEBERRY CRUMBLE

This blueberry pie has a crisp and crumbly oat topping with a tapioca-thickened filling. Use fresh or frozen berries.

Filling

4 cups blueberries
½ cup tapioca, quick-cooking granules
½ cup maple syrup or honey
½ teaspoon cinnamon
½ teaspoon nutmeg

Serves 8
Prep: 15 minutes
Bake: 40–45 minutes

Crust

1 cup rolled oats
¼ cup whole-grain flour
¼ cup oat bran
¼ cup fructose or sugar
4 tablespoons unsalted butter or margarine, melted

1 tablespoon honey
¼ teaspoon cinnamon
¼ teaspoon nutmeg

ᴥ§ Preheat oven to 375°F. Lightly oil a 9- to 10-inch pie plate.
ᴥ§ Gently mix all the filling ingredients in a medium bowl. Set aside.
ᴥ§ Mix all crust ingredients in a small bowl.
ᴥ§ Spread a thin layer of the crust mixture on the bottom of the pan and slightly up the sides.
ᴥ§ Gently pour the filling into the crust and smooth out the top. Sprinkle the remaining crust mixture on top and spread it out to cover the filling. Gently pat down the crust.
ᴥ§ Bake the pie for 40 to 45 minutes. Let cool slightly before cutting. Serve warm or well chilled.

Nutritional Analysis: 1 serving
cal 271; chol 16 mg; fat-total 7 g; fat-mono 1.7 g+; fat-poly 0.4 g+; fat-sat 3.6 g+; protein 3.44 g; carbo 50.9 g; fiber 3.44 g; calcium 40 mg; sodium 10 mg; fat 23%; protein 5%; carbo 72%

◆ With margarine instead of butter: chol 0; fat-mono 2.6 g+; fat-poly 2 g+; fat-sat 1.2 g+

APPLE CRISP

Apples, cinnamon, and raisins are surrounded by a granola crust. Serve warm with a scoop of low-fat or nonfat frozen yogurt. Yum!

Filling
6 – 8 tart apples (peeled if skin is thick or bitter), sliced
Juice of 1 lemon
¾ cup raisins
2 tablespoons whole-grain flour
1 teaspoon cinnamon
1 teaspoon nutmeg
1 teaspoon vanilla

¼ teaspoon cloves
¼ teaspoon allspice

Serves 12
Prep: 20 minutes
Bake: 1 hour

Crust
2 cups rolled oats
¾ cup oat bran
4 tablespoons unsalted butter or margarine, melted

½ cup whole-grain flour
½ cup fructose or sugar
2 tablespoons honey
2 teaspoons cinnamon

◄§ Preheat oven to 350°F. Lightly oil a 9 × 13-inch baking pan.
◄§ Mix the filling ingredients in a very large bowl.
◄§ Mix the crust ingredients in a medium bowl. Firmly pat half the crust on the bottom of the prepared baking pan. Spoon filling evenly over crust, making sure to fill corners.
◄§ Firmly pat the remaining crust on top of the filling.
◄§ Cover the pan with aluminum foil and bake for 45 minutes. Uncover and bake for another 15 minutes or until the top is lightly browned. Let cool slightly before serving.

Nutritional Analysis: 1 serving
cal 255; chol 10 mg; fat-total 5.4 g; fat-mono 1.1 g+; fat-poly 0.3 g+; fat-sat 2.5 g+; protein 4.85 g; carbo 49.6 g; fiber 3.67 g; calcium 39 mg; sodium 6 mg; fat 18%; protein 7%; carbo 75%
◆ With margarine instead of butter: chol 0; fat-mono 1.7 g+; fat-poly 1.3 g+; fat-sat 0.9 g+

BROWNIE PUDDING

This dessert is a combination of brownie flavor and soft, pudding texture. Serve Brownie Pudding à la mode with a scoop of low-fat or nonfat frozen yogurt and smother with Raspberry Coulis (page 312).

1 cup whole-wheat pastry flour
1¼ cups fructose or sugar
¼ cup + 2 tablespoons carob
   powder
2 teaspoons baking powder
¼ cup chopped walnuts
½ cup evaporated skim milk
3 tablespoons unsalted butter or
   margarine, melted
1 tablespoon vanilla
1½ cups boiling water

Serves 9
Prep: 15 minutes
Bake: 30–40 minutes

◆§ Preheat oven to 350°F.
◆§ In a large bowl, mix the flour, ½ cup of the fructose, 2 tablespoons of the carob powder, baking powder, and walnuts.
◆§ Stir in the milk, butter, and vanilla and pour into an ungreased 8 × 8-inch baking dish.
◆§ Combine the boiling water, remaining ¾ cup fructose, and ¼ cup carob. Pour this liquid over the batter in the baking dish. Bake for 30 to 40 minutes or until the pudding is set on top.

Nutritional Analysis: 1 serving
cal 229; chol 11 mg; fat-total 6 g; fat-mono 1.6 g; fat-poly 1.6 g; fat-sat 2.6 g; protein 3.56 g; carbo 44.8 g; fiber 1.46 g+; calcium 120 mg; sodium 89 mg; fat 22%; protein 6%; carbo 72%
◆ With margarine instead of butter: chol 1 mg; fat-mono 2.2 g; fat-poly 2.6 g; fat-sat 1 g

LEMON TAPIOCA PUDDING

A family favorite in our house, this cool, refreshing, low-fat dessert or snack is easy to make. You can substitute any flavor extract for lemon.

4 cups skim milk
6 tablespoons tapioca, quick-
  cooking granules
4 tablespoons maple syrup or
  honey (or to taste)
4 teaspoons vanilla
½ teaspoon lemon extract
Dash of nutmeg

Serves 4
Prep: 10 minutes
Chill: 2 hours or more

◦§ Mix all the ingredients in a medium saucepan.
◦§ Cook over medium heat, whisking until the mixture comes to a
   boil.
◦§ Let boil for 3 minutes while stirring constantly.
◦§ Remove pudding from the heat and pour into 4 serving cups.
   Refrigerate until well chilled.

Nutritional Analysis: 1 serving
cal 184; chol 4 mg; fat-total 0.5 g; fat-mono 0.1 g+; fat-poly 0; fat-sat
0.3 g+; protein 8.10 g; carbo 37 g; fiber 0; calcium 324 mg; sodium
128 mg; fat 2%; protein 18%; carbo 80%

PERFECT PUMPKIN PUDDING

This is really a recipe for pumpkin pie without the crust, to keep the
fat content low. The whole eggs help to create the creamy texture.

2 cups pumpkin purée
½ cup fructose or sugar
¼ cup honey
1 tablespoon molasses
1½ teaspoons cinnamon
¼ teaspoon ginger
¼ teaspoon nutmeg
¼ teaspoon cloves
1½ cups evaporated skim milk
3 eggs, lightly beaten

Serves 8
Prep: 10 minutes
Bake: 45 – 50 minutes

◦§ Preheat oven to 425°F. Lightly oil 8 ovenproof 1-cup dishes.
◦§ Beat all the ingredients in the order given.

◄§ Pour the mixture into the prepared dishes and bake for 10 minutes. Lower the oven temperature to 350°F and bake for another 35 to 40 minutes or until the top is lightly browned and the pudding is solid. Serve warm or chilled.

Nutritional Analysis: 1 serving
cal 176; chol 104 mg; fat-total 2.7 g; fat-mono 0.9 g+; fat-poly 0.3 g+; fat-sat 0.8 g+; protein 6.6 g; carbo 33.8 g; fiber 1.1 g+; calcium 188 mg; sodium 87 mg; fat 13%; protein 14%; carbo 73%

FRUIT COULIS

Coulis (kuli) is a special French sauce or purée. Fresh-tasting and mildly sweet, this *coulis* is 90 percent fruit and only about 10 percent sweetener. You can spoon *coulis* over frozen yogurt, plain yogurt, pudding, cakes, pancakes, and even French toast.

Here's a recipe for Raspberry Coulis, one of my favorites. Raspberry seeds are a great source of fiber and add a fresh feeling to the coulis. Strain the sauce if you would prefer not to have seeds. And for a special touch, add a few drops of framboise liqueur before cooking. Remember, the alcohol evaporates when heated — only the special taste remains. Try using peeled peaches, apricots, or other berries in place of raspberries. Adjust the sweetener as needed. You may have to purée some fruits like peaches in a blender after cooking.

3 cups raspberries, fresh or
    unsweetened frozen, packed
¼ cup sweetener, or to taste

Serves 6
Cook: 20 minutes

◄§ Heat the berries and sweetener in a heavy saucepan over medium heat for 20 minutes. Stir often.
◄§ Let the sauce cool. Store in a covered jar in the refrigerator until ready to use.

Nutritional Analysis: 1 serving
cal 62; chol 0; fat-total 0.5 g; fat-mono 0.1 g; fat-poly 0.2 g; fat-sat 0; protein 0.50 g; carbo 15.3 g; fiber 4.55 g; calcium 14 mg; sodium 0; fat 7%; protein 3%; carbo 90%

LEMON RICOTTA ICING

Icing is usually very high in fat, made with butter, whipped cream, or cream cheese. This recipe is different. It's made with part–skim milk ricotta cheese. It has the flavor of traditional icing but without all the fat and cholesterol. You can substitute other naturally flavored extracts for lemon.

½ cup part–skim milk ricotta
   cheese
4 tablespoons fructose or honey
1–2 tablespoons lemon juice
2 teaspoons grated lemon rind or
   lemon extract
1 teaspoon vanilla

Serves 16
Prep: 5 minutes
Chill: 1 hour

◦§ Combine all the ingredients. Beat until smooth with an electric mixer.
◦§ Chill for 1 hour or until thickened.

Nutritional Analysis: 1 serving
cal 23; chol 2 mg; fat-total 0.6 g; fat-mono 0.2 g; fat-poly 0; fat-sat 0.4 g; protein 0.89 g; carbo 3.6 g; fiber 0; calcium 21 mg; sodium 10 mg; fat 23%; protein 15%; carbo 62%

CREAMY LOW-FAT DESSERT TOPPING

Nonfat yogurt is used to create this creamy, syrupy topping, which transforms a bowl of fresh fruit into a very special dessert. Try it on baked goods too.

1½ cups nonfat yogurt
¼ cup nonfat dry milk
2 tablespoons honey
1 teaspoon grated lemon rind
¼ teaspoon nutmeg
Dash of ginger

Serves 10
Prep: 5 minutes
Chill: 30 minutes or
more

◆§ Combine all the ingredients in a bowl. Beat with an electric mixer for 3 to 5 minutes.

◆§ Place in a covered container and chill until ready to use. This sauce keeps well.

Nutritional Analysis: 1 serving
cal 38; chol 1 mg; fat-total 0.1 g; fat-mono 0; fat-poly 0; fat-sat 0.1 g; protein 2.56 g; carbo 6.9 g; fiber 0; calcium 89 mg; sodium 36 mg; fat 2%; protein 27%; carbo 71%

Snack Ideas and Options

One of the most important steps you can take for good health is eating light, nutritious between-meal snacks every 2½ to 3 hours. Prepare these snacks in advance and take them to work or school, or make them on the spot.

Here are some simple snack ideas:

- Homemade whole-grain baked goods*
- Whole-grain low-fat cookies*
- Bagels, plain or with low-fat cottage cheese and/or fruit spread*
- Whole-grain muffins or breads*
- Spreads on whole-grain bread or crackers* (one of our family favorites: Whole-Grain Pita Chips with Cinnamon, Raisin, and Nut Spread)
- Pita chips with salsa*
- Air-popped popcorn, plain or with very small amounts of unsalted butter or margarine, nutritional yeast, and/or herbs
- Whole-grain crackers: brown rice or rye, with little or no added fats (try these with one of the spreads in the "Additional Recipes" section)
- Fresh fruits and vegetables (generally eaten with a whole grain)
- Canned fish, packed in either water, mustard, or tomato sauce
- Puffed grains: cereals and cakes
- Melon filled with low-fat cottage cheese or nonfat yogurt, topped with berries and lemon or lime wedges
- Cottage, Fruits, and Nuts*
- Chilled Fresh Peach Soup*
- Fresh strawberries or raspberries sprinkled with balsamic vinegar and fructose. Cover and refrigerate for a couple of hours. A real Italian treat.

---

* Recipes are included in this cookbook.

Additional

Recipes

•◆•

◆•◆

COTTAGE CREAM

Cottage Cream is a great substitute for high-fat sour cream. Try mixing in some chopped chives and serve on top of baked potatoes.

½ cup low-fat cottage cheese
2 tablespoons nonfat plain yogurt

Makes ⅔ cup
Prep: 5 minutes

ᥫ᭡ Whip the cottage cheese and yogurt in a food processor or blender until it's very smooth and creamy. Store in a covered container as you would regular cottage cheese.

Low-Fat Cream Cheese–Style Spreads

The following 3 spreads are delicious substitutions for high-fat cream cheese. They are made with nonfat yogurt and low-fat cottage cheese and flavored with a variety of ingredients. For a thicker spread, drain the cottage cheese and yogurt to remove the excess liquid before mixing. Try one of these spreads on a bagel, whole-grain crackers, pita chips, soda bread, or whole-grain bread. It's a great snack.

BLACK OLIVE AND PIMIENTO SPREAD

¾ cup low-fat cottage cheese
¼ cup nonfat plain yogurt
½ teaspoon basil
¼ teaspoon garlic powder
15 black olives, thinly sliced
4 tablespoons pimientos, diced
1 tablespoon chives

Serves 6
Prep: 10 minutes

319

◄§ Mix the first 4 ingredients in a food processor or blender until smooth and creamy.

◄§ Stir in the remaining ingredients and refrigerate in a tightly covered container. This spread will thicken as it cools.

Nutritional Analysis: 1 serving
cal 49; chol 3 mg; fat-total 2.3 g; fat-mono 1.2 g+; fat-poly 0.2 g+; fat-sat 0.6 g; protein 4.61 g; carbo 3 g; fiber 0.39 g+; calcium 51 mg; sodium 183 mg; fat 40%; protein 36%; carbo 24%

VEGETABLE CREAM SPREAD

To speed chopping, use a food processor to mince the vegetables. And to make this spread even thicker, drain the chopped vegetables before adding them to the mixture.

¾ cup low-fat cottage cheese   *Serves 6*
¼ cup nonfat plain yogurt   *Prep: 10 minutes*
½ teaspoon garlic powder
½ teaspoon basil
½ teaspoon thyme
1 carrot, very finely chopped
½ red onion, very finely chopped
1 green pepper, very finely
  chopped
2 tablespoons minced fresh
  parsley
2 tablespoons diced pimientos

◄§ Mix the first 5 ingredients in a food processor or blender until smooth and creamy.

◄§ Stir in the remaining ingredients and refrigerate in a tightly covered container. This spread will thicken as it cools.

Nutritional Analysis: 1 serving
cal 48; chol 3 mg; fat-total 0.7 g; fat-mono 0.2 g+; fat-poly 0.1 g+; fat-sat 0.4 g+; protein 5.05 g; carbo 5.5 g; fiber 1.05 g+; calcium 53 mg; sodium 130 mg; fat 13%; protein 42%; carbo 45%

CINNAMON, RAISIN, AND NUT SPREAD

¾ cup low-fat cottage cheese   *Serves 6*
¼ cup nonfat plain yogurt   *Prep: 10 minutes*
1 teaspoon maple syrup or honey,
    to taste
¼ teaspoon grated lemon rind
¼ teaspoon cinnamon
⅛ teaspoon nutmeg
¼ cup raisins
¼ cup finely chopped walnuts or
    almonds

◈ Mix all the ingredients, except the raisins and nuts, in a food processor or blender until smooth and creamy.

◈ Stir in the raisins and nuts and refrigerate in a tightly covered container. This spread will thicken as it cools.

Nutritional Analysis: 1 serving
cal 84; chol 3 mg; fat-total 3.7 g; fat-mono 0.9 g; fat-poly 2 g; fat-sat 0.7 g; protein 5.34 g; carbo 8.2 g; fiber 0.68 g; calcium 48 mg; sodium 123 mg; fat 38%; protein 24%; carbo 38%

GUACAMOLE

Guacamole is made from mashed avocados. Most recipes also call for mayonnaise or sour cream. Avocados are high in fat — 30 grams in 1 fruit — and when other high-fat ingredients are added to make guacamole, it becomes a food best left out of our diets. But when used as a condiment and in small quantities, this Guacamole can be an enjoyable addition to a Mexican meal.

3 ripe avocados   *Serves 20*
⅓ cup minced red onion   *Prep: 15 minutes*
½ green pepper, minced
½ red pepper, minced
1 small tomato, finely chopped
1 tablespoon picante sauce or
    salsa
1 tablespoon parsley
1 teaspoon lemon juice
Freshly ground black pepper

⋑ Cut the avocados in half lengthwise and remove the pits (but save one). Scoop the flesh into a bowl and discard the skin.

⋑ Add the remaining ingredients and chop everything together with a knife to form a lumpy spread.

⋑ To prevent the Guacamole from turning brownish, push the reserved avocado pit into the top of the mound. Cover the bowl very tightly and refrigerate. Remove the pit and stir well before serving.

Nutritional Analysis: 1 serving (approximately 2 tablespoons) cal 50; chol 0; fat-total 4.5 g; fat-mono 2.9 g+; fat-poly 0.5 g+; fat-sat 0.7 g+; protein 0.75 g; carbo 2.6 g; fiber 0.74 g+; calcium 5 mg; sodium 5 mg; fat 75%; protein 6%; carbo 19%

PESTO SAUCE

Traditionally, this sauce is made from fresh basil leaves and has quite a bit of olive oil along with pine nuts and Parmesan cheese, making the fat level relatively high. I've created a recipe that keeps the traditional flavor but reduces the fat. I've also included a Winter Pesto variation,* which uses spinach instead of basil. Pesto freezes very well, so it's a good idea to make a few batches and freeze some in small containers to be used throughout the winter. A stew or Minestrone Soup tastes special with a spoonful or two of pesto. Try spreading it on pizza, baked potatoes, lasagna, or thinning it with a little water or skim milk and using it as a dip or dressing. This recipe makes enough for 12 servings, or 2 pounds of pasta. A pound of pasta serves about 6 people.

4 cloves garlic
3 tablespoons grated Parmesan
 cheese
3 tablespoons pine nuts
½ cup fresh parsley
3 cups fresh basil, packed
6 tablespoons olive oil

Serves 12
Prep: 15 minutes

---

* *Winter Pesto:* When winter hits and fresh basil is no longer available or becomes outrageously expensive, try making pesto with a package or two of frozen spinach and a few tablespoons of dried basil. It's lacking in the fresh basil flavor, but it's nice in its own right.

◄§ Combine the garlic, Parmesan cheese, and pine nuts in a food processor.

◄§ Add the remaining ingredients and combine until the basil is coarsely chopped (don't overprocess; a coarse texture is nice).

◄§ If the pesto seems too thick, add a tiny bit of water and mix.

Nutritional Analysis: 1 serving
cal 84; chol 1 mg; fat-total 8.6 g; fat-mono 5.7 g+; fat-poly 1.1 g+; fat-sat 1.4 g+; protein 1.31 g; carbo 1.4 g; fiber 0.49 g+; calcium 37 mg; sodium 37 mg; fat 88%; protein 6%; carbo 6%

◆ Analysis is based on spinach instead of fresh basil due to a lack of data from the United States Department of Agriculture.

WHITE BEAN DIP

Navy beans are puréed into a smooth, flavorful dip that's wonderful with raw vegetables. The garlic's bite is tamed by boiling or baking it for 5 to 10 minutes before mixing with the remaining ingredients.

1 cup cooked navy beans (⅓ cup raw)	*Makes ¾ cup*
	Prep: 10 minutes
2 cloves garlic, cooked	
1½ tablespoons olive oil	
½ teaspoon lemon juice	
Tabasco sauce to taste	
Salt to taste (optional)	

◄§ Combine all the ingredients in a food processor or blender and purée until smooth.

◄§ Refrigerate until ready to serve.

Nutritional Analysis: 1 serving (approximately 2 tablespoons)
cal 68; chol 0; fat-total 3.7 g; fat-mono 2.6 g; fat-poly 0.4 g; fat-sat 0.5 g; protein 2.4 g; carbo 6.7 g; fiber 1.03 g+; calcium 17 mg; sodium 3 mg; fat 48%; protein 14%; carbo 38%

BABA GHANOUSH (EGGPLANT SPREAD)

There are as many spellings for this Mediterranean dish as there are ways to make it. Traditional recipes include eggplant, garlic, and large amounts of olive oil. Here's my lower-fat interpretation. Serve with thick slices of whole-grain bread.

2 medium eggplants

2 cloves garlic, unpeeled

2 tablespoons lemon juice

2 tablespoons olive oil

2 tablespoons minced fresh
  parsley

Salt to taste

Freshly ground black pepper to
  taste

Makes 2½ cups
Cook: 15 – 30 minutes
Prep: 5 minutes

◆§ Slice the eggplants and place them on a lightly oiled broiling pan or grill along with the garlic. Brush the eggplant slices very lightly with oil.

◆§ Broil several minutes until the garlic peel is browned. Turn the garlic to brown the other side and then remove. Cook the eggplant until light brown. Turn the slices over and continue broiling until browned.

◆§ Remove skin from the garlic and eggplant and purée in a food processor. While the processor is on, add the remaining ingredients.

◆§ Taste to adjust seasoning and serve at room temperature.

Nutritional Analysis: 1 serving (approximately 2 tablespoons)
cal 20; chol 0; fat-total 1.9 g; fat-mono 1.4 g; fat-poly 0.2 g+; fat-sat 0.3 g+; protein 0.12 g; carbo 0.8 g; fiber 0.08 g+; calcium 5 mg; sodium 1 mg; fat 82%; protein 2%; carbo 16%

TZATZIKI (CUCUMBER AND YOGURT SPREAD)

The first time I tasted this refreshing, nonfat dish was in a fabulous Greek restaurant. As we were seated, *tzatziki* and thick slices of hearty bread were placed on the table. I found it addictive and can't even remember the other dishes I ate that afternoon. The spread's thickness comes from draining the yogurt and the cucumbers — an important step.

2 cups nonfat plain yogurt
1 large cucumber, peeled
½ teaspoon salt
2 small cloves garlic, minced

Serves 5
Prep: 20 minutes
Drain: Several
   hours – overnight

- ◈ Place the yogurt in cheesecloth, a yogurt funnel, or other device to drain in the refrigerator for at least several hours or overnight. Place a cup under the yogurt to catch the whey that drips.
- ◈ Grate or finely chop the cucumber. Place in a colander, sprinkle with salt, and let drain for 20 minutes.
- ◈ Rinse the cucumbers and drain.
- ◈ Mix a small amount of drained yogurt with minced garlic in a deep bowl. Stir in the remaining yogurt and fold in the cucumbers.
- ◈ Chill. Serve with thick slices of whole-grain bread.

Nutritional Analysis: 1 serving
cal 60; chol 2 mg; fat-total 0.2 g; fat-mono 0; fat-poly 0; fat-sat 0.1 g; protein 5.57 g; carbo 8.8 g; fiber 0.37 g; calcium 192 mg; sodium 284 mg; fat 4%; protein 37%; carbo 59%

HOMEMADE BREAD CRUMBS

Bread crumbs are so easy to make and are a great way to use leftover bread. Store slices in the freezer until you have 5 or 10 pieces. Process them all at once into crumbs. For herbed bread crumbs, put thyme, basil, oregano, sage, and garlic powder in the food processor, too.

1 slice whole-grain bread makes
   approximately ½ to 1 cup of
   bread crumbs

Prep: 5 minutes

- ◈ Cut the bread into several pieces. Put in a food processor with the knife blade. Process until bread is in fine crumbs. If the crumbs seem a bit moist, spread them out on a baking sheet and bake several minutes until fully dried.
- ◈ Store in a tightly covered container. If frozen, the bread crumbs will last up to a year, and you can use them directly from the freezer.

HOMEMADE CROUTONS

Homemade croutons have a big nutritional advantage over store-bought — no added fat, sodium, or artificial ingredients.

Several pieces of leftover bread
Optional:
  Olive oil or nonstick cooking
    spray
  Garlic powder
  Grated Parmesan or Romano
    cheese
  Soy sauce
  Italian seasonings
  Cayenne pepper
  Freshly ground black pepper

Prep: 5 minutes
Bake: 20 minutes

- Preheat oven to 375°F.
- Cut the bread into small cubes.
- If you want to make flavored croutons, place the bread cubes in a bowl, very lightly coat them with olive oil or cooking spray, and sprinkle them with any of the other optional ingredients.
- Place the cubes on a baking sheet and bake for 20 minutes or until lightly browned and crisp.
- Store in a tightly covered container and freeze. The croutons will keep in the freezer from 6 months to a year.

HOMEMADE NONFAT BUTTERMILK

When cultured nonfat or low-fat buttermilk isn't available, try making your own. It doesn't have the thick, creamy texture of store-bought, but it works well in many recipes.

1 cup skim milk
2 tablespoons lemon juice

Prep: 15 minutes

- Warm the milk slightly. Add the lemon and let sit at room temperature for 10 minutes. Use as you would store-bought buttermilk.

Resources

References

Indexes

Resources

Shopping for Hard-to-Find Items

Are you having trouble finding an ingredient needed for one of the recipes? Or is the quality of ingredients in your supermarket not as good as you would like? This list of resources can help you find what you need without searching all over town and may actually save you dollars in the long run.

Mail order has become a tremendous business. And for good reason: shopping for quality items in the comfort of your own home. I love it! If you know what you want and have a credit card, many stores, companies, and restaurants without catalogues will take telephone orders and ship direct to you as well.

Here's a list of some of my favorite and most useful resources for everything from organic whole grains, spices, canned products, and wine to balsamic vinegar, quality cooking utensils, and computerized machines that make and bake bread while you sleep. Write or call for catalogues.

American Spoon Foods, Inc., 411 East Lake Street, Petosky, Michigan 49770; (800) 222-5886, (616) 347-9030

Tucked away in rural northern Michigan, this company sells a treasure trove of unique American products. The owners began by preserving the best of Michigan's wild and domestic fruits, and they have grown to include wild mushrooms, a variety of honeys, special nut meats, and cofounder (and owner of the New York restaurant An American Place) Larry Forgione's line of products. Along with fruit preserves, jellies, and conserves, American Spoon Foods has a selection of fruit butters (rich reductions of puréed fruits and concentrated fruit juices) and dried fruits (including wild blueberries, cranberries, and my favorite, tart red cherries), all made without added sugar. If gooseberry marmalade, wild elderberry jelly, black cherry spoon fruit, or the strawberry preserves that were judged "best in America" in 1986 sound enticing, this catalogue will be a treat.

329

The Catalogue of Healthy Food by John Tepper Marlin, Ph.D. (Bantam, 1990)

A comprehensive resource guide to understanding, finding, selecting, and eating healthful food. This book begins by describing what healthful food is and isn't, and continues with who produces it and where you can buy it — from restaurants, retail suppliers, farms, and food co-ops in a state-by-state listing.

The Chef's Catalog, 3915 Commercial Avenue, Northbrook, Illinois 60062; (800) 338-3232

This catalogue carries professional-style kitchen equipment for the home chef as well as other household items — from knives and wine racks to pasta machines, recycling bins, and all sorts of gadgets.

Dean & Deluca, 560 Broadway, New York, New York 10012; (800) 221-7714, (212) 431-1691

One of New York's most exciting specialty food shops has a mail order catalogue that carries many of the items available in the store. This company began in 1977 in a small storefront in SoHo. It now occupies a full city block and has a huge inventory of imported foods as well as high-quality domestic products. The mail order catalogue includes everything from pastas, grains, beans, teas, oils, and specialty vinegars to elite cookware, caviar, and miscellaneous kitchen tools. They even offer beautiful gift baskets, abundant with valuable and delicious items.

Four Chimneys Organic Winery, R.D. 1, Hall Road, Himrod-on-Seneca, New York 14842; (607) 243-7502

Since 1979 this winery has offered a wide selection of wines. The grape-growing and wine-making are totally organic, adhering to the standards of the International Federation of Agriculture Movements and the Natural Organic Farmers Association of New York. Four Chimneys products are sold in New York stores only, but individuals can call to inquire about shipping. Call or write for this year's selections.

Frey Vineyards, 14000 Tomki Road, Redwood Valley, California 95470; (800) 345-3739 in California, (707) 485-5177 outside the state

This small, family-run winery is managed in accordance with California Certified Organic Farmers standards and uses careful, traditional wine-making techniques. To find Frey wine near you, call the winery for the name of your state distributor, who will know the closest retail outlet.

Frieda's Finest, P.O. Box 58488, Los Angeles, California 90058; (213) 627-2981

Frieda's Finest is a marketer and distributor of new and unusual fruits, vegetables, and complementary items. The mail order business is for gift baskets only, but Frieda's sells its specialty items in supermarkets across the country. Shoppers can purchase any of Frieda's products simply by asking their local supermarket produce manager to order the item they want. Call or write to find out more about Frieda's unusual foods, and which market in your area carries these products, and to receive a nice sampling of brochures, newsletters, and recipes.

G. B. Ratto & Company, 821 Washington Street, Oakland, California 94607; (800) 325-3483, (800) 228-3515 in the state

This international grocery has supplied the Oakland area with ethnic foods since 1897. Founded by an Italian immigrant and still run by his descendants, G. B. Ratto has a large mail order catalogue that includes a wide selection of ethnic and specialty items from olives, mushrooms, oils, vinegars, mustards, herbs, beans, and grains to great Spanish pimientos and more. Call or write for a catalogue — it's entertaining reading.

The Herb & Spice Collection, P.O. Box 118, Norway, Iowa 52318; (800) 365-4372

This mail order catalogue is from a company that has been in the herb and spice wholesale business since 1976. Now this collection of culinary herbs and spices, teas, essential and fragrance oils, potpourris, and natural body care products is available through mail order. The listing of some 140 culinary herbs and spices is quite complete.

Ideal Cheese Shop, 1205 Second Avenue, New York, New York 10021; (212) 688-7579

This shop carries an impressive line of imported and domestic low-fat, low-cholesterol, and low-sodium cheeses. The owner and buyer, Edward Edelman, reportedly chooses only those with the finest flavor and insists on nutritional analyses for all his low-fat products. Call or write for a price list and order form. Edelman ships via UPS throughout the country.

Walnut Acres, Penns Creek, Pennsylvania 17862; (800) 433-3998

Walnut Acres has been farming organically since 1946. Today the catalogue includes over 40 pages filled with foods grown on their farm or by carefully selected, reputable outside suppliers. The selection is so broad (more than 500 products) that one could use it to stock an entire pantry — from fruits and vegetables (canned, dried, juices, and preserves), flours, grains, legumes, cheeses, nuts, oils, pastas, spices, and sweeteners to bread and cookie mixes, baby products, cereals, soups, nut butters, and sauces.

Williams-Sonoma, P.O. Box 7456, San Francisco, California 94120; (415) 421-4242

The Williams-Sonoma mail order catalogue features a large selection of high-quality cookware, kitchen supplies, and other cooking and kitchen-related products. The retail stores are located in many cities.

Nutrition Periodicals

Contact these periodicals for a sample issue and subscription information. To stay up to date in the field of diet and nutrition, it's beneficial to subscribe to one or more periodicals.

Environmental Nutrition, 2112 Broadway, Suite 200, New York, New York 10023; (212) 362-0424

Nutrition Action Healthletter, Center for Science in the Public Interest, 1501 Sixteenth Street N.W., Washington, D.C., 20036-1499; (202) 332-9110

Tufts University Diet & Nutrition Letter, P.O. Box 57857, Boulder, Colorado 80322-7857; (800) 274-7581, (303) 447-9330 in Colorado

References

The nutritional analyses in this cookbook were calculated using the following scientific references:

USDA Nutritive Value of Foods, Home and Garden Bulletin No. 72 (Washington, D.C.: U.S. Government Printing Office, revised November 1985).

USDA Composition of Foods . . . Raw, Processed, Prepared, Agriculture Handbook No. 8 (Washington, D.C.: Consumer and Food Economics Institute, Agricultural Research Service, reprinted October 1975).

USDA Composition of Foods . . . Raw, Processed, Prepared, Agriculture Handbook Revisions (Washington, D.C.: Consumer and Food Economics Institute, Human Nutrition Information Service).

And additional revisions:

USDA Composition of Foods: Dairy and Egg Products . . . Raw, Processed, Prepared, Agriculture Handbook No. 8-1, November 1976.

USDA Composition of Foods: Spices and Herbs . . . Raw, Processed, Prepared, Agriculture Handbook No. 8-2, January 1977.

USDA Composition of Foods: Fats and Oils . . . Raw, Processed, Prepared, Agriculture Handbook No. 8-4, June 1979.

USDA Composition of Foods: Soups, Sauces, and Gravies . . . Raw, Processed, Prepared, Agriculture Handbook No. 8-6, February 1980.

USDA Composition of Foods: Breakfast Cereals . . . Raw, Processed, Prepared, Agriculture Handbook No. 8-8, July 1982.

USDA Composition of Foods: Fruits and Fruit Juices . . . Raw, Processed, Prepared, Agriculture Handbook No. 8-9, August 1982.

USDA Composition of Foods: Vegetables and Vegetable Products . . . Raw, Processed, Prepared, Agriculture Handbook No. 8-11, August 1984.

USDA Composition of Foods: Nut and Seed Products . . . *Raw, Processed, Prepared,* Agriculture Handbook No. 8-12, September 1984.

USDA Composition of Foods: Finfish and Shellfish . . . *Raw, Processed, Prepared,* Agriculture Handbook No. 8-15, September 1987.

USDA Composition of Foods: Legumes . . . *Raw, Processed, Prepared,* Agriculture Handbook No. 8-16, December 1986.

Nutrition Wizard Computer Software by Michael F. Jacobson, Ph.D. (Washington, D.C.: Center for Science in the Public Interest, 1986).

The Food Processor II: Computerized Nutrition Analysis System (Salem, Oregon: ESHA Research Corporation, 1987).

Total Nutrition Guide by Jean Carper (New York: Bantam, 1987).

Note:
◆ Product manufacturers provided nutritional values for ingredients not available from the United States Department of Agriculture or in the computer software programs.

◆ Optional ingredients listed in the recipes are not figured into the nutritional analyses.

◆ Wine is occasionally used in the recipes. Because the alcohol (and calories) evaporate when heated, it is not figured into the analyses.

◆ Some marinades are not completely absorbed by foods. The unabsorbed marinade has been deducted from the nutritional analyses where necessary.

◆ When a recipe gives a choice of ingredients, the nutritional analyses is figured using the first ingredient listed.

Fast-Meal Index: Recipes That Take 45 Minutes or Less

An asterisk indicates that a dish requires additional time to soak, chill, marinate, or set.

Recipe Index

General Index

Salad dressings: (*cont.*)
  Buttermilk, Creamy, 100–101
  Garlic, Creamy, 184–85
  Ginger Horseradish, 104
  Lemon Mustard Vinaigrette, 213
  Parsley Parmesan, 121–22
  Pignoli, 219–20
  Poppy Seed–Tahini, 198–99
  Red Pepper Vinaigrette, Sweet,
    125
  in restaurants, 34–35, 36
  Tomato
    Spicy, 203
    Tangy, 215–16
  Vinaigrette Fines Herbes, 260–61
  Watercress, Creamy, 233–34
Salmon
  Loaf with Lemon Mustard Sauce,
    207–8
  Sauce, Linguine with, 248–49
Salt, 10–11
  daily allowance, 2, 11
  in recipes, 14–15, 31
Sandwiches
  Beanwiches, 26
  Cutlet Parmesan Hero, 99–100
  Hummus-in-Pita, 171–72
  Vegetable Tofu Spread, 164–65
Sauce
  Cucumber Dill, 264
  Lemon Mustard, 208
  Marinara, 218–19
  Peperonata, 106–7
  Pesto, 322–23
    in Lasagna Rolls, 211–12
    Ricotta Pecan, 148–49
  Red Raspberry Yogurt, 158–59
  Salmon, 248–49
  Sweet Pea and Pimiento, 259–60
  Tomato, 25
    Fresh, Relish, 251–52
    Fresh, Sauce, 239–40
    in Lasagna Rolls, 211–12
    Marinara, 218–19
    Tuna, 189–90
    Turkey, 226–27

Scones, Raspberry Currant, 288–89
Seafood. *See* Fish
Shakes, Frosty Strawberry, 81–82
Sherbets, 35, 36
Snacks and light meals, 42, 44, 61,
    279–315
Soda Biscuits, Whole-Grain, 110
Soda Bread, Whole-Grain Irish, 25,
    132–33
Sodium. *See* Salt
Sorbets, 35, 36
Soup
  Acorn Cheddar, 91–92
  Black Bean, Caribbean, 102–3
  Borscht, Cool Magenta, 165–66
  Bouillabaisse, Saffron, 179–80
  Cabbage Caraway, German, 114–15
  canned, 25
  Corn Chowder, Creamy, 131–32
  Gazpacho, Thick and Zesty, 151–52
  Hot and Sour Ramen, 111–12
  Minestrone, 109–10
  Pea, Chilled Sweet, 145–46
  Peach, Chilled, 174
  Split Pea and Wild Rice, 126–27
  Tomato
    Cucumber, Chilled, 265
    Rice, Herbal, 120–21
Soybeans au Gratin, Savory, 193–94
Soy sauce, 16
Spa cuisine, 39
Spanish cuisine, 38
Spanish Rice, 205
Spinach
  and Garlic Sauté, Fresh, 180–81
  Mushroom Salad, 219–20
  Salad, Warm, 187–88
Split Pea and Wild Rice Soup, 126–27
Spread
  Baba Ghanoush (Eggplant
    Spread), 323–24

Vinegar, 21, 34
  Balsamic Splash, Tossed Greens
    with, 190
  Raspberry-Marinated Tomatoes
    and Onions, 149–50

Whole-grain(s), 19, 45
  bread recipes, 96, 107–8, 110,
    116, 118–19, 132–33, 142–
    43, 146–47, 152–53, 156–
    57, 159–60, 162–63, 169–
    70, 175–76, 181–82, 188,
    191, 195–96, 199–200,
    209–10, 216–17, 224–25,
    237–38, 250–51, 254–55,
    266–67, 288–89, 294–95
  breakfast recipes, 75–85
  cake, pie, and pudding recipes,
    298–302, 304–10
  cookie recipes, 281–88
  cooking chart, 48–49
  cooking method, 45–47
  muffin recipes, 93–94, 175–76,
    289–92
  quick bread recipes, 292–97
  pasta recipes, 129, 148–49,

Whole-grain: (cont.)
    168–69, 173–74, 183–84,
    211–12, 214–15, 218–19,
    226–27, 232–33, 239–40,
    248–49, 259–60, 268–69,
    275–76
  rice recipes, 112–13, 123–24,
    158–59, 166–67, 186–87,
    205, 246–47, 256–57
  soup recipes, 120–21, 126–27
  vegetable recipe, 193–94
Wines for cooking, 11, 15

Yogurt, 16
  Dessert Topping, Creamy Low-
    Fat, 314
  frozen, 35, 36
  Sauce, Red Raspberry, 158–59
  Spread, Cucumber and (Tzatziki),
    324–25
  -Tahini Dressing for Falafel, 137–
    38

Zucchini
  -Oat Bran Burgers, 243–44
  Spice Bread, 296

ABOUT THE AUTHOR

For more than a decade, Leslie L. Cooper has been developing *America's New Low-Fat Cuisine.* She has many years of experience studying international cuisine, throughout Europe and North America, and has worked for health-oriented gourmet restaurants as a chef, manager, and consultant.

From the first, Ms. Cooper has been committed to creating a collection of new and traditional recipes that are light but hearty and have a lively emphasis on simplicity and great taste. Every recipe and meal plan is low in fat, high in fiber, free of artificial ingredients, and designed to meet two seemingly contradictory standards — to equal or exceed the current guidelines of leading health organizations while capturing the sought-after variety of gourmet tastes found in the most renowned international cuisine.

Leslie Cooper spent years testing and using the recipes and meal plans in this cookbook and has helped thousands of people transform the recipes they know and love into more healthful variations.

She is vice president of Advanced Excellence Systems, a corporate training and consulting firm, and she directs programs on women's fitness, nutrition, cooking, and applications of diet to health, fitness, and performance. In addition, Ms. Cooper has spent several years teaching fitness to handicapped children. She is a professional member of the Women's Sports Foundation and serves on the board of directors of Better & Better, Inc., a nonprofit foundation dedicated to researching and promoting health education and wellness. Leslie Cooper lives on Lake LaSalle in Minnesota with her husband, Robert, and children, Christopher and Chelsea.